A Christian Introduction to the History of Philosophy

By

FRANCIS NIGEL LEE

THE CRAIG PRESS
Nutley, New Jersey
1978

UNIVERSITY SERIES: Historical Studies

Rousas J. Rushdoony, Editor

Library of Congress Catalog Card No. 79-107146

Printed in the United States of America

ABOUT THE AUTHOR

Francis Nigel Lee was Professor of Philosophy and Chairman of the Department of Philosophy and Religion at an American college from 1967 through 1969.

A South African, Dr. Lee received the B.A., LL.B., and M.A. (Philosophy) degrees from the University of Cape Town, and the B.D., M.Th., and Th.D. degrees from the University of Stellenbosch. He is a minister of the Reformed Church (D.R.C.) and an advocate of the Supreme Court of South Africa.

The author of the books *Communism versus Creation, The Covenantal Sabbath*, and *A Christian Introduction to the History of Philosophy*, Dr. Lee has also written several philosophical and theological booklets on culture, education, nationality, etc.

CONTENTS

INTRODUCTION

"Philosophy was born in Ancient Greece." "Thales was the first philosopher." Christian philosophy is impossible."
It is widespread misstatements like these which have prompted the writing of this work as a rebuttal. Our book is a modest one, both in its scope and in its content. But it would anchor the history of philosophy in God and His pre-creational eternity and unfold it towards the final advent of God's new earth. It would root the entire subject in a thoroughly Christian life and world view. It would attempt, however feebly, to glorify the Triune God and Lord of *all* history Who is the Lord of the history of philosophy too.

The writer admits his extreme prejudice in dealing with this subject. He is, thank God, incurably prejudiced in seeing the Lord in *all* things; for in Him we *all* live, and move, and have our very being—whether we realize is or not.

The reader may disagree with this analysis, but he will not be able to escape its main thrust. For in this analysis, the rather inferior and very fallible philosopher writing these words will repeatedly appeal to the Words of the only really authoritative thinker—the infallible and Supreme Philosopher Himself.

FRANCIS NIGEL LEE
Professor of Philosophy
September 1969

Chapter I

PROLEGOMENA TO THE HISTORY OF PHILOSOPHY

An Outline of the Subject

Many thinkers superficially imagine that philosophy and
the Bible have nothing at all to do with one another. Philosophy, they (quite correctly) say, is the universal science
of man's love of wisdom; whereas the Bible, they (incorrectly) add, is nothing more than a source-book for the particular science of theology alone.

However, this erroneous view not only somewhat "de-
universalizes" philosophy by separating it from that part of
the universe known as the Bible, and not only blasphe-
mously restricts God's Word to the science of theology
alone, but it also forgets that man's love of wisdom, as
well as the universe which wisdom-loving philosophers investigate, have both been obscured by the advent of *sin*
(which is of universal scope), whereas the Bible as God's
Own Word has been wonderfully preserved from the effects
thereof, so as to be able to be a lamp unto man's feet and
a light unto his path.[1]

Accordingly, the true philosopher now needs to wear the
"spectacles of the Bible" (thus Calvin), the glasses of God's
special revelation, in order to obtain a correct view of the
whole (sin-obscured) universe as God's general revelation.
Whereas true *theology* looks *at* the spectacles of the Bible
and at them alone, true *philosophy* looks *through* the spec-

[1] Ps. 119:105.

1

tacles of the Bible *at* the entire universe. For without the use of the spectacles of the Bible, philosophy can only arrive at a distorted view of the universe. And so true philosophy needs the Bible too.

At the beginning of this prolegomena, this preparatory first chapter to our Christian introduction to the history of philosophy, we will now define "philosophy," and then successively describe its Source, the origin of the objects it studies, its task, its deformation by sin, its pluriformity, its redemption, its renewal, its present state and its future goal—all in the light of the Bible alone.

1. *Definition of philosophy*

"Philosophy," the love of wisdom—first so-called by Pythagoras—may be defined by us as: "man's scientific total-view of all created reality."

Philosophy is *man's* view, a view qualified by human capabilities and *limitations*; for man, God's earthly viceroy, while divinely appointed as lord of the earth, is not the omniscient and omnipotent Lord of the universe.

Now philosophy is not man's simple knowledge, but rather his *scientific* knowledge of creation. In this respect, philosophy is to be distinguished from the simple or naive or pre-scientific outlook of man's non-scientific common sense —which simple knowledge is more extensive yet less intensive than is scientific knowledge.

Again, philosophy is man's scientific *total-view* of all created reality. It is not only man's partial view of merely some aspects of created reality (such as that offered by the special sciences like astronomy, physics, art, law, or ethics, etc.), but it attempts to account for their inter-relationship as parts of the cosmic *whole*.

Furthermore, philosophy is man's scientific total-view of all *created* reality. It deals with the crea*ted* universe and

2

all the creatures in that creation. It is not (and does not include) man's scientific view of Crea*tive* Reality, of God the Crea*tor* of the universe. (It is theology that gives us man's scientific view of the Creator [and of the Re-Creator or Redeemer] to the extent to which He has graciously revealed Himself, and true theology confines its field of scientific study to God's [partial yet adequate and wholly gracious] direct and indirect Self-Revelation in the Bible alone.) But true philosophy gives us man's scientific view of the whole crea*tion* (and all of its creatures), not confining itself to its principal field of scientific study—namely that major part of creation found *outside* of the Bible—but even investigating such creational material as is found *in* the Bible too, and interpreting the former in the light of the latter.

It may perhaps be added that philosophy is also man's *fallible* scientific total-view of created reality. Like the special sciences and even theology, philosophy too is fallible. Hence philosophy, theology, and the special sciences all need the corroborative and supplementary support of one another. But above all, all these fallible sciences continually need to test themselves by and to build on the foundations of the infallible Bible and infallible God-given faith.

Philosophy is therefore the human science of all created reality, and accordingly the science of all its sub-sciences. It is the encyclopaedia of all the sub-sciences in their interrelation and separate demarcation; the scientific survey and summary of the meaning and place of mathematics, mechanics, physics, chemistry, biology, zoology, psychology, analytical thought, history, geography, linguistics, sociology, economics, aesthetics, law, education, and ethics (amongst many other disciplines). Philosophy is the omnibus science of all the many facets of an integrated world outlook, and *Christian* philosophy is the scientific study of God's entire creation as revealed in all of His works and as interpreted according to all of His Word.

3

2. Source of philosophy

According to the Bible, philosophy, the love of wisdom, has as its Source the all-wise Lord Jehovah, the Triune God, the Supreme Philosopher. For God alone perfectly understands the totality of His creation as it really is, as only He Who designed and sustains it can.

The Fountainhead of the wisdom-loving Trinity is God the Father, "God only *wise*." [2] The Word or Outgoing Communication of the wisdom-loving Trinity is God the Son, "Christ the Power of God, the Wisdom of God," [3] Who "of God is made unto us *wisdom*." The Spirit or Living Principle of the wisdom-loving Trinity is God the Holy Ghost, "for the Spirit searcheth all things, yea, the deep things of God . . ., the things of God knoweth . . . the Spirit of God." [4] But these three wise Persons of the Trinity are all one and the same God, namely "the King eternal, immortal, invisible, the only *wise* God, [to Whom] be honor and glory for ever and ever." [5] Accordingly, all true philosophy will necessarily be trinicentric—will emphasize the recognition of the Triune God as its most important Principle and as its ultimate Prophet, Priest, and King.

3. Origin of philosophical objects

Philosophy is the human scientific investigation of the whole of created reality, and the first page of the Bible describes the origin of created reality, the origin of the objects of philosophical investigation.

"In the beginning God created the heaven and the earth." [6] In this first sentence of the Bible we are given the foundation of all the objects of philosophy and, more particularly, the basis for philosophical ontology (the study of being), genesiology (the study of origins), cosmogony (the study of the process of formation of the universe), and cos-

---

[2] Rom. 16:27. [4] I Cor. 2:10-11. [6] Gen. 1:1.
[3] I Cor. 1:24,30. [5] I Tim. 1:17.

4

mology (the study of the present structure of the world). In addition, this verse also points to the origin of the objects of all philosophical reflection on causation, time, number, and space.

"And the earth was without form and void; and darkness was upon the face of the deep. And the Spirit of God moved upon the face of the waters. And God said: 'Let there be light!' And there was light. And God saw the light, that it was good." [7] Here we are given the basis for philosophical epistemology (the study of knowledge, of which the Spirit and the Logos or the Word of God are the enlightening Principles),[8] and axiology (the study of values, of the determination of what is good); and here we also have the origin of the objects of all philosophical reflection on matter and motion.

"God divided the light from the darkness . . ., and divided the waters which were under the firmament from the waters which were above the firmament." [9] Here we meet with the principle of division, the selection of some facts from their equally factual background, and the distinguishing of some things from their contrary opposites. So this represents the basis of both philosophic methodology and of logic.

"Let there be a firmament"; "let the dry land appear"; "let the earth bring forth grass"; "let the waters bring forth abundantly the moving creature that hath life, and fowl . . . after their kind." [10] Here we see the germ of all the objects analyzed by physics, geology, botany, zoology, and many other sciences; all of them (relatively speaking) sovereign in their own created spheres, all of them mutually underivable from one another, and all of them capable of philosophical analysis.

Finally, the Triune God said: "Let Us make man in Our image, after Our likeness: and let them have dominion over

[7] Gen. 1:2-4.
[8] Cf. Job 32:8 and John 1:9.
[9] Gen. 1:4,7.
[10] Gen. 1:6-21.

5

the fish of the sea, and over the fowl of the air, and over the cattle, and over all the earth, and over every creeping thing that creepeth upon the earth." [11] So God created man in His Own image, in the image of God created He him; male and female created He them. And God blessed them, and God said unto them: "Be fruitful, and multiply, and replenish the earth, and subdue it! And have dominion over the fish of the sea, and over the fowl of the air, and over every living thing that moveth upon the earth!" [12]

The above text should be regarded as God's mandate to Adam (and Eve) as the federal or covenantal head(s) of the entire human race,[13] and therefore as God's mandate to all men, their descendants, to whom it was later substantially repeated.[14] This mandate is God's revelation of what He would have man do on earth; it is God's instructions as to what man's life's work should be. As such, this text reveals the God-ordained and total task of man; the *total* task, both at the common sense level and the scientific level. And so, at the scientific level, this text is not only God's mandate to man to develop the special sciences, and not only the basis of philosophical anthropology, but it is also God's mandate to man to pursue the task of philosophy as such.

4. *The task of philosophy*

The task of philosophy, then, is indicated in God's mandate to His image man to subdue the earth and the sea and the air and all their inhabitants, to study the totality of all created reality. As the image of God, man was to image the divine Prophet, Priest, and King even in his subjection of the cosmos as God's vicegerent: as His deputy prophet, deputy priest, and deputy king or "viceroy." As a prophet man was to describe the cosmos and as a priest he was to

[11] Gen. 1:26.   [13] Cf. Hos. 6:7 marg.
[12] Gen. 1:28.   [14] Cf. Gen. 9:1-6; Ps. 8; Matt. 28:18-20; Heb. 2-4.

6

serve God in the cosmos; [15] whereas as a king, man was to rule over the cosmos to God's glory.[16]

Now this prophetic, priestly, and kingly task of man, even at the scientific and philosophical level, necessarily covers the human analysis of the universe of *natural* phenomena, as well as man's pursuit of all the *humanitarian* sciences too. Primordial man, the earthly lord of nature, created as the image of the Lord God of nature, was to analyze *natural* phenomena. Man was to dominate and therefore also to count and to measure the fowl and the fish and every living thing—a mathematical task; he was to proceed from Eden and to replenish or fill the earth—a spatial as well as a kinematical (or movemental) task; he was to subdue and to have dominion over the earth (a physical task), over the plants (a botanical task), and over the animals (a zoological task).[17] And man was also to react to his own natural feelings, such as his desire for a mate when he saw the animals pairing off together—a psychological task.[18]

But primordial man, the image of the Lord God of culture, was also to *cultivate* creation and himself as a part thereof. And this he would do in his pursuit of the *humanitarian* sciences, amongst other things. For man would pursue logic as, for example, he reflected on the differences between the various kinds of trees; [19] he would make history as he multiplied and filled the earth; [20] he would develop linguistics as he gave names to the animals, and he would expand his social life in his companionship with his wife.[21]

Furthermore, man would practice economics in his exploitation of gold and bdellium and the onyx stone;[22] he would develop the art of aesthetics as he dressed the garden of Eden and the discipline of law as he kept it safely from the illegal transgression of the devil.[23] And finally, we also

[15] Cf. Gen. 2:15-24.
[16] Gen. 1:26-28.
[17] Gen. 1:28-29.
[18] Gen. 2:18-25.
[19] Gen. 2:9.
[20] Gen. 1:28-29.
[21] Gen. 2:18-25.
[22] Gen. 2:12.
[23] Gen. 2:15.

7

see Adam's ethical task in his love of his wife.[24] In every respect, then, primordial man was a wise philosopher in his total-view of all created reality.

5. *Sin and philosophy*

However, the advent of sin and its consequence of God's punitive cosmic curse brought about a profound change in all this. Sin deformed the universe, distorted man's wisdom, and broke his total-view of all created reality, for even his understanding was darkened on account of his alienation from the life of God.[25] "Where is the wise?" it may now be inquired for by "worldly wisdom the world knew not God." [26] Hence, after the fall, "profane and vain babblings, and oppositions of science falsely so called" abound; [27] and we must now "beware lest any man spoil you through philosophy and vain deceit," [28] through the vain deceit which even (unregenerated) philosophy has now become as a result of the sin of the first human philosopher.

So, as the result of sin, critical elements are now found in philosophy and elsewhere. Although the Logos or God the Son and God the Holy Spirit continue to enlighten both external objects[29] and man's inner-mind[30]—thus explaining how even unbelievers are often capable of true if superficial insights into reality[31]—nevertheless the harmony of knowledge was now shattered. So that if man now seeks of his own accord to reconstruct such harmony, he necessarily absolutizes some or other aspect of creation (at the expense of others) into an "-ism" as the fulcrum for his epistemological synthesis.

However, the Christian philosopher, who recognizes his own sinful limitations, but who also recognizes the Logos or God the Son and God the Holy Spirit as the enlightening

[24] Gen. 2:18-25.
[25] Eph. 4:18.
[26] I Cor. 1:20-21.
[27] I Tim. 6:20.
[28] Col. 2:8.
[29] Col. 1:13-17 and Job 26:13.
[30] John 1:5-9 and Job 32:8.
[31] Prov. 20:27.

8

Principles in this sin-darkened universe, is in a much better position epistemologically than his non-Christian counterpart. Although the Christian philosopher's true insight into cosmic reality is right now restored only in principle— yet his insight into reality, albeit only in principle, is nevertheless truly restored.[32] The Christian's knowledge is not as unbroken as was the unfallen Adam's, for the Christian is still hampered by sin, whereas the unfallen Adam was not.[33] Yet the Christian's knowledge is greater in scope than was the unfallen Adam's and has progressed from Eden towards the knowledge which Adam would ultimately have attained, had he not sinned.[34] This is because God the Son, the Wisdom of God, incarnated Himself as the Second Adam. Through His shattered body, He substitutionarily restored the harmony of the shattered body of the cosmos, and thenceforth leads His elect descendants through His divine Spirit into all truth and into all true knowledge.[35]

Although God the Son mediated knowledge to man both before and after the fall, and finally through His own incarnation gave man the greatest insight into true knowledge, yet man's darkened mind continually misinterpreted the true knowledge which God revealed to him in nature, in history, in conscience, and in religion.[36] Moreover, man even misinterpreted the radical nature and cosmic scope of sin as well as God's remedy for sin—His own restorative incarnation.[37] To act as the primary permanent epistemological criterion for sinful fallen man, then, God inscripturated His dealings with man, culminating in the Word of God made Book about the Word of God made flesh.[38] The spectacles of Holy Scripture can now largely correct shortsighted fallen man's epistemological construction of the sin-blurred outer world. The non-Christian philosopher

[32] Col. 2:2.
[33] Rom. 5:14; 8:22-24.
[34] Gen. 3:22; Heb. 4:4-10.
[35] John 16:13.
[36] Ps. 19; Ps. 78; Rom. 2:15; Acts 17:23f.
[37] Col. 1:20; Eph. 1.

who rejects Holy Scripture, however, remains short-sighted and consequently operates epistemologically in a relative darkness.

6. *Pluriformity and philosophy*

Partly as a result of the development of the patent and latent variety of principles in God's creation, and partly as a result of the divisive power of sin, philosophy now underwent a *pluriform* development—particularly after the destruction of the tower of Babel.

In the divine destruction of the tower of Babel, we see God checking the unbridled spread of sin by confusing the tongues of the human race and dispersing men from one another by separating them into different nations.[39] Although the different nations would probably have come into being in any case as men would have left their parents and filled the earth even if sin had never taken place,[40] national and racial differences were certainly intensified (and, of course, very adversely affected) as a result of the fall and the subsequent Babelic dispersion. So, after the destruction of the tower of Babel, we see three main cultures developing in different parts of the world (the "Semitic," "Hamitic," and "Japhethitic" cultures).[41]

Each of these three differently developing main cultures necessarily had its own basic kind of philosophy. In "Semitic" philosophy we see man's one true total-view of all created reality as it developed in the generations of Abraham, the Israelites, and the early Christian Church—the only true philosophy of trinicentrism. In "Hamitic" philosophy, however, we see the development of such false Eastern systems of thought as Melanesian animism, African Negro polytheism, and Hinduistic pantheism; whereas in "Japhethitic" philosophy we detect the unfolding of both Indo-

[38] John 17:17.   [40] Gen. 1:28 and 2:24.
[39] Gen. 11.   [41] Gen. 9:18 and 10:32.

10

Aryan Vedism as well as such false Western systems of thought as pre-Socratic and post-Marxian materialism, Platonic idealism, American pragmatism, and Western European existentialism.

Then there are also syncretistic or "hybrid" philosophies such as Hamitico-Semitic deism as in Muhammadanism, Japhethitico-Semitic supranaturalism as in Romanism and possibly Japhethitico-Hamitic immanentism as in Confucianism. But in our opinion, it is the task of Western man to avoid such syncretistic philosophies, and to see to it that Japheth humbly dwells in the philosophical tents of Shem (as in Bible-believing Protestantism) instead of adapting and absorbing Shem's tents into his own enlarged domains (as in Western humanism) or, worse still, allowing Japheth to become the servant of Ham and Canaan (as in the current cosmopolitan orientalization of the West, e.g., in the United Nations Organization).[42] For Western man (and, indeed, man everywhere) can only fulfill his God-given philosophical task if he is first and foremost redeemed in the tents of Shem.

7. Redemption of philosophy

This brings us to the philosophical importance of the Master Builder of the tents of Shem Who Himself came down to earth to dwell therein—the Redeemer or Re-Creator, Jesus Christ.[43]

When man unphilosophically ceased to love true wisdom and became unwise as a result of the fall and man's accompanying loss of his total-view of reality, God the Son, the Logos or Word of God, immediately arrested and controlled the developing process of human degeneration in the protevangelium or the prophecy of the coming Seed of the woman.[44] In this and subsequent promises, God the Son

42 Cf. Gen. 9:27; 10:6-10; 11:1-8; Rev. 18:1f.   44 Gen. 3:15.
43 Heb. 3:1-6.

11

undertook to incarnate Himself and bruise the head of that master sophist and pseudo-philosopher, Satan.[45] Hence, throughout the Old Testament, we see God instructing His separated people in the true wisdom of God, in true philosophy, cf. the Biblical books of Job, Proverbs, and Ecclesiastes.

Then, in the fullness of time, God the Son showed the true wisdom of God and the true wisdom of man in His own human body during His incarnation. During His earthly life, He philosophized about the lilies of the field and the fowls of the air and the beasts of the field and the fishes of the sea (cf. the cultural mandate!)[46] with far greater wisdom then even Solomon did;[47] and Solomon's philosophic wisdom had excelled that of all the children of the east.[48] And then Christ the Second Adam[49] died for the re-establishment of cosmic harmony and the restoration of elect mankind's total-view of all created reality; died on that second tree of life known as the cross of Calvary, where the horizontal beam crossed the vertical, where the human met the divine, where the immanent met the transcendent—and all by virtue of the infinite wisdom and matchless merits of the Supreme Philosopher crucified thereon, "Christ Jesus, the Power of God and the Wisdom of God,"[50] Christ Jesus, our great Prophet, Priest, and King![51]

8. *Renewal of philosophy*

After elect man and his philosophy were redeemed or re-created on Calvary, they were both renewed and energized on the day of Pentecost not many days thereafter.

Pentecost indeed principially cancelled the disruptive ef-

[45] Cf. Gen. 9:1-6; Ps. 8; Heb. 2.
[46] Gen. 1:28.
[47] Matt. 6:26f; 7:6f; 12:42 and 13:47f.
[48] II Ki. 4:29-34.
[49] I Cor. 15:22,45-49; cf. Gen. 1:26-28 and Heb. 2.
[50] I Cor. 1:24,30.
[51] John 6:14; Heb. 6:20; Rev. 19:16.

12

fects which the destruction of the tower of Babel had brought down on man and his philosophy, but it did not cancel the principle of pluriformity as such. To the contrary, at Pentecost "every nation under heaven" heard in their *own* "tongues the wonderful works of God." [52] And in the renewing work of the outpoured Spirit of God, in the comprehensive cosmic signs of wind and fire and smoke and darkness and rain and blood,[53] we are presented with a philosophical total-view of the recreation of created reality, namely the principial renewal of the metaphysical universe and of elect men as parts of the universe and its prophets, priests, and kings.[54]

Thenceforth the Creator Spirit would not destroy His pluriform creation and renewed man as the crown thereof, but rather sanctify each regenerated separate personal and national insight into created and recreated reality. The national philosophical insights of the Athenians[55] and of the Cretians,[56] for example, are preserved and sanctified, as too are the different personalities of the Apostles Peter and Paul and John. The Spirit of the Lord cleanses not only our hearts and our bodies, but our intellects too, for He is "the Spirit of wisdom and understanding, the Spirit of counsel and might, the Spirit of knowledge and of the fear of the Lord"; and when "the Spirit of the Lord shall rest upon him," upon him who is sanctified by the Spirit (that is, primarily the Lord Jesus, but, by implication, also His sanctified children who possess the same Spirit, albeit in lesser measure), the Spirit "shall make him of quick understanding in the fear of the Lord." [57] Hence the Spirit-filled Christian philosopher too should be equipped with God-given wisdom, understanding, counsel, knowledge, and (above all) the fear of the Lord—even in (or rather, especially in) his philosophy!

[52] Acts 2:5,11.
[53] Acts 2:1-20.
[54] I Pet. 2:9-10; Rev. 1:3,6.
[55] Acts 17:23,28.
[56] Tit. 1:12-13.
[57] Isa. 11:2-3.

13

9. *Philosophy today*

This necessarily brings us to a consideration of the task of the redeemed and Spirit-renewed philosopher in the world today.

In our modern world, man is shaken to his very foundations by unbelief, uncertainty, and fear. Today very many doubt the existence of Creative Reality, of God—especially the communists, many socialists, and all the other varieties of atheists. Many people also doubt the very existence even of created reality (as also of reality as such, quite apart from its createdness or not). This denial of the objective existence of the universe is encountered particularly among the subjective existentialists and all kinds of functionalists, phenomenalists, and extreme idealists. Others again doubt the possibility of the true knowledge of reality and of fixed values, such as the agnostics and the skeptics. And yet others are tortured by a consuming pessimism—the nihilists.

In these critical days, the true Christian philosopher is called by God to proclaim that all created reality points to the eternal Creative Reality, points to the fact that "the Lord liveth!" [58] He is also called to proclaim the objective existence of all created reality, to proclaim that "God is in the heaven, and thou upon the earth"; [59] and to proclaim the certainty of the Christian's correctly acquired knowledge, incomplete though it must of necessity be. For although "we know in part," yet nevertheless "we know"! "When I was a child . . . I understood as a child," yet even then I nevertheless understood. And "when I became a man, I put away childish things," and now I know as an adult, now I understand and know still better. And one day "shall I know even as also I am known." [60]

As much as is humanly possible the imperfect yet regenerated Christian philosopher is to be an intellectual

[58] Ps. 18:46.   [59] Eccl. 5:2.   [60] I Cor. 13:9-12.

14

prophet, priest, and king—sanctified unto the service of the Creator and Recreator of the whole of created and recreated reality.

Perhaps most important of all, the true Christian philosopher is also called by God to proclaim an anti-nihilistic cosmic optimism—an optimism amidst and in spite of the discouraging chaos of earth's last days, an optimism rooted in the Eternal and in His promises for the future of the cosmos. "For I reckon that the sufferings of this present time are not worthy to be compared with the glory which shall be revealed in us. For the earnest expectation of the creature waiteth for the manifestation of the sons of God. For the creature was made subject to vanity, not willingly, but by reason of Him Who hath subjected the same in hope. Because the creature itself also shall be delivered from the bondage of corruption into the glorious liberty of the children of God. For we know that the whole creation groaneth and travaileth in pain together until now. And not only they, but ourselves also which have the first-fruits of the Spirit, even we ourselves groan within ourselves, waiting for the adoption, to wit, the redemption of our body. For we are saved by hope." [61]

10. *Philosophy and the future*

We are saved by hope. And this thought brings us to another consideration, namely the ultimate goal of philosophy.

"Where is the promise of His coming?" taunt the "last day's scoffers," the anti-Christian philosophers, peripatetically "walking after their lusts. . . . For this they willingly are ignorant of, that . . . the day of the Lord will come, like a thief in the night, in the which the heavens shall pass away with a great noise, and the elements shall melt with fervent heat, the earth also and the works that are therein shall be burned up, . . . all these things shall be dissolved,

[61] Rom. 8:18-24.

. . . the heavens being on fire. . . . Nevertheless we [including the Christian philosophers amongst us!] look for new heavens and a new earth, wherein righteousness dwelleth" [62] —a new creation, the recreation of the whole of created reality.

Now this new creation will include and even deepen the present totality of all created reality. For the new creation and the city of the new Jerusalem will continue to exist in the cosmic dimension of time—behold the *monthly* yield of the fruit of the tree of life.[63]

The city will have a numerical aspect—behold its twelve gates and angels and foundations; [64] a spatial aspect—behold its foursquare dimensions of twelve thousand furlongs each; [65] a kinematic aspect—behold the movement of the kings of the earth into it;[66] a physical aspect—behold its precious stones and pearls and gold; [67] a botanical aspect— behold the fruit and the healing leaves of the tree of life; [68] and a psychical aspect—behold the wolf and the lamb feeding together, and the joyous feelings of all of the city's inhabitants.[69]

Yet not only will nature be exalted, but man and his culture too. There will be a glorification: of logic, even in the analytical distinctions between the varieties of precious stones in the new Jerusalem; [70] of history, even in the glory and honor of the nations there; [71] of linguistics, even in the song of the redeemed, the song of Moses and the Lamb; [72] of sociology, even in the fact that saved kings will be the servants of God; [73] of economics, for God's elect shall long enjoy the work of their hands, and they shall build houses, and they shall plant vineyards; [74] of aesthetics, for eye hath not seen nor ear heard the things which God hath prepared

[62] II Pet. 3:3f.
[63] Rev. 22:2.
[64] Rev. 21:12-14.
[65] Rev. 21:6.
[66] Rev. 21:24.
[67] Rev. 21:18-21.
[68] Rev. 22:2.
[69] Isa. 65:25; Rev. 21:3-7.
[70] Rev. 21:18f.
[71] Rev. 21:24.
[72] Rev. 15:3.
[73] Rev. 21:24; 22:3.
[74] Isa. 65:21-22.

for them that love Him; [75] of law, for God's elect shall reign with Christ and sit every man under his (own) vine and under his (own) fig tree; [76] and of ethics, in the life of the whole family of God, for love or charity never faileth.[77]

And faith? Faith is the substance of things hoped for, the evidence of things not seen.[78] Now we walk by faith, not by sight.[79] Now we see through a glass darkly, but on the new earth we shall see face to face.[80] There we shall have no temple, for the Lord God Almighty and the Lamb are the temple of it, and we shall see His face.[81] And under Him, we ourselves shall be prophets, priests, and kings over the renewed cosmos unto all eternity.[82]

And the whole totality of this recreated reality will be sustained forever by the Triune Lord God Almighty, in Whom it will live and move and have its very being; [83] for the city will have no need of the sun or the moon to shine in it, for the glory of God will lighten it, "and the Lamb is the light thereof." [84]

Now all this will come about after the Supreme Philosopher Jesus Christ, the Wisdom of God, confounds the worldly wisdom of scoffing worldly philosophers by returning to this earth with power and great glory on the clouds of the heavens. In great wisdom He will unify the sin-riven cosmos and His sin-stricken children, and reward them all—including the Christian philosophers among them—according to their works[85]—according to their philosophical and all their other works. The present life of the Christian philosopher is thus inspired by his future destiny, the glorious goal towards which both he and the entire cosmos are heading, namely the new heaven and the new earth as the renewal of all created reality; which, of course, includes

[75] I Cor. 2:9.
[76] Rev. 22:5; Mic. 4:4.
[77] Eph. 3:14-15; I Cor. 13:8.
[78] Heb. 11:1.
[79] II Cor. 5:7.
[80] Cf. I Cor. 13:12.

[81] Rev. 21:22; 22:4.
[82] Rev. 21:24 - 22:7.
[83] Acts 17:28.
[84] Rev. 21:23.
[85] Rev. 14:13; 20:13.

17

even his own true human insight into the totality of God's created and recreated reality, the true philosophical insights of "trinicentrism." Even his future life and his future works will be built upon the foundation of his true insights achieved in this present life. And so true philosophy, true human wisdom concerning the total created reality, is therefore of importance for both time and eternity.

* * *

11. *Aim of this subject*

On the basis of the Biblical principles enunciated in the above pages, the Christian philosopher must next proceed to the colossal task of examining the totality of God's creation as revealed in all of His works outside of His Word —as revealed in nature as well as in culture. This may be done in various ways—for example, in an analytical manner, as in the subject known as "Systematic Philosophy"; or in a more or less chronological account of the views presented by great philosophers, as in the subject known as "History of Philosophy," the subject here under discussion.

The aim of this subject known as "History of Philosophy," then, is to give a historical and descriptive account of the major influential thinkers down through world history— from the Supreme Triune Philosopher in the counsels of eternity before the creation of the universe, right down to the ever-increasing apostasy of the present day.

12. *Value of this subject*

This is a presentation of the chief thinkers in each period of the world's cultures, whose insights reflect (and indeed also help mold) the views of their times. By studying the views of leading thinkers in the history of philosophy, we may:

(a) see their mistakes and learn where not to look for solutions to the problems of philosophy;

(b) see the elements of truth in their proposed solutions, and thus expand our own understanding of the truth;

(c) obtain insight into the growth and development of the world's cultures;

(d) achieve a better understanding of our own times, its problems and their causes as rooted in past history.

Thus we may discover the factors which have contributed to make our world the way it is, and which will continue to help mold the world of tomorrow. Whether we will like that world or not, we will probably still have to live in it—and to witness to the Lordship of Christ in it.

Equipped with this knowledge, our Christianity should then become more relevant to the times in which we live, and we should then so much the better be able to testify clearly and effectively to modern man concerning the eternal claims of the Triune God.

13. *Limitations of this subject*

Two considerations in particular which limit the presentation of this subject are:

(a) the introductory, non-comprehensive and necessarily selective nature of the material to be discussed; and

(b) the available sources, which are limited to the *writings* of philosophers. There are probably no extant writings anywhere from before the great flood,[86] nor from before about 3000 B.C., from which time the oldest yet discovered specimens of writing date, nor even since then amongst illiterate primitive peoples (who may nevertheless have had great though now unknown philosophers in their midst).

14. *Presuppositions of this subject*

A Christian Approach to the history of philosophy presupposes:

[86] Gen. 6-8.

19

(a) that the Bible is the infallible Word of God and contains reliable historical and philosophical information;

(b) that available non-Biblical documents of a philosophical nature are more or less historically accurate; and

(c) that one has already acquired an adequate knowledge of philosophical terminology and problems, as generally presented in the subject known as "Introduction to Philosophy."

15. *Methods of this subject*

The subject has been divided into a number of subsequent chapters, each dealing with a historical period in the largely chronological development of philosophy (see section 20, below).

Usually, for each successive period of philosophical development under discussion:

A. A short introduction is given about the period and its main philosophical problems.

B. Accounts are then given of the major influential philosophers of each period—more or less according to their locality of operation, and then more or less in the chronological order of their appearance.

C. The views of each philosopher discussed are then set out under the various philosophical disciplines, viz.: ontology or the doctrine of being (subdivided into theontology, the doctrine of the being of God, and existontology, the doctrine of the being of all that is not God), cosmogony or the doctrine of the origin of the cosmos, cosmology or the doctrine of the structure of the cosmos, anthropology or the doctrine of man, federology or the doctrine of the relationship between God and man, hamartiology or the doctrine of sin, epistemology or the doctrine of knowledge, axiology or the doctrine of values, soteriology or the doctrine of redemptive re-creation, and eschatology or the doctrine of the end of all things. Where necessary, remarks will also be made about a thinker's logic, politics, social views, etc.

D. Often the philosopher under discussion will be dealt with under only some of these categories, and not under all of them. In such cases, this will be because (i) the philosopher concerned did not express himself on these topics; or (ii) the philosopher's views were similar to those of his contemporaries, previously discussed.

16. *Scope of this subject*

Although philosophy is the *human* science systematizing creation in its totality, so that the whole of creation must here be studied by man, it must also be remembered that creation could be studied even before the creation of the first man—viz., studied by God and the angels.

Accordingly, for completeness' sake, this subject will first give a short initial survey of the understanding of the totality of creation in the mind of God, the good angels, and the fallen angels—to the extent that these matters have been revealed to us. Only after that will we proceed to consider the human philosophy of the first man and all his human philosophical successors right down to the present time—or at least the main ones. Our initial survey of the philosophy of God and the angels, however, will even be helpful in understanding Adam's philosophy—for Adam, the first human philosopher, is the image of God the Supreme Philosopher and was deceived by the Satanic (philo)-soph*ist*, a fallen angel.

17. *Perspective of this subject*

The subject is here presented from a radically and Biblically Christian perspective. No apology is offered for this, for this perspective is the *only* true and objective and correct one. However, this presentation not only deals with

Christian thinkers. It deals with *all* leading thinkers, both Christian and non-Christian—but it deals with them all only from the correct point of view, the Christian viewpoint. Accordingly, this presentation does not seek to give an introduction to the history of Christian philosophy, but it seeks to give a Christian introduction to the whole of the "History of Philosophy."

18. *Contrast between true and false philosophy*

Throughout this presentation, the contrast between true philosophy and false philosophy should be kept in mind, for it should be remembered that the Bible encourages true philosophy[87] but condemns all philosophy which is not according to Christ.[88]

Philosophers may perhaps be classified into four groups, according as to whether they are:

(a) *true philosophers*, i.e., thinkers whose views are more or less in accordance with the Biblical viewpoint;

(b) *radically false philosophers*, whose views are totally at variance with the teachings of the Bible;

(c) *synthesis philosophers*, who attempt to combine the true Biblical viewpoint with one or more false viewpoints; and

(d) *enlightened heathen philosophers*, who received very much common grace in spite of their unregenerated condition.

A. The history of true philosophy—bearing in mind human imperfections — would run more or less as follows, presenting the thinkers in the approximately chronological order of their appearance: GOD, the good angels, Adam (before the fall and after his redemption therefrom), Noah, Job, Abraham, Joseph, Moses, David, Solomon, Isaiah, Jeremiah, Daniel, JESUS CHRIST AND HIS HOLY SPIRIT, Paul, John, Justin Martyr, Irenaeus, Athanasius, Augustine,

[87] Eccl. 1:13; 3:11.   [88] Col. 2:8; I Tim. 6:20.

22

Isidore, Anselm, Calvin, Ursinus, Alsted, Voetius, Cotton Mather, Jonathan Edwards, Sr.; and various relatively modern philosophers, such as the Dutchmen Groen van Prinsterer, Steketee, Kuyper, Woltjer, Bavinck, Hepp, Dooyeweerd, Vollenhoven, Kohnstamm, etc., the South Africans Stoker, Venter, Potgieter, Strauss, Kock, Brümmer, etc., and the Americans Van Til, Runner, Rushdoony, Clark, etc.

B. The history of radically false philosophy, on the other hand, is far more extensive than is the history of true philosophy, and is almost unsurveyable. However, by confining our attention only to the main thinkers, it would include names like the following: Satan, Cain, Nimrod; various Egyptian and Babylonian manuscripts; Chinese thinkers like Confucius, Mencius, Lao-tse, and Lu-wang; Zoroaster the Persian; Indian philosophers like Charvak, Vardhamana, Buddha, Nagarjuna, and Shankara; thinkers of Ancient Greece such as Thales, Anaximander, Anaximenes, Heraclitos, Empedocles, Democritus, Protagoras, Gorgias, Diogenes, Zeno the Stoic, and Epicurus; Gnostics like Valentine and Plotinus; Heathen anti-Christians like Lucian, Celsus, and Porphyry; apostates from Christianity like Marcion, Tatian, and Pelagius; Moslem thinkers like Muhammad, Avicenna, and Averroës; Jewish philosophers such as Saadia, Gabirol, Maimonides, and Spinoza; Mediaeval thinkers like Eriugena, Ockham, and Duns Scotus; Mystics like Eckhart, Tauler, and Boehme; and a whole assortment of various kinds of Post-Renaissance humanists such as Bacon, Descartes, Hobbes, Locke, Hume, Kant, Fichte, Wolf, De Lamettrie, Diderot, Voltaire, Rousseau, Hegel, Schelling, Moleschott, Feuerbach, Marx, Engels, Lenin, Comte, Wundt, Nietzsche, Husserl, Windelband, James, Dewey, Bergson, Gandhi, Radhakrishnan, Bultmann, Tillich, Carnap, Ayer, Heidegger, and Sartre.

C. Then there are the protagonists of synthesis philosophy, who combine truth and falsehood, such as the Romanistic philosophers who seek to combine the Bible with Aristotle. A lot of what is taught here is relatively true, but even such truth has a good deal of injurious falsehood mixed up with it. Examples are: Philo, Clemens Alexandrinus, Origen, Boëthius, Albert Magnus, Thomas Aquinas, Kierkegaard, Tolstoy, Berdyaev, Blondel, Marcel, Smuts, Toynbee, Teilhard du Chardin, Buber, and Barth.

D. Finally, there are several enlightened heathen philosophers, who, in spite of their principial errors, nevertheless possessed a great amount of truth too on account of God's common revelation to and common grace bestowed upon them. Among such are Socrates, Plato, Aristotle, Cicero, Seneca, and Plutarch of Chaeronea.

As the above four classifications are often fluid and overlap one another, it will be best rather to treat the history of philosophy basically in accordance with the land of origin and time of appearance of the philosopher concerned.

19. The various religious basic motives

All human life is religious.[89] Religion is a necessary and unavoidable bond between every man and his true or pretended Origin, which determines his whole life. Consequently, even all philosophical life and thought is religiously determined, for the religion of a man's heart also determines the philosophy of his mind.[90] The question is therefore not *whether* a man's philosophy is religiously determined, but *which* religion determines a man's philosophy—true religion or false religion.

Now each kind of religion is governed by a certain religious basic motive, which influences the entire life and world view and the philosophy of the person embracing that religion. True religion (and therefore also *True Philosophy*, i.e., Hebrew philosophy before Christ's incarnation and

[89] Cf. Acts 17:4,22.
[90] Cf. Ps. 36:10; Prov. 4:23; Matt. 15:18f.

Christian philosophy thereafter) is governed by the triune *creation-fall-recreation* religious basic motive (re-creation= redemption *and* consummation)[91] and the dialectical tension between creation and sin is completely dissolved by God's radical recreation, whereby He completely purges His creation from sin and perfects that creation—in principle, at least. False religion (and therefore also false philosophy), however, is radically governed by sin; but this sin motive manifests itself differently in different kinds of false philosophy.

Ancient Eastern philosophy, for example, is governed by the sinful motives of *"too-this-worldliness"* and *"too-other-worldliness"* (*Ueberdiesseitigkeit* and *Ueberjenseitigkeit*), and contains an unresolved dialectical tension whereby first the one and then the other religious basic motive dominates such philosophical development: largely *jenseitige* or other-worldly Egyptian philosophy fluctuates between too-this-worldly social ethics and too-other-worldly and anti-social post-mortal speculation; largely other-worldly Indian philosophy fluctuates between too-other-worldly Brahman or Nirvana and an occasional too-this-worldly reaction thereagainst as in Charvak and Vivekananda; and largely this-worldly Chinese philosophy fluctuates between a similar too-this-worldly emphasis (as in Confucius, Mo-ti, and Mencius) and a too-other-worldly trend (as in Chuang-chou, Lao-tse, and Lu-wang).

Ancient Greek philosophy, however, is dominated by the dialectical tension between the religious basic motives of *form and matter*, between the Mycenaean matter motive of the older nature-gods on the one hand and the Olympian form motive of the newer culture-gods on the other. This leads to the alternation between the philosophical primacy of the matter motive (as in Thales, Democritus, Protagoras,

[91] Cf. Col. 1:20; Eph. 1:10,20-23.

etc.) and the philosophical primacy of the form motive (as in Pythagoras, Parmenides, Plato, etc.).

Roman-Catholic or *scholastic philosophy* attempted to combine the True Philosophy (of Eden, the Old Testament Israelites, and the New Testament Church) with Ancient Greek philosophy—and especially with Aristotle. Consequently, a new dialectical tension was introduced as a result of this attempted synthesis between the true creation-fall-recreation motive on the one hand and the false form-matter motive on the other.

The false form-matter motive was reduced to *"nature,"* and the true creation-fall-recreation motive was telescoped into *"supra-nature"* or *"grace"*— and these two thus reduced motives were then combined into the scholastic *"nature-grace"* religious basic motive developed by Thomas Aquinas in particular. (As if grace could be *limited* to the *"supra-natural"* [which was also *created* and *sustained* by grace!] And as if "nature" could exist for a moment without God's grace! And as if grace—essential for both the "natural" and the "supranatural"—could ever be anything other than supra-supranatural or divine, and could ever be anything but "natural" or rather "not-anti-natural" in respect of the entirety of God's creation, in respect of things both material *and* spiritual!)

Now this scholastic hierarchical superiority of the "supra-natural" above the "natural" led to the typically Romanistic elevation of the ("supranatural"?) clergy above the ("natural") laity, the elevation of the ("supranatural"?) "religious" monks above the ("natural") "secular" parish priests, the elevation of "sacred" or religious (Church) work above the "secular" work of subjecting the earth and the sea and the sky to God's glory, and the elevation of *"soul*-winning" as opposed to winning the soul, body, mind, *and* culture of man for the Kingdom of Christ.

The *humanistic philosophy* of the Renaissance agreed

with the "nature-grace" dichotomy of the scholastics—Rome was quite right that the supranatural realm of grace was radically different from the realm of nature, they argued. Let Rome then have her "sacred" field to her heart's content; the humanists would have the "secular" field and develop it to their heart's content—develop it independently of "sacred" things: a philosophy without God! And nature (as opposed to the "supranatural") and nature's sciences, the "natural" sciences, would be used to do this.

But the more the natural sciences (mathematics through psychology) were developed, the more were the humanitarian sciences (logic through ethics) neglected. When "nature" thrived, then "culture" died! So that the more the natural sciences were developed, the more was human freedom threatened precisely by such development and by the concomitant neglect of pursuing the humanitarian sciences.

This led some thinkers to react by asserting the superiority of man and his freedom over against nature and her regularity and determinism.

Yet the problem still remained as to the relationship between science and freedom. So once again, a dialectical tension resulted. Some philosophers stressed the primacy of the science motive (e.g., Hobbes, De Lamettrie, and Engels), others stressed the primacy of human freedom (Montaigne, Rousseau, Marx, and Sartre), and yet others (unsuccessfully!) tried to stress both by combining them into the humanistic *freedom-science* religious basic motive (e.g., Kant, Dilthey, Lenin, etc.).

Amidst all this confusion, *True Philosophy* rose again from the dead, and re-affirmed the triune *creation-fall-recreation* religious basic motive of the Triune God and His children—while nevertheless gladly acknowledging the *elements* of truth which God by His common grace had preserved even in the various false philosophies. And so True Philosophy, after first thoroughly subjecting all the false philosophies to a radically Biblical critique, incorporates into its own basic scheme of creation-fall-recreation the elements of truth in (i) the "too-this-worldly" - "too-other-worldly" motive of ancient Eastern philosophy, (ii) the form-matter motive of ancient Greek philosophy, (iii) the nature-grace motive of scholastic philosophy, and (iv) the freedom-science motive of humanistic philosophy. In this way, True Philosophy combines the fruits of special grace and common grace without falling into Romanistic syncretism on the one hand or into Pietistic anti-intellectualism on the other.

21. *Chapter divisions*

This presentation rather automatically falls into a number of more or less successive periods of historical thought. Accordingly, the chapter divisions to be adhered to are as follows:

Chapter I: *Prolegomena to the History of Philosophy* (with which we are at this moment engaged)

Chapter II: *Pre-Babelic Philosophy*—from Creation to the Origin of the Nations (i.e., down to about 3000 B.C.)

Chapter III: *Ancient Eastern Philosophy*—the Hegemony of the Orient (from about 3000 B.C. onwards)

Chapter IV: *Ancient Greek Philosophy*—the Hegemony of Hellas (from about 800 B.C. onwards)

Chapter V: *Early Christian Philosophy*—The Thinkers of the Ancient Church (from 4 B.C. – A.D. 500)

Chapter VI: *Medieval Western Philosophy*—Stagnation and Synthesis (from A.D. 500 – 1300)

Chapter VII: *Western Philosophy in Decline*—the Apostasy of Humanism (from 1300 – the present day)

Chapter VIII: *The Rebirth of True Philosophy*—the Continuing Reformation (from 1300 – the present day)

In the light of the above scheme, we now present a more detailed account of a Christian introduction to the history of philosophy.

Chapter II

PRE-BABELIC PHILOSOPHY

From Creation to the Origin of the Nations

1. *Survey*

This second chapter of our presentation deals with the beginning of the history of philosophy in the remote past prior to the development of all the nations of humanity, and will successively present the philosophies of God, the good angels, the fallen angels, Adam, Cain, Noah, Shem, Ham, Japheth, and Nimrod.

2. *God*[1]

The Triune God is not only unique in that He alone thoroughly and eternally understands the totality of Himself and of His own uncreated deity (*theologia archetypa*), but He is also unique in that He is the only Thinker Who equally thoroughly and eternally understands the totality of His universe and understood it even before He created it (*philosophia archetypa*). As such, God is the Supreme Philosopher; [2] and although there once was a "time" when the creation, the object of study of the science of philosophy, did not actually exist (viz., before creation) [3] nevertheless, even then, in that timeless eternity, the (as then unactualized) creation was clearly understood in the unchanging mind of

[1] First read again chapter I, secs. 2 and 3.
[2] Cf. I Tim. 1:17; Jude 25.
[3] Gen. 1:1; Ps. 90:1f.

the Eternal Triune God—understood by Him right down to its smallest detail.

In the act of creation, it was not God that changed, but it was the creation itself which was changed from potentiality to actuality[1]—namely when the potential yet eternally preplanned creation was actualized, when it was brought forth out of the eternal mind of God and given an objective existence over against God—although nevertheless eternally and continually dependent upon God.

So then, God, the Supreme Philosopher, eternally and perfectly knows the whole of His creation. His understanding of all creation has never changed, and never will; it does not need to, for it is perfect.

This is perhaps an appropriate point at which to say something about theontology and existontology. By "theontology" is meant the philosophical science or knowledge of the Divine and Independent Being Who *never becomes* or changes and Who therefore always unchangeably *is*—the Ground of the universe, on Whom all created being depends. And by "existontology" is meant the philosophical science or knowledge of dependent being, of that which becomes and changes, of the existence of the whole creation.

Theontologically, God as the Supreme Philosopher unchangeably recognizes His Triune Self as the Ground and necessary Back-Ground of all created being. God the Father is "the Father of lights, with Whom is no variableness, neither shadow of turning"; [5] God the Son shared the Father's glory before the world was; [6] and God the Holy Spirit searcheth all things, yea, even the depths of God.[7] The Triune God is neither form nor matter, existence nor becoming. He just *is*[8]—and He *alone* is, for all else merely exists or "ex-sists" or resides in and from *Him*. He is, and He

[1] Gen. 1:1; Ps. 33:6-9; Rom. 4:17; Heb. 11:3.
[5] Jas. 1:17.　　　[7] I Cor. 2:10.
[6] John 17:5.　　　[8] Ex. 3:14.

31

is eternally and actively energetic, both in His blessed Triune Self-love as well as in His eternal potential and actual counsel for His universe, grounded as it is in Himself. And through the Second Person of the Trinity, the divine *Log*os, the entire universe is *"log*-ically" articulated—(exist)onto-*log*-ically, cosmo-*log*-ically, anthropo-*log*-ically and federo-*log*-ically, etc., as described below.

Existontologically, God perfectly understands the tensionless ontic dual*ity* (which is not a dual*ism*!) between Himself as the sole Creative Being on the one hand and the objectively dependent created being (or "ex-sistence") of everything else on the other. And He also perfectly understands the further non-dualistic ontic duality between the material and spiritual elements of all created being itself.

Ontologically, the Triune God thus entirely comprehends all the created tri-unities of the universe—such as in time (past, present, and future), space (length, breadth, and height), physics (matter, energy, result), logic (thought, word, meaning), the so-called "normative sciences" (the good—ethics, the true—logic, and the beautiful—aesthetics), beauty (in the artist's mind, in the work of art, in the eye of the beholder), and music (cf. the triadic chord), etc. —as well as all the other humanly uncomprehended or incomprehensible mysteries which reflect His perfect Self.

Cosmogonically, the Triune God Elohim created the universe from nothing: He created time as the first creature and as "the beginning" of creation; and then, in time, He created the heavens and the earth and all their hosts of angels[9]—His universe, which, by His Providence, He then continued and still continues to maintain. God the Father spoke His creative Word God the Son, and God the Holy Spirit moved over the face of the deep.[10] Then, in six subsequent divine days of formation, the Triune God changed

[9] Gen. 1:1; 2:1; Job 38:4-7.
[10] Gen. 1:1-3; Ps. 33:6-9; II Cor. 2:10; Col. 1:13-17.

the unformed and unadorned chaos into the finished and adorned cosmos—He progressively fashioned that part of the already created universe known as the *earth*, and progressively enacted and sustained its cosmic laws of time, number, space, movement, matter, life, animality, and humanity—and then made the subjects of all these laws.[11]

Cosmologically, God's cosmos is now structured into functional (or "abstract"), material (or mineral), biotical (or botanical), psychical (or zoological), and anthropological (or human) kingdoms, which are all subjected to the divinely ordained cosmic laws, in terms of which laws each kingdom, both collectively and individually, analogically reflects the entire universe (man presupposes animals, plants, rain, etc.[12]).

Anthropologically, God the Supreme Philosopher created His image, the first human philosopher, and called him "man" or "Adam." [13] God first created this one human person, the historical Adam, His own image, in the tensionless *uniduality* of body and soul (which is not a dualism!).[14] Then God distinguished man into the further and subsequent tensionless uniduality of man and woman, the historical Adam and Eve.[15]

Federologically, the Lord created man to execute the covenant of works to His glory, which covenant God made with Adam and all his descendants.[16] God created man male and female, Adam and Eve, created them so that they should both themselves as well as through their descendants keep the moral law and also philosophize about and subject the totality of all created terrestrial bodies to God's glory, which no single man, nor single man and woman like Adam and Eve, but only all mankind, their descendants, can do.[17]

[11] See chapter I, sec. 3, above.
[12] Cf. Ps. 104.
[13] Gen. 5:1-3.
[14] Cf. Gen. 2:7!
[15] Gen. 1:26-28; 2:18-25; I Cor. 11:7-12; I Tim. 2:8-15.
[16] Gen. 1:26-28; 2:15f; Hos. 6:7 marg.; Rom. 5:12f.
[17] Gen. 1:26-28.

To this end, God created man as the image of God: as a *mikrotheos* (or "small god") as well as a *mikrokosmos* (or "small universe"); and He created man as lord and viceroy of the universe. Whenever man touches nature, it becomes culture (e.g., when man touches nature's field or agri-nature, it becomes man's field or agri-culture). Out of the *chaos* or form-less void of creation,[18] God proceeded to form the *kosmos* or orderly world, form it for man His image, so that man would take that *kosmos* and "cosmify" or adorn or cultivate it still further, by way of his obedience to the covenant of works as expressed in the cultural mandate[19] and as implied in his *positive* obedience to *inter alia* especially the fourth, sixth, seventh, and eighth commandments of the decalogue divinely stamped into his supralapsarian heart.[20]

First there was a covenant of works in eternity between the different Persons of the Trinity.[21] Then the Triune God proceeded to execute that covenant of works, each divine Person doing His own share of the work. The Father created, the Son illuminated and spoke, and the Spirit moved over the face of the deep.[22] Then the Triune God progressively formed: light, air, sea, dry land, plants, earthly time, sea creatures, air creatures, and land creatures,[23] so that man, created immediately thereafter and created in God's image, could immediately set about subjecting the previously created light, air, sea, dry land, plants, earthly time, sea creatures, air creatures, and land creatures to God's glory.[24] And so, after and on the basis of the first covenant of works in eternity between the different Persons

[18] Gen. 1:2.
[19] Gen. 1:26-28.
[20] Cf. Ex. 20:8-15; Eccl. 7:29; Rom. 2:14f; Westminster Confession IV:2, VI:2-4, VII:2; Westminster Larger Catechism, Q. 17-20, 91-151.
[21] Cf. Ps. 111:2-9; Zech. 6:12-13; John 17:1-5,24; Acts 15:18; I Cor. 2:9-11; Heb. 9:14; 13:20.
[22] Gen. 1:1-3.
[23] Gen. 1:3-25.
[24] Gen. 1:26:28.

of the Triune God to "cultivate" the world, God made a second covenant of works in time between Himself and His image man (that is, Adam and all his descendants), whereby He required and still requires man to "cultivate" the world further by virtue of *all* mankind's obligation to (try to) keep the covenant,[25] each person according to his own special gifts.[26]

To this end, God then proceeded to structure and unfold man (a *mikrokosmos* or small universe) into individual, marital, family, kinship, educational, social, political, national, international, religious, and other societal spheres— and the Triune God did all this by His original revelation to man through His Word and Spirit,[27] by His common revelation and common grace through His Word and Spirit,[28] and, after the fall, also by His special revelation and His special grace through His Word and Spirit.[29]

Hamartiologically, God ordained (but did not effectively morally cause) sin—first in the reprobate angelic world and then amongst men, the results of such sin being of cosmic scope (John 3:16f; Rom. 8:19f) yet to His own ultimate glory.[30]

Soteriologically, God also ordained (and effectively morally caused) the salvation of His elect, through the covenantal incarnation of the Logos or the Second Person of the Trinity as Jesus Christ, and through the covenantal operation of the Third Person of the Trinity as the Holy Spirit, for the restoration and consummation of the elect cosmos through Their works of particular revelation and particular grace, built on the foundation of Their works of common revelation and common grace.

25 Hos. 6:7 marg.; Ps. 8.
26 I Cor. 7:17-24; 12:1-31; Eph. 4:1-16.
27 Gen. 1:28; 2:7-18.
28 Cf. Gen. 4:15f; 6:3f; John 1:9 and Job 32:8.
29 Gen. 3:8-15.
30 Job 1:8-12; Prov. 16:4; Isa. 45:7f; 54:16.

35

Epistemologically, the Triune God exhaustively knows the entire totality of created reality, which He illuminates in His Son and Word; [31] and which He searches through with His Spirit.[32] And none of God's creatures can know anything save by the operations of His Son and His Spirit.

Logically, God structures the cosmos according to His Logos, according to His spoken Word as the accurate expression of His innermost rational thought.[33] And axiologically, God sees that the whole cosmos is in accordance with Himself as the Highest Good.[34]

And eschatologically, God from the very beginning creates and forms and unfolds the cosmos teleologically towards Adam as its initial goal,[35] and then, after Adam's sin, God further unfolds Adam down through history towards the Second Adam, towards Jesus Christ as the Supreme Philosopher of these last days,[36] Who, after His incarnation as the Second Adam, by His human labors subjected the totality of all created reality,[37] and Who, in spite of the deepening apostasy, is nevertheless even now leading this principially redeemed cosmos[38] towards the consummation of all things,[39] a (re)new(ed) earth under or united with a re-new-ed heaven(s), where redeemed men will reign with Him as philosopher kings forever.[40]

3. *The good angels*

Theontologically, the unfallen angels recognize the Triune God alone as the Ground of all created being.[41]

Existontologically, they doubtless recognize the universe's dual nature as spiritual and material, and recognize themselves as non-material spirits which can, however, take on a temporary material form at the Lord's command.[42]

[31] John 1:4,9; II Cor. 4:6.
[32] I Cor. 2:10.
[33] Gen. 1:3f; John 1:1-9.
[34] Gen. 1:31.
[35] Gen. 1:1-28.
[36] Heb. 1:1-3.
[37] Matt. 1 - John 21; cf. Gen. 1:26-28.
[38] Col. 1:15-20.
[39] Rom. 8:19f.
[40] Cf. II Pet. 3 and Rev. 21-22.
[41] Rev. 4:8-11; 5:11f; cf. Isa. 6:2f.
[42] Luke 1:26-29,38; Heb. 1:13-14.

36

Cosmogonically, they themselves were created probably before and were present during the formation of the earth.[43]

Cosmologically, they are purely spiritual or non-material creatures, divided up into various orders such as archangels,[44] cherubs,[45] seraphs,[46] thrones, dominions, principalities, and powers,[47] and various individual angels such as Gabriel[48] and Michael.[49] Their work is to obey God's commandments,[50] and particularly to control the natural elements,[51] to bring messages to and to minister to elect men,[52] and especially to take care of small children.[53]

Hamartiologically, the good angels are eternally elect,[54] and they successfully passed the single and unrepeatable test of loyalty by not revolting against God with Lucifer.[55] Accordingly, the good angels are not direct subjects of salvation, because they have nothing to be saved from. However, they are intensely interested in the salvation of each human being[56] and of the cosmos.[57]

Epistemologically, angels have a limited knowledge; [58] and axiologically, their highest good is to obey the Lord; [59] whereas eschatologically, they will be instruments in pouring out the last curses of God on the earth,[60] in gathering God's elect humanity from the four winds,[61] in praising God in heaven,[62] and in keeping the gates of the new earth, and particularly of the new Jerusalem.[63]

4. *The fallen angels*

Perhaps one third of the created angels fell into sin[64]

[43] Job 38:4f.
[44] Jude 9.
[45] Gen. 3:24.
[46] Isa. 6:2f.
[47] Col. 1:16.
[48] Dan. 8:16; 9:21.
[49] Dan. 10:13-21; Jude 9; Rev. 12:7.
[50] Ps. 103:20f.
[51] Rev. 7:1.
[52] Luke 1:26f; Heb. 1:14.
[53] Matt. 18:10.

[54] I Tim. 5:21.
[55] Rev. 12:7.
[56] Luke 15:10.
[57] Rev. 5:11f; 21:9f.
[58] I Pet. 1:12.
[59] Ps. 103:23.
[60] Rev. 8:2f.
[61] Matt. 24:31.
[62] Rev. 5:11f.
[63] Rev. 21:9,12; 22:8.
[64] Cf. Rev. 12:3-9.

under the leadership of Lucifer, who thereupon became Satan when he egotistically tried to make himself equal to God.[65]

Theontologically, when he failed in his attempt to seize power, Lucifer thenceforth hated, but had to accept, the fact that God was still the Ground of his being.[66]

Cosmologically, his fall into sin affected the whole cosmos —the heavens and the earth and the sea and the air,[67] so that he now became the god of this world[68]—not the God of God's world-as-such, but only the god of this present sin-stained world which now lay in his power.[69]

Anthropologically and federologically, Satan is the enemy of man,[70] and he jealously tried to stop man from subjecting the earth, sea, and air which he, the devil, sought to control.[71] Alas, Satan succeeded, and so, instead of man dominating the devil,[72] man now became dominated by Satan,[73] until Christ the Son of man and Second Adam broke that dominion.[74]

Hamartiologically, the devil sinned from the beginning,[75] and he thus disturbed the cosmic order,[76] bringing death into the world.[77] Soteriologically, he is unsavable and was in principle crushed by Christ; and epistemologically he knows that his time is short.[78] Axiologically he has completely perverted the scheme of true values,[79] and eschato-

[65] Cf. Isa. 14:2f and Ezek. 28.
[66] Jas. 2:19.
[67] Isa. 14:1-2; Rev. 12:9-12; 21:1; Job 1:7f; 2:2f; Eph. 6:12.
[68] II Cor. 4:4; Matt. 4:8-9.
[69] I John 5:19.
[70] I Pet. 5:8.
[71] Gen. 2:15-17; 3:1f.
[72] Gen. 2:15-17; 4:7; cf. Jas. 4:7.
[73] John 8:44.
[74] Gen. 3:15; Isa. 28-16; cf. Acts 4:10-12; Col. 1:13.
[75] John 8:44.
[76] Gen. 3:15f.
[77] Rom. 6:23.
[78] I John 3:8; Rev. 12:12.
[79] Jas. 3:6-9,13-17.

logically his doom in the lake of everlasting fire is certain.[80]

In short, Satan is the first sophist, the master (philo)soph*ist* who absolutized or "ism"-ized his created self instead of his Creator.[81]

5. *Adam*[82]

As philosophy is particularly *man's* scientific understanding of creation, philosophy proper only really begins with Adam.

Now Adam is the *image* of God the Supreme Philosopher, although he is only the *finite* image. Yet Adam, like all his fallen descendants, remains this image *throughout*—in spite of sin.[83] We may, however, distinguish three successive stages in the development of Adam, viz.: (i) *Adam Dei imago supralapsarius* (before the Fall); (ii) *Adam Dei imago infralapsarius* (after the Fall); and (iii) *Adam Dei imago ultralapsarius* (beyond the Fall). It is to a consideration of these three successive stages to which we must now proceed in some detail, if we would obtain a good grasp of the very foundation of True Philosophy.

A. *Adam supralapsarius*—Adam before the fall

Theontologically, before the fall Adam recognized the Triune God as the Ground of all created being. Existontologically, he believed that creation existed as a materiospiritual duality,[84] and cosmogonically, Adam believed the account of the progressive formation of the earth before his own creation, which account probably was revealed to him by God.[85] Cosmologically, Adam distinguished the cosmos into many parts, realizing that it was comprised of at least matter, plants, animals, and humans. Adam probably even

[80] Rev. 20:10.
[81] Cf. Rom. 1:25.
[82] First read again chapter I, sections 3-5.
[83] Cf. Gen. 5:1f; 9:5f; Jas. 3:9.
[84] Gen. 2:1f.
[85] Gen. 1:1 - 2:3.

distinguished as many as fifteen spheres of creation together with the laws for and the subjects of those spheres (see chapter I, section 4, above).

Anthropologically, Adam knew himself to be the image of God, created in perfect knowledge, righteousness, holiness, and dominion, yet subject to further growth.[86] And federologically, Adam knew himself to have been in covenant with God,[87] to have been the federal head of the entire human race,[88] and to have received the covenant of works and its "cultural mandate"—that is, Adam knew that he had been created for the purpose of obeying the decalogue and (thereby) subjecting the whole earth, sea, and sky to God's glory.[89]

Epistemologically, supralapsarian man knew both God the Creator and God's creation—instinctively,[90] empirically,[91] and rationally.[92] Logically, Adam could think consistently on account of the divine Logos or Word Who spoke to Adam both outwardly and inwardly and in Whose divine image he had been created.[93] And axiologically, Adam was perfect, and accepted only God's values as good.[94]

Eschatologically, although Adam had been created with unlosable, everlasting *existence*, he initially possessed only losable, everlasting *life*. Yet he knew that he was expected to earn unlosable everlasting life and to receive it as his ultimate reward should he yield perfect obedience to God by way of meticulously executing the covenant of works; and he also knew that, should he fail and break the covenant, he would earn that *other* form of unlosable, everlasting existence

[86] Gen. 1:26-28; Eccl. 7:29; Ps. 8; Eph. 4:24 and Col. 3:10.
[87] Gen. 1:28; 2:15f; Hos. 6:7 marg.
[88] Gen. 1:26-28; 2:23f; 3:20; Rom. 5:12f.
[89] Gen. 1:26-28; Ex. 20:8-15; Ps. 8.
[90] Gen. 2:23.
[91] Gen. 2:19a.
[92] Gen. 2:19b.
[93] Gen. 1:26-28; John 1:1; I Cor. 15:45f.
[94] Eph. 4:24; Gen. 1:31.

known as unlosable, everlasting *death* as his punishment.[95]

B. *Adam infralapsarius*—Adam after the fall

As a result of his sin, Adam ceased to be the image of God in the narrower sense,[96] but he still remained God's image in the broader sense.[97] Accordingly, theontologically Adam still had to acknowledge God as the Ground of all created being.[98]

Anthropologically, previously perhaps even unaware of any tensionless duality between his soul and his body, Adam was infralapsarianally informed of his earthly origin and destiny.[99] Ultimately, and on account of sin, his soul and his body would be separated from one another in death.[100] Yet even though both body and soul were now totally depraved, neither would ever be annihilated,[101] for both bear the image of God,[102] the soul functioning intellectually (intuitively, rationally, and empirically), voluntatively, emotionally, vitally, and physically, etc., and the body functioning as the living mantle of the soul,[103] yet both soul and body now functioning disharmoniously in all their parts as a whole as a result of the fall.

Federologically, Adam broke his covenant with God[104] by entering into a new covenant with the devil and against God; [105] and hamartiologically, Adam knew that he had sinned and (as federal head of the whole earth) had caused the entire cosmos and all his own descendants to

[95] Gen. 1:26-28; 2:15-17; 3:22; Hos. 6:7 marg.; Rev. 2:7; Rev. 20-22.
[96] Gal. 3:10; cf. Eph. 4:24 and Col. 3:10.
[97] Gen. 5:1-3; 9:6; Acts 17:28; Jas. 3:9.
[98] Gen. 3:10.
[99] Gen. 2:7; cf. 3:19.
[100] Eccl. 3:17-21; 12:7; Luke 23:46,52; John 19:30-31; Acts 7:59; II Cor. 5:1-8; Phil. 1:21-23; I Pet. 3:18f.
[101] Gen. 3:19; Matt. 10:28; I Cor. 15:42-54; Phil. 3:21; I Tim. 4:8; Rev. 20:11-15.
[102] Gen. 1:26-28; 2:15; 9:5-6.
[103] II Cor. 5:1-8.
[104] Hos. 6:7 marg.; Gen. 1:28 and 2:15.
[105] Cf. Gen. 3:1-7.

41

be cursed on account of his sin—and he would be reminded of this every time he saw the thorns and thistles as the wages of his sin while he struggled to try to execute the covenant of works and its cultural mandate—henceforth, in the sweat of his face! [106]

Epistemologically, Adam's mind now became darkened;[107] axiologically, his values became perverted; [108] and eschatologically, he himself became deserving of everlasting death.[109]

C. *Adam ultralapsarius*—Adam beyond the fall

Beyond the fall we encounter Adam graciously restored to the image of God in the narrower sense,[110] and here we may distinguish: *Adam regeneratus*, the born-again Adam; *Adam coelestinus*, the heavenly Adam; and *Adam reincarnatus*, the re-embodied Adam.

As regards *Adam regeneratus* or the born-again Adam, he was regenerated in his soul (and principially according to both soul and body) right after the fall—regenerated through faith in Jesus Christ the Logos and the Seed of the woman, Who would come as the Second Adam in Adam's place and break Adam's covenant with the devil and execute Adam's covenant with God.[111] Even though Adam would still have to suffer all the above infralapsarian effects of the fall (such as death or the separation of the soul from the body), he was nevertheless principially renewed to repossess all he had ever possessed before the fall, as well as in principle given all he did not possess before the fall but which (by executing the covenant of works and its cultural mandate) he would ultimately have earned had he been obedient and never fallen, including unloseable everlasting life.[112]

---

[106] Gen. 3:17-18.
[107] Eph. 4:17; I Tim. 6:5; Tit. 1:15.
[108] Gen. 2:25; 3:7.
[109] Gen. 2:17; Rom. 6:23.
[110] Cf. II Cor. 3:18; Eph. 4:24; Col. 3:10.
[111] Gen. 3:15f; Isa. 28:14-18; 42:1-7; Rom. 5:12f; I Cor. 15:22f.
[112] Gen. 3:22; Rev. 2:7; 22:2.

As regards *Adam coelestinus* or the heavenly Adam, i.e., Adam between his death and the Second Coming of Christ: After his earthly death, the regenerated Adam went to heaven and there enjoyed the above covenantal benefits— not only principially (as he had done while regenerated yet still only on earth), but now also in practice too—albeit only according to his disembodied soul.[113]

And as regards *Adam reincarnatus* or the re-embodied Adam: When Adam's soul ultimately either leaves heaven forever or otherwise comes with heaven onto the new earth forever, his soul will be re-united with his resurrected body. Then he will forever dwell on the new earth, where he will enjoy all the promised covenantal benefits not only in principle, but also in practice, and not only according to his soul (as previously in heaven), but now also according to his body too.[114] Amen, even so, come Lord Jesus![115]

* * *

From all that has so far been said,[116] the essential truth of the triune *creation-fall-recreation* religious basic motive at the root of True Philosophy should now be quite evident. And as regards the elements of truth in the religious basic motives at the roots of the various kinds of false philosophy such as Oriental, Greek, Romanistic, and humanistic philosophy, it may be remarked that there is indeed a state of dialectical tension between infralapsarian man and ultralapsarian man, between the degenerate and the regenerate. The originally healthy and tensionless *this-worldly* and *other-worldly* expectations of supralapsarian man who was originally *form*-ed from the *matter* or material of the earth, who was originally both a part of *nature* yet also *supra-naturally* the image of God so that he possessed both a created *free-*

113 Gen. 2:7f; 3:19f; Eccl. 3:21; 12:7; Heb. 12:23; Rev. 4:1; cf. 6:9-10 and 14:13.
114 Matt. 5:5; I Cor. 15:22,44-54; Rev. 20:12-15; 21:1-6,24-27; 22:1-5.
115 Rev. 22:20.
116 See especially chapter I, sections 3-10 and 20.

dom and *science* or systematized knowledge of all he beheld—now all became misdirected from their divine source and dialectically opposed to one another, when man fell into sin. But through the restorative and consummative work of the Second Adam Jesus Christ, all these categories have now been reconciled with God and with one another, so that saved man—at least in principle—can now serve the God of Re-creation in all of the creational dimensions.

6. Cain

Here we may distinguish *Cajinus depravatus* or the depraved Cain, *Cajinus damnatus* or the damned Cain, *Cajinus anathematus* or the accursed Cain, and *Cajinus ornatus* or the adorned Cain.

(a) *Cajinus depravatus* was born a sinner on account of the federally imputed unrighteousness of his father, *Adam infralapsarius*, as are all the other descendants of the latter.[117] This means that the entire human race, like Cain, is *by nature* in the position of *Adam infralapsarius* (q.v.).

(b) *Cajinus damnatus*. Like all other reprobates, Cain was sentenced to be banished forever from the presence of the Lord—firstly, in body and soul, for the rest of his days on earth; [118] secondly, in soul only, after his death, in the realm of the dead; [119] and thirdly, in body and soul in the lake of fire, after the bodily resurrection of the wicked.[120]

(c) *Cajinus anathematus*, however, is distinguishable from the vast majority of the rest of mankind. Because he did not dominate sin,[121] but murdered his brother Abel, he was particularly anathematized by God. The ground would not give its yield to Cain, and he was sentenced to be a

117 Gen. 5:3f; Job 14:4; 15:14-16; 24:4; Ps. 51:7; Eph. 2:1f.
118 Gen. 4:14.
119 Luke 16:23.
120 I John 3:12f; cf. Rev. 20:12-15.
121 Gen. 4:7.

nomad, all of which would make his required execution of the cultural mandate so much the more difficult.[122]

(d) *Cajinus ornatus.* Yet notwithstanding Cain's punishment, he was still required (and, by the donated common grace with which God adorned him, to some extent empowered) to try to execute the cultural mandate. Accordingly, he begins to try to subject and dominate the earth and the sea and the sky by being fruitful and multiplying and by building the city of Enoch.[123] And his descendants continued to try to execute the cultural mandate—Jabal by weaving tents and herding cattle, Jubal by musically mastering the harp and the flute, and Tubal-Cain by fashioning all kinds of implements in copper and iron.[124] But although some of these endeavors did to some extent objectively glorify God, Cain and his descendants did not by such endeavors intend to glorify God, Whom they hated. Their endeavors were objectively of some value, but their motives were subjectively totally depraved.

7. *Noah*

The cultural mandate to subject the totality of created reality[125] is clearly repromulgated to Noah and to all his descendants.[126] Like Cain, Noah received common grace to enable him to continue executing this mandate—as *Noachus ornatus* or the adorned Noah. But unlike Cain yet like Adam, Noah also received special or saving grace, which enabled him to continue executing the cultural mandate consciously to God's glory. To God's glory, unlike Cain —to God's glory, as *Noachus regeneratus* or the regenerated Noah.[127] And in these two capacities, Noah is the postdiluvian prototype of all subsequent Christian philosophers. His subjection of much of created reality by architecturally

---

[122] Gen. 4:11f.
[123] Gen. 4:17.
[124] Gen. 4:20-22.

[125] Gen. 1:28.
[126] Gen. 9:1-6; cf. Ps. 8 and Heb. 2-4 and 11-12.
[127] Gen. 6-9; I Pet. 3:18-22; II Pet. 2:4-5.

building the gigantic ark,[128] by zoologically conserving all the animals and birds,[129] by genealogically multiplying and filling the earth,[130] and by agriculturally developing grape-farming[131] are examples for all of us, his descendants, to follow. And this is much easier for us to do, now that God then (i.e., during the lifetime of Noah, and right after the flood) instituted regular ploughing and harvest times, summer and winter,[132] human government with its laws and sanctions and protection from wild animals,[133] and the rainbow covenantal guarantee of no future flood catastrophes of such totally destructive dimensions.[134]

8. Shem

Shem, one of the three sons of Noah, was blessed by his father. "Blessed is the Lord, the God of Shem," exclaimed Noah, thus implying that Shem was thoroughly orthodox in his theontological and soteriological outlook.[135] Even Shem's descendants, the Semites, were the least henatheistic and sometimes even monotheistic. E.g., the true world outlook of Abraham and his Old Testament descendants,[136] as well as the Semitic Job.[137] Cf. too, the much less true yet equally Semitic monotheism of Muhammad and his Islamic followers.

9. Ham

Ham, the second son of Noah, who was not blessed by him, and whose son Canaan—yet not Canaan's brothers—was positively cursed,[138] became the father of his descendants, the Hamites. These include not only the animistic Negroes and Melanesians, etc., but also henatheistic Egyp-

[128] Gen. 6:14f.
[129] Gen. 7:2-3.
[130] Gen. 9:1.
[131] Gen. 9:20.
[132] Gen. 8:22.
[133] Gen. 9:2-6.
[134] Gen. 9:11f; cf. II Pet. 3.
[135] Gen. 9:26f.
[136] Gen. 12:10-26.
[137] Gen. 10:21-23; 22:21; cf. Job 1:1f.
[138] Gen. 9:25-27.

tians and even theistic Ethiopians.[139] Of course, Ham's decendants richly share in the Messianic blessings![140]

10. *Japheth*

Noah expressed the desire that Japheth, his third son, might be "enlarged," and also that he might dwell in the tents of Shem.[141] It is a remarkable fact that the Caucasian sons of Japheth—the Russians, Germans, Persians, Greeks, Spaniards, etc., and their descendants[142]—have (since the earthly coming of Jesus Christ the Son of Shem[143] and until comparatively recently) by and large believed in God and thus "dwelt in the tents of Shem." As a result, God has truly "enlarged" Japheth. The Caucasians have, until recently, enlarged their domains throughout most of the earth, and in this way they have fulfilled much of the cultural mandate, at least outwardly, in being fruitful and multiplying and filling or replenishing the earth and dominating the earth and the sea and the sky—in all fields, and especially in the fields of (Western) technology, (European) literature, (Roman) law, and (Greek and German) philosophy. However, it is probable that God is now no longer "enlarging" Japheth, but "shrinking" him (cf. the process of decolonization), because the Japhethites have by and large apostasized from the tents of the Lord God of Shem. "Righteousness exalteth a nation: but sin is a reproach to any people." [144]

11. *Nimrod*

Nimrod the Hamite is one of the most important figures in ancient history. A son of Cush, he became famous in the days immediately after the flood and before as well as after

[139] Gen. 10:6; cf. Ps. 105:26-27; Jer. 13:23; Acts 2:10; 8:27f.
[140] Matt. 28:19; Acts 2:10; 8:27f.
[141] Gen. 9:27.
[142] Cf. Gen. 10:2-4.
[143] Luke 3:23,36.
[144] Prov. 14:34.

47

the dispersion of mankind into the different languages and nations.[145] Even then, he was a mighty warrior and a hunter of proverbial fame.[146] Theontologically, however, he rejected God, and exalted himself by inciting all mankind to defy God's cultural mandate to spread out and to fill the earth. This he did by persuading men to build the tower of Babel in Shinar to keep them all together in a cosmopolitan one-world state, "lest we be scattered over the whole earth." [147] In this way, Nimrod was the world's first great imperialist, and the beginning of his empire was in Babel and Erech and Akkad and Calneh and Shinar.[148]

But God would not be frustrated. Man must obey His cultural mandate and subject the whole earth. So God destroyed the tower of Babel in Shinar, and divided mankind into different nations and languages, and scattered them over the face of the earth,[149] causing Nimrod to move on to Asshur or Assyria and to build Nineveh, Rehoboth City, and Calah.[150]

12. *Summary*

From creation to the destruction of the tower of Babel and the origin of the nations, then, there are two philosophical lines: True Philosophy, dominated by the triune basic religious motive of creation-fall-recreation, which developed through God, the good angels, Adam, Noah, and Shem; and false philosophy, dominated by sin, which developed through Satan and the fallen angels, Cain and his descendants, and Nimrod.

From Adam onwards, all men would continue to attempt to subject the world and all its fullness, to dominate the earth and the sea and the sky in (philosophical) thought, (rhetorical) word, and (act-ual) deed. Hence, all men are

---

[148] Gen. 10:10.
[149] Gen. 11:9.
[150] Gen. 10:11; cf. Micah 5:5f.

[145] Gen. 10:8.
[146] Gen. 10:9; I Chr. 1:10.
[147] Gen. 11, especially verse 4.

involved, either consciously or unconsciously, in the divine covenant of works and its cultural command. *That* is unavoidable.

The question, however, is whether men are faithfully living in the power of Christ the Second Adam's fulfilment of the covenant of works, and whether they are thinking to His glory as True Philosophers. Are thinking men then True Philosophers, are they regenerate and also dominating the world to the glory of God? Or are they false philosophers, consciously or unconsciously dominating the world not to the glory of God and therefore to the glory of Satan?

Chapter III

ANCIENT EASTERN PHILOSOPHY

The Hegemony of the Orient

1. *Survey*

After the destruction of the tower of Babel, mankind went into all the world and was dispersed into the various nations, each of them perverting the covenant of works[1] by philosophizing about the earth and the sea and the sky in their own sinful manner.

Broadly speaking, we may perhaps divide all the nations into Semites, Hamites, and Japhethites, according as to whether such groups of nations descended from Shem, Ham, or Japheth. Thus the Semitic nations would be comprised of the Babylonians, Jews, and Arabians; the Hamitic nations would include the various dark-skined peoples of Africa, South India, and Australia; and the Japhethitic nations would consist of the Caucasian peoples of Europe, Russia, Persia, and Northern India, etc. Some nations are undoubtedly of mixed Semitico-Hamitic descent (e.g., the Egyptians and the Ethiopians), others of mixed Semitico-Japhethitic origin (e.g., the Afghani's), and still others of mixed Japhethitico-Hamitic descent. Perhaps the Chinese and the Redskins, for example, fall into this latter category.

From the Babelic dispersion of mankind into the various nations onwards, up to the time of Jeremiah, we see true philosophy developing only amongst the descendants of

[1] Gen. 1:26-28; Hos. 6:7 marg.

50

Shem—and almost disappearing from the earth after that time, until the birth of Christ. Again, for perhaps one thousand years or more from the time of Shem onwards, no major Semitic true philosopher is known to have existed, and so we start our survey of true Semitic philosophy with Job and Abraham, dating them both at perhaps 2000 B.C. However, we do have records of (both Semitic and non-Semitic) *false* philosophy from before that date. From shortly after the destruction of the tower of Babel or from about 3000 B.C. onwards, we have a series of documents from Egypt, and from about 2400 B.C. onwards we have extant documents from Mesopotamia—both areas located in the anciently civilized "fertile crescent" formed by the Nile, Tigris, and Euphrates Rivers. Our presently available records of Indian philosophy hardly date back to 1400 B.C., at which time Moses and the Israelites were planning to enter Canaan. And as regards the West, our extant records of even the crudest beginnings of Greek philosophy do not go back beyond Homer or about 850 B.C.—and more properly begin only from Thales or about 600 B.C. onwards. And although Chinese civilization and an ancient philosophical tradition dates from perhaps at least 2500 B.C., we have no reliable philosophical records from before about 600 B.C., i.e., approximately about the time of Jeremiah.

In this chapter, it will perhaps be best to study the various philosophers in their national setting rather than to study them in a strictly chronological order irrespective of their nationality. Yet nevertheless, we may perhaps distinguish five periods in the history of ancient Eastern philosophy, in each of which periods different nations have successively (though not necessarily exclusively) led in the global development:

1. *Egyptian* philosophy, from about 3000 B.C. onwards;
2. *Mesopotamian* philosophy, from about 2400 B.C. onwards;

51

3. *Hebrew* (or true) philosophy, from about 2000 B.C. onwards;

4. *Indian* philosophy, from about 1400 B.C. onwards; and

5. *Chinese* philosophy, from about 600 B.C. onwards.

These various philosophies did indeed have some common features, but they also clearly diverged from one another on many points. What, then, were the reasons for such similarities and divergences?

2. *Why the philosophies of different nations exhibit both similarities and dissimilarities*[2]

The following principles or explanations are offered as some of the reasons why philosophy has developed both similar and different characteristics amongst the various nations:

(a) *Principle of original revelation.* God's original theontological, existontological, cosmogonical, cosmological, anthropological, hamartiological, soteriological, epistemological, logical, axiological, and eschatological revelations to Adam were doubtless handed down by tradition and preserved (in varying degrees of purity) amongst the various nations. E.g., the Babylonian account of creation; the Bechuana account of the flood; the Zulu account of the tree of life; the Buddhist eight-day week, and the Chinese six-day week.[3]

(b) *Principle of natural variety.* The phenomenon of natural variety[4] would have led to a variety amongst men both on an individual basis[5] and on a national basis,[6] even had sin never taken place.

(c) *Principle of common revelation.* God's common rev-

---

[2] First read again chapter I, section 6.
[3] Cf. Gen. 2:1-3f. and 8:6-12.
[4] Gen. 1:11,21,24, etc.
[5] Gen. 1:27.
[6] Gen. 1:28 cf. Acts 17:26.

elation in nature to all men[7] obviously varies from nation to nation and even within each nation, depending on what kind of natural environment He places each nation in.[8] E.g., jungle or prairie, desert or lakeland, island or continent, tropical or temperate zone, plain or mountainous area, fertile or barren land, coastland or interior, in a riverless territory or in one with navigable or unnavigable rivers, etc.

(d) *Principle of common grace.* God gives different nations different degrees of common grace with which to understand his common revelation.[9]

(e) *Principle of special revelation.* Pharaoh and his Egyptians obviously received more light about God's saving acts than did the rest of the heathen, even though he still hardened his heart.[10]

(f) *Principle of special grace.* Moses and the Israelites, who received special grace to believe in God's special revelation, obviously had a different national outlook than did the Egyptians.[11]

(g) *Principle of isolation.* A nation isolated from others (e.g., ancient India, isolated by the Himalayas) will obviously have a different cultural outlook from a nation open to foreign influences, e.g., ancient Egypt from 2000–1400 B.C.[12] and later Mesopotamia from 600 B.C. onwards. Both Egypt and Mesopotamia were exposed to the true Semitic philosophy of the Israelites. Egyptian and Mesopotamian philosophy are thus not as apostate as, e.g., Indian and Chinese philosophy, which never came into contact with God's ancient covenant people.

(h) *Principle of sin.* A nation which deliberately turns its back on whatever revelation God gives it (e.g., the Jews,

[7] Acts 14:17.
[8] Cf. Deut. 32:8-14.
[9] Cf. Mal. 1:11; Acts 17:28; Rom. 2:14-16.
[10] Ex. 5-10.
[11] Ex. 10-15.
[12] Cf. Gen. 12-50.

after the coming of Christ)[13] will obviously differ in world outlook from a nation which welcomes such light (e.g., the Assyrians during the time of Jonah)[14]

3. General characteristics of the various Oriental philosophies

In spite of mutual differences, it may perhaps be said of all Oriental philosophies (e.g., Egyptian, Mesopotamian, Hebrew, Indian, and Chinese) that they are collectively *more ethical* yet *less systematic* than the various Western philosophies (e.g., the Ancient Greek, Renaissance, German, etc.). Only in Christian philosophy do we see both the ethics of the East and the systematic nature of the Western mind. Apart from this, however, the various Oriental philosophies differ from one another too.

Egyptian philosophy from 3000 B.C. onwards, for instance, specialized in (a too-other-worldly) eschatology; Mesopotamian philosophy from 2400 B.C. onwards, in fantastic cosmogonies; Indian philosophy from 1400 B.C. onwards, in too-other-worldly ontology, epistemology, and soteriology; Hebrew philosophy in theontology, anthropology, and soteriology, etc., and Chinese philosophy in too-this-worldly social ethics.

4. Egyptian philosophy

Egypt is the oldest country of whose philosophy we have written records dating back to about 3000 B.C., or shortly after the destruction of the tower of Babel and the dispersion of mankind into the various races and nationalities.

The Egyptians trekked southwestwards from Babel into Egypt, where they became pre-occupied with a characteristic too-other-worldly eschatology, towards which even their social ethics were oriented—as a means to achieve, as some

[13] Cf. Matt. 27:25; 28:15.
[14] Cf. Jonah 3:5f; Matt. 11:20f; 12:42f.

would say, "a pie in the sky bye-and-bye." E.g., the *Book of the Dead* teaches the immortality of the soul, and the writings of the Priest of Seneferu describe the importance of being ethical in one's this-worldly social relationships. Ptahhotep's advice to his son is even more interesting. He not only advises his son to rule wisely and with justice and courtesy, but also that "*God* forbids the suppression of the people" and that "to be loved by *God*, is to obey." Here the remaining traces of originally revealed theontology can still be seen.

Soon, however, the sun was worshiped instead of the Creator God, even though the sun alone was worshiped, and henatheistically worshiped as creator: "We worship Thee Who renewest Thyself, Who dost rise into the heavens, to look at all which thou hast created. . . . We worship Thee Who created the gods, o hidden God." This was the religion of Ra-ism. In other cities, however, not the sun, but the moon was worshiped as the one and only God(dess) of time —the religion of Thotism (Thot = moon).

Some five hundred years after Ptahhotep, we encounter a document known as the *Admonitions of Ipuwer*, about 2000 B.C. In a time of laziness and skepticism, Ipuwer pseudo-messianically advocated the need of a "shepherd of the people" who would bring peace to his people. Perhaps we should regard this as a perverted version of the *protevangelium* impurely handed down from Eden, eschatologically (mis)-oriented.[15] It should also be noted that the Messianically oriented Abraham visited Egypt at least once at about this time,[16] and it is conceivable that Ipuwer's pseudo-messianism could have been acquired from Abraham, if it was not handed down from Eden—or from both.

Even more remarkable resemblances to the Biblical data are found in Baba and Amenemope. Baba advocated cour-

---

[15] Gen. 3:15f; cf. Isa. 9:6.
[16] Gen. 17:7 cf. Gal. 3:16; cf. Gen. 13:1f.

tesy towards one's family and relatives, and prepared for future times of famine in Egypt. Living about 1600 B.C., it is even conceivable that he may have been the same person as the Joseph of the Bible.[17] Again, a certain resemblance is detected between Amenemope (who, about 1400 B.C., condemned the exploitation of the poor and advocated the protection of private property and respect for religious things) and Moses.[18] At about the same time, Amenophis IV, king of Egypt, alias Ikhnaton, attempted to reform Egyptian heathendom towards a solar monotheism, cf. Ra-ism, above. The sun-god was then supposed to be provident toward all his creatures.

5. *Mesopotamian philosophy*

Although Mesopotamia, "the-land-between-the-rivers" (the Tigris and the Euphrates), was originally inhabited by pre-Semitic Sumerians, the Babylonians were the first Semitic descendants of those who, after the Babelic dispersion after the destruction of the tower of Babel, did not trek very far from the site of that tower, but remained nearby, in Ur of the Chaldees, where Abraham was born.[19] Consequently, the Mesopotamian proximity to the cradle of the human race and contact with godly pre-Abrahamic Semites helped the Mesopotamians in general and the Semitic Babylonians in particular to preserve the accounts of creation and the flood to a remarkably authentic extent. This is not in the least to say that their cosmogony (and hamartiology) was not perverted, but it is probably true to say that these accounts are perhaps less perverted than those of any other heathen people; and many of these ancient Semitic Mesopotamian accounts (whether Chaldean, Accadian or later Babylonian, and Assyrian), themselves derive from even more ancient pre-Semitic Sumerian accounts.

[17] Cf. Gen. 41-46.
[18] Cf. Ex. 2:10-15; 5:1-8; Ex. 22, etc.
[19] Gen. 11:2f,28f.

The *Enuma elish* Babylonian account of creation is one of the most interesting of the heathen cosmogonies. It deals with the birth of the gods, the battle between Marduk and Tiamat, and man's creation in a divinely sustained universe. Marduk, the local god of Babylon, became "the King of the gods of heaven and earth, the King of all the gods." But then the demon-god Tiamat with all her monsters fought against Marduk and the good gods. Tiamat was also the great primaeval sea,[20] and conceived other gods such as the Silts, the Horizons, and, later, the Sky and the Earth. And then, Marduk "decided to create another wonder of wonders: Opening his mouth, he spake forth to Ea(rth), inviting him to comment on the theory he proposed. 'Blood will I compose, bring a skeleton into being, produce a lowly primitive creature. 'Man' shall be his name: I will create *lullu-amelu*—an earthly 'puppet'-man. To him be charged the service, that the gods may then have rest. . . .' Thereupon from his blood (he cre)ated mankind (and) imposed the service upon him, releas(ing) the gods who must else have served." Cf. the Genesis account,[21] of which original revelation this is perhaps a perverted version rather than a totally unrelated outright human fabrication.

The *Gilgamesh* Epic was written later, perhaps around 2000 B.C., or more or less at the time Abraham was born. Part of the Epic deals with Utnapishti, sometimes referred to as the "Babylonian Noah." Utnapishti told Gilgamesh, the hero of the Epic, how "the great gods decided to bring on a deluge," and how they advised Utnapishti to "build a vessel" and to "load in the vessel the seed of all creatures." So Utnapishti related how he made the vessel of pitch and timber, and how "of the species of all living creatures, all that I had did I load aboard her. I made enter the vessel all my family and kindred; beasts wild and domestic and all

20 Cf. Gen. 1:2.
21 Gen. 1-2.

of the craftsmen I made to enter the vessel. It was Shamash (the Sun-god) who set the time appointed: 'Who sendeth the bane, on the previous evening will pour down the rain: then enter the vessel and close down thy doorway!'" Then the storm came, the dam-stays were torn down, the weirs overflowed, so that "even the gods were afeared at the deluge, took to flight and went up to the heaven . . . , (and) cowered . . . like dogs," while "for six days and (seven) nights the wind blew, and the flood and the storm swept the land. But the seventh day arriving did the rainstorm subside and the flood," and "I opened a vent . . . and I looked . . . —but the whole of mankind had returned unto clay." Then, "when I looked out again . . . across the expanse of the sea, mountain ranges had emerged . . . and on Mount Nisir the vessel had grounded. . . . On the seventh day's arriving, I freed a dove . . . the dove came back to me: there was not yet a resting-place and he came returning. Then I set free a swallow and did release him . . . but (he) came back to me. . . . So I set free a raven . . . and he . . . came not returning. So . . . I poured a libation, and scattered a food-offering, on the height of the mountain. . . . And the gods smelled the savor, . . . the gods gathered like flies about the priest of the offering. Then, as soon as the Mother-goddess arrived, she lifted up the great jewels which, (in childhood, her father) Anu had made as a plaything for her: 'O ye gods here present, as I still do not forget these lapis stones of my neck, so shall I remember these days— shall not forever forget them! If it please now the gods to come here to the offering, never shall Enlil come here to the offering, for without any discrimination he brought on the deluge.'" One should compare this account very carefully with the Biblical account of the flood.[22] As in the case of the Enuma elish described previously, the resemblances between the Babylonian "Noah" and the Biblical

[22] Gen. 6-9.

Noah should be attributed to the principles of original revelation, common revelation, common grace and/or special revelation, whereas the differences are on account of the principles of special grace, isolation, and sin (see section 2, above).

The *Hammurabi* stele, written about 1750 B.C. in the Accadian or later Babylonian language, contains a legal code (cf. the Mosaic Deuteronomy) which ameliorates the position of the poor, prescribes appropriate punishment of the various kinds of crime, and, in general, perhaps presupposes some kind of *Jus gentium* or international law, or even some kind of *Jus naturale* or natural law, as the inspired root of both the inspired Mosaic code and the uninspired yet remarkable code of Hammurabi. E.g., Codex Hammurabi, item 250: "If an ox has gored a citizen, while going along the road, and has occasioned his death, there shall be no penalty attached to this case," cf. the Mosaic law.[23] The closing sentence of the previous paragraph, then, probably applies here too.

Many of these early Mesopotamian ideas are found much later in Zoroaster (perhaps about 1000 B.C.). Repudiating priestcraft and idolatry, he exalted Ahura Mazda, the "Wise Lord," as the only deity and source of all cosmic order. Men everywhere are enjoined to oppose evil and do good for the sake of Ahura Mazda. After Zoroaster's death, however, his ideas were corrupted into Zoroastrianism.

Zoroastrianism represents an attempt to combine the thought of Zoroaster with the ancient Japhethitic polytheistic nature worship of ancient Persia (cf. Indian Vedism, below), and, possibly, with some Israelitic influences later. In Zoroastrianism, the whole of world history is developing against the background of a titanic struggle between the god of light Ahura Mazda or Ormazd, and the god of darkness Angra Mainya or Ahriman. The whole cosmos is in-

[23] Cf. e.g., Ex. 21:28.

59

volved in this struggle. Ormazd is assisted by his divine attributes which were later personified as angels, just as Ahriman is aided by his demons. Ormazd is not the creator of all things, but only of that which is good—evil was created by Ahriman. Ormazd did, however, create time, sun, moon, and stars. And he also created the first man as the blossom of the world-tree Haomo, from which the elixir of immortality could be obtained. Fire is the element which best reveals Ormazd, and he is incapable of defeating Ahriman without the aid of all his creatures.

The evil god Ahriman was originally the disorderly chaos known as Druzd, a female demon. Ahriman was the creator of devils and all evil things such as fleas. Zoroastrianism therefore teaches a radical dualism between good and evil.

Eschatologically, however, good finally triumphs. At death each man goes either to heaven, hell, or an intermediate place, according to his own works. Ultimately, however, all three places will terminate, and all souls will be purged by fire. Then follows a new heaven and a new earth on which righteousness shall dwell, while Ahriman is relegated to the eternal darkness from which he emanated.

Throughout, Zoroastrianism—as indeed most Mesopotamian philosophy—shows many traces of God's original revelation to man, however perverted this revelation later became on account of man's misinterpretations and elaborations.

6. Hebrew philosophy [24]

The word "Hebrew" may have been derived from Eber, the son of Shem [25] and the forefather of Abr(ah)am and Jacob or Israel; [26] at any rate, the word is currently used to

[24] First read again chapter I, sections 6-7.
[25] Gen. 10:21-25.
[26] Do., cf. Gen. 11:17-26 and I Chr. 1-2.

denote all those who genealogically descend from Abraham, and, more particularly, from his grandson Israel.[27]

The general characteristics of Hebrew philosophy are its sound theontology, cosmogony, anthropology, and ethics and—to a somewhat lesser extent—its soteriology and eschatology.

Perhaps around about 2000 B.C., Job, a Semite,[28] and perhaps even a Hebrew in the wider sense of the word,[29] lived in the land of Uz. Theontologically, he knew the true God;[30] cosmologically, he learned about the wonders of God's creation;[31] anthropologically, he knew of man's origin and nature;[32] and soteriologically and eschatologically, he expected man's salvation and perfection.[33]

Abraham was perhaps contemporary to Job. Theontologically, Abra(ha)m, although born near the site of the previously destroyed tower of Babel,[34] and although apparently raised in idolatry,[35], came to worship the true God as the Ground of all being.[36] Ethically and anthropologically, he obeyed God and was full of compassion towards his fellow man.[37] Soteriologically, he believed in the Messianic Seed Who was to come,[38] and eschatologically, he journeyed towards the heavenly country and longed for the city of God[39] on the new earth.[40]

Joseph shared the life and world view of his great-grandfather, Abraham. In addition, however, Joseph also

[27] Ex. 1:1-16 and Phil. 3:4-5.
[28] Job. cf. Gen. 10:21-25.
[29] Do., cf. Gen. 22:19-21 and 36-28.
[30] Job 1-2.
[31] Job 26-28; 38-42.
[32] Job 31:33; 33:4-6; 14-15.
[33] Job 19:25-27.
[34] Gen. 11:9-31.
[35] Josh. 24:2-3.
[36] Gen. 12f. cf. 24:3.
[37] Gen. 18; 23; and 26:5.
[38] Gen. 3:15f; 17; cf. Gal. 3:16 and John 8:56f.
[39] Heb. 11:16 cf 13:14 and 12:22.
[40] Gen. 17:6,8 cf. Rev. 21:23-24 and Matt. 8:11.

had the epistemological gift of intuitive interpretation of dreams.[41] He also achieved great acuteness in political science, rising to the position of viceroy of Egypt; [42] and ethically, he was extremely forgiving of the shortcomings of others.[43]

Moses was a major figure in Hebrew philosophy. As the writer of the Pentateuch,[44] he was theontologically thoroughly acquainted with the one true God;[45] and cosmologically, he himself wrote the inspired Genesis account of the creation of heaven and earth.[46] Anthropologically, he wrote the Genesis account of man's origin,[47] and the ethical duties of man to man in the book of Deuteronomy. Hamartiologically and soteriologically, he recorded the gravity of sin and how it could be expiated, especially in the book of Leviticus. And in addition to all this, even more so than Joseph before him, he was thoroughly schooled in the common grace and the treasures of Egypt,[48] which, again like Joseph, adequately equipped him to be a great political leader and ruler and lawgiver when God called him to that high and holy office.[49]

David—with the exception of his own son Solomon—was perhaps the greatest Hebrew philosopher of all time. In many of his Psalms, written from about 1000 B.C. onwards, he touched on matters of profound philosophical importance. This is especially true of his theontology,[50] but his writings also present us with a cosmology and an anthropology,[51] an hamartiology,[52] and a soteriology.[53] In addition, there is much of ethical importance in his writings.[54]

[41] Gen. 37 and 41.
[42] Gen. 41f.
[43] Gen. 45f.
[44] Gen.-Deut.
[45] Cf. Deut. 6:4.
[46] Gen. 1:1 - 2:3.
[47] Gen. 2.
[48] Heb. 11:26.
[49] Acts 7:35 cf. Ex. 3:1f; cf. Westm. Confession chapter XXIII:II and Calvin's Inst. IV:20:4.
[50] E.g., Pss. 3-7, etc.
[51] Pss. 8 and 19, etc.
[52] Pss. 25, 32 and 51.
[53] Pss. 22, 69 and 89.
[54] E.g., Pss. 34-37.

He was also successively a shepherd, musician, general, prophet, and king, and—in spite of many sinful failings—nevertheless a man after God's own heart.

Solomon was the greatest thinker Israel ever produced. For "God gave Solomon wisdom and understanding exceeding much, . . . and Solomon's wisdom excelled the wisdom of all the children of the east . . . and all the wisdom of Egypt"; [55] philosophical wisdom to help execute the Adamic cultural mandate to "have dominion over the fish of the sea, and over the fowl of the air, and over the cattle, and over all the earth, and over every creeping thing that creepeth upon the earth." [56] For Solomon "spake three thousand Proverbs: and his Songs were a thousand and five. And he spake of trees, from the cedar tree that is in Lebanon, even unto the hyssop that springeth out of the wall: he spake also of beasts, and of fowl, and of creeping things, and of fishes." [55] The probable author of many of the Psalms,[57] of most of the highly philosophical Proverbs,[58] and, according to some, perhaps even of the book of Ecclesiastes (which describes man's philosophical search for the meaning of life in wisdom, pleasure, sex, riches, moderation and obedience),[59] Solomon was a wise emperor who promoted economic expansion and architecture and international goodwill.[60]

Isaiah the prophet (740 B.C.) theontologically magnified the Lord God,[61] soteriologically announced the coming of the cosmic Messiah,[62] and eschatologically opened up cosmic perspectives.[63] And the prophets Jeremiah[64] and Daniel

[55] I Ki. 4:29-34.
[56] Gen. 1:26.
[59] Eccl. 1:1 - 12:14 cf. Song of Sol. 1:1 - 8:14.
[60] E.g., I Ki. 4-10.
[61] Isa. 40-43.
[62] Isa. 42 and 53.
[63] Isa. 44:23-24; 45:5-18; 49; 60; 64:1-4 cf. I Cor. 2:9; Isa. 2, 11 and 65-66.
[64] Jer. 10:10-13; 23:5f, etc.
[57] Pss. 72, 127 and 128 (q.v.).
[58] Prov. 1-29 (q.v.).

(both about 610–570 B.C.) opened up similar perspectives. In addition, Daniel, like Joseph (q.v.), also had the epistemological gift of intuitive interpretation of dreams as well as a flair for political science.[65]

As regards Hebrew philosophy after Malachi (about 420 B.C.) yet before the beginning of Christian philosophy (4 B.C.), mention must be made of Jesus Sirach, Pseudo-Solomon, and Philo in particular.

Jesus Sirach (about 180 B.C.) was the author of the apocryphal book of Ecclesiasticus (not to be confused with the canonical book of Ecclesiastes), which is an ethico-philosophical and poetical treatise somewhat resembling the book of Proverbs. *Pseudo-Solomon* or the book of the so-called "Wisdom of Solomon" (about 150–50 B.C.) praises the personalized Wisdom who in the beginning reigned with God;[66] although it claims to be of Solomonic authorship,[67] it betrays itself as a synthesis between Hebrew theology and Greek philosophy, and Luther therefore not without reason assumed Philo to be its author. Philo (25 B.C. – about A.D. 50), a most important philosopher, will be dealt with later under ancient Greek philosophy.[68]

Hebrew philosophy, then, was largely true philosophy, and developed in particular a characteristically theocentric theontology, anthropology, and ethics.

7. *Indian philosophy*

It was probably a branch of the Hamitic race which originally traveled southeastwards from the tower of Babel in southern Mesopotamia, arriving perhaps before 2500 B.C. in south India, where this group became known as the Dravidians. But from about 1500 B.C. onwards (i.e., just before Moses was born in Egypt), tribes of the Japhethitic

---

[65] Cf. Dan. 2:28f, etc.
[66] Wisd. 9:4; cf. Prov. 8-9 and John 1:1f.
[67] Wisd. 8:10f; 9:7f.
[68] See chapter IV, section 13 below.

race known as the Aryans invaded India from the north, subjugated the Dravidians, imposed the caste system on them, and developed a corresponding life and world view, a view which particularly and increasingly developed its own mystical ontology, epistemology, and soteriology.

The first expression of this life and world view is encountered in the *Vedas* or "books of wisdom," and they present an optimistic and polytheistic nature-worship of the gods of the sky, storms, sun, etc. (Cf. the ancient religions of Mesopotamia and Greece). This polytheism, however, gradually degenerated through the *Brahmanas* and especially through the *Upanishads* (from about 800 B.C. onwards) into the pessimistic pantheism so characteristic of Indian thought—cf. especially *Yajnavalkya*. The further development of Indian ethics and particularly of the Vedic priesthood, is related in the *Mahabharata* epic, and especially in that part thereof known as the *Bhagavad-gita*.

Materialistic opposition to the priesthood developed especially around 600 B.C. under Chavak or Carvaka, and the authority of the Vedas was repudiated by his contemporary Vardhamana, the father of Jainism. The *Samkhya* system, reputedly of Kapila, advocated the theory of evolution, and Buddha, about 500 B.C., repudiated the caste system and taught salvation by knowledge rather than by ritual; it was his teachings which spread particularly into Ceylon, Burma, Thailand, China, Indo-China, and, in the form founded by Daruma and known as Zen-Buddhism, into Japan. A peculiar system of Buddhist logic and metaphysics of a negative character was developed by Nagarjuna around 425 B.C., whereas shortly thereafter, Patanjali developed a system of self-perfection known as Yogism, and the Vedas were rounded off by the *Vedanta* or "end of the Vedas."

Centuries later, Harirarmen (A.D. 250–350) nihilistically denied the existence of personality, physical objects and ideas, but Vasubandhu (A.D. 420), while denying the existence of the former, did at least accept the existence of the latter. At that time, Isvarakrsna also perfected the pessimistic and dualistic Samkhya system.

Around A.D. 800, Shankara or Samkara systematized the Upanishads and expounded the Vedanta. He was undoubtedly one of India's greatest philosophers, and advocated a tolerant social life and pantheistic intellectualism. From this time onwards, Indian thought to some extent crystallized out into that system now known as Hinduism. Around A.D. 1000, Ramanuja taught a cosmogonical emanationism, and two centuries later Madhva upheld a dualism between the human soul and the cosmic soul.

In the fifteenth century A.D., one encounters Sri Vallabhacharya, an accomplished Vedantist and metaphysician, and from 1850 onwards, influential thinkers such as the universalistic Sri Ramakrishna, the rationalistic and agnostic Vivekananda, the politicians Sri Aurobindo and Mohandas Ghandhi, and the great agnostic humanist Sarvepalli Radhakrishnan. Some of the latter men were undoubtedly somewhat influenced by Western Christian missionaries in their ideas.

On the whole, it may be stated that Indian philosophy is steeped in mysticism and pantheism, and has largely been too-other-worldly and epistemistic.

8. Chinese philosophy

The Chinese, perhaps Japhethites with a Hamitic admixture, probably arrived from the Babelic dispersion in China around 2500 B.C.—although such a great antiquity is really steeped in myth, and genuinely historical evidences go back only to about 1700 B.C. Political confederation from about 1000 B.C. ultimately disintegrated, however, and this caused violent socio-political insecurity in China, which was opposed in about 500 B.C. by the first and best-known of all Chinese philosophers, the understandably too-this-worldly Kung-fu-tse (or Confucius).

The remnants of ancient ritualism and fatalism in Confucianism were soon opposed especially by the rationalistic Mo-tzu or Mo-ti around about 450 B.C.; but from the fourth century B.C. onwards, there was a reaction to Confucian too-this-worldliness—a reaction which took the form of the development of an obscurantistic system of nature-worship known as Taoism which was progressively formulated by Yang-chu, Lao-tse or Lao-tsu, and Chuang-tzu. At the same time, however, the idealist Meng-tse (alias Meng-tzu, alias Mencius) further developed Confucianism around 300 B.C., as did the realists Tzu-szu, Hsün-tzu (Hsüng-ching) and Hui-shih, and as did the legalist Han-fei-tzu and the skeptic Wang-ch'ung around A.D. 200.

From about A.D. 800 onwards, Neo-Confucianism developed, with a lively interest in cosmogony—and here an attempt to reach a balance between this-worldliness and other-worldliness can be seen. Then, around 1150, Lu-wang tried to synthesize Confucianism and Buddhism (which latter had arrived in China probably about the time of Christ), while Chu-hsi (Cho-shi) and his school show some affinity to Platonic idealism.

China long withstood Western influence, but since 1900 she has produced powerful Westernized thinkers of the calibre of the nationalists Sun-yat-sen and Chiang-kai-shek. Other thinkers, such as Yu-lan-fung, for instance, continued to promote orthodox Neo-Confucianism. Today, however, China, under a very extreme form of its traditional too-this-worldliness, suffers under the galling strictures of the totalitarian communist philosopher Mao-tse-tung, the most influential living thinker of the whole socialist world. Will Mao succeed in permanently stultifying the further philosophical development of the great Chinese nation? The world of philosophy looks on with interest and anxiety.

9. *Summary*

Post-Babelic Oriental thought can be divided into true philosophy, the philosophy of the Hebrews; and false philosophy—everything else. It was seen that Hebrew philosophy not only developed particularly the areas of theontology, cosmogony, anthropology, ethics, and soteriology in terms of the triune *creation-fall-recreation* religious basic motives of true philosophy, but that it also maintained a perfect balance between the this-worldliness and the other-worldliness motives which kept false philosophy in a state of unresolved dialectical tension, and even caused it to vary from place to place and from time to time.

Hence: Egyptian thought was ethical, yet, on the whole, too other-worldly; the Mesopotamians were highly cosmogonical, yet polytheistic; the Indians were ontological, yet, on the whole, too other-worldly; and the Chinese were highly ethical, yet, on the whole, too this-worldly. Only Hebrew philosophy had the right balance—and even Hebrew philosophy was destined to be enriched by the systematic Western mind of the Greeks and, funneling that latter gift of God's common grace into God's special revelation, to produce that great system of true thought known as Christian philosophy.

Chapter IV

ANCIENT GREEK PHILOSOPHY

The Hegemony of Hellas

1. *Introduction*

After the destruction of the tower of Babel, that tribe of the Japhethites known as Javan went to live in "the isles of the Gentiles" to the west of Palestine, including that territory now know as Greece (cf. Gen. 10:1-5).

Although Greece, or at least parts of it, was originally inhabited by the ancient Minoan civilization, it was later subjected to one wave of Japhethites after the other who invaded it from the north. First were the Mycenaeans, whose civilization in Greece flourished from at least 1600 B.C. onwards. Next came the Achaeans, from about 1300 B.C. onwards. And lastly came the Dorians, who invaded Greece from about 1100 B.C. onwards.

The Mycenaean Greeks had religiously worshiped many *material* nature-gods and nature-demons, gods of seasonal change and movement (a perversion of common revelation),[1] gods of life, death, and resurrection (a perversion of the protevangel),[2] gods which arose from the formless and eternal flux or flowing matter, and which obtained merely a temporary form in time, but which "fate" (*Anangke*) destined only to return to the "divine" ground of all being, the formless eternal flux from which the gods themselves

---

[1] Acts 14:15-17.
[2] Gen. 3:15.

69

had arisen, and from which raw material other nature gods would arise after them (cf. the polytheism and nascent pantheism of the Indian Vedas and the Upanishads—indeed, the ancient Greeks and the ancient Aryans of India were themselves kindred Japhethitic peoples).

However, it was especially the invasions of the post-Mycenaean peoples in general, and the Dorians in particular, which brought about the "Dark Ages" of Ancient Greece when the world became "without form and void, and darkness was upon the face of the deep." [3] Even some of the Achaeans fled the Doric mainland; some went eastwards and colonized Ionia (on the western coast of what is now Turkey) from about 1000 B.C. onwards, whereas other colonists went westwards to places in Sicily and southern Italy like Elea from about 800 B.C. onwards.

Escaping the darkness of Doric domination, Ionian culture began to develop, stimulated by trade links with the east, increasing urbanization, a rising standard of living, and more leisure time for contemplation. Kings were supplanted by popular tyrants, who created an atmosphere of greater freedom and who patronized the arts and sciences. Religion developed, and so did culture—and the old nature-gods (which continued to be worshiped in *private*) were relegated from *public* worship in favor of the official Olympian gods in an attempt to make the scores of city-states where they were worshiped conscious of their common Greek affinities with one another. These were the Olympian culture-gods of form and harmony, and especially the divine trio Hades (the god who dominates the earth), Poseidon (the god who dominates the sea), and Zeus (the god who dominates the sky)—a perversion of the trinity and a perversion of the cultural mandate; [4] perverted and mis-*form*-ed by the men of culture (cf., once again, a perverted

[3] Cf. Gen. 1:2.
[4] Cf. Gen. 1:1,26-28.

70

culture mandate!)[5]—a new religious basic motive, the *form* motive, had arrived.

At first, Homer, the great Ionian poet (about 850 B.C.), sang chiefly of bygone days—of the former destruction of Tory (in the *Iliad*) and of the erstwhile foreign journeyings of Greek adventurers (in the *Odyssey*)—but even amidst much mythologizing, he emphasized absolute values such as law and fate. But it was particularly Hesiod, about a century later, who set the stage for the beginning of Greek philosophy.

Relegating the public use of the old Mycenaean material nature-gods of change and movement in favor of the new official Olympian culture-gods of human form which proceeded from the former, the poet Hesiod subjected the old religious basic motive of matter and nature to the new motive of form, order, and culture. This is particularly seen in Hesiod's pessimistic philosophico-historical "Theogony," in which—under the influence of Ionia's orderly legal justice and orderly social ethics—he gives an orderly account of the orderly origin of the gods and of their orderly mutual relationship, and also of the orderliness of the world of sub-human creatures too.

It was this love of orderliness and systematization which was to make Greek thought great. Increasing development of the different branches of knowledge (trade, mathematics, warfare, art, poetry, religion, etc.) led to the need of generalizing knowledge and of developing an encyclopaedic science. A search for basic principles (and especially for an ultimate basic [monistic] principle) was underway, and soon—Greek philosophy was born!

2. *Survey*

Although the new form-religion which worshiped the Olympian culture-gods *publicly* replaced the old matter-

[5] Gen. 1:28; 2:15!

religion which worshiped the Mycenaean nature-gods, the latter religion nevertheless continued to be observed in *private*. Consequently, the Greeks thenceforth practiced *two* different religions simultaneously—two religions which were dialectically opposed to one another. Hence too the entire development of Greek philosophy, itself religiously determined, was dominated by the fluctuating religious basic motives of form and matter.

Sometimes the matter motive dominated that of form, as in the case of Mycenaean religion, and at other times the reverse was the case, as in Hesiod's Theogony. But whichever basic motive was monistically subsumed under the alleged primacy of the other, the subsumption was always only apparent, and it only created and perpetuated an unresolved dialectical tension between the two motives. This was because both basic motives are ontically false philosophical attempts to characterize the ground and the nature of the world order monistically. For the Fixed *Ground* of the world order is not monistic or even dual(istic), but is the uniplural Triune God 'Elohim alone; and the *nature* of the world order is not monistic or even dual(istic) either, but can only be truly grasped in terms of the uniplural Christian philosophical triune religious basic motive(s) of creation, fall, and re-creation. (See too section 4 below, on Pythagoras and Parmenides).

The development of Greek philosophy may perhaps be traced through three periods—the *Pre-Socratic Age* (about 600–450 B.C.); the *Golden Age* (about 450–300 B.C.); and the *Post-Aristotelian Age* (from about 300 B.C. onwards).

The Pre-Socratic Age was the age of *ontology*. Theontologically, the "atheists" opposed the "theists," the matter motive of the Ionian materialists (Thales, Anaximander, Anaximenes, and Heraclitos) and the atomists (Leucippus and Democritus) opposed the form motive of Pythagoras and the Eleatics (Xenophanes, Parmenides, and Zeno Elea-

72

ticus)—while Empedocles and Anaxagoras sought an intermediate position.

The Golden Age was the age of *epistemology*. Here the false epistemists (cf. the matter motive) opposed the great epistemologists (cf. the form motive). Epistemists like the sophists (e.g., Protagoras and Gorgias) and the later skeptics (e.g., Pyrrho and Carneades) were opposed by the cynics (like Antisthenes and Diogenes Sinopus) and especially by the three greatest philosophers of Greece, the Athenian trio—Socrates, Plato, and Aristotle.

The Post Aristotelian Age was the age of *existentialism*, the age of the individual on the one hand and of world government on the other. Both parties had to come to terms with one another and with themselves—existentially. This was the age of the philosophy of (human) life, the age of the matter-motivated pleasure-seeking hedonists (like the Greeks Aristippus and Epicurus and the Roman Lucretius). It was the age of the form-motivated politically indifferent yet cosmopolitan stoics (like the Greeks Zeno Stoicus, Cleanthes, and Chrysippus, and the Romans Seneca, Epictetus, and Marcus Aurelius). And it was also the age of syncretistic non-Christian philosophy, of neo-Platonism and neo-Aristotelianism (e.g., Pliny the Elder, Plutarch of Chaeronea, and Plutarch of Athens). It was the age of increasing dissatisfaction and speculative Logos-doctrines (cf. Philo and Plotinus). And it was the age when God answered that dissatisfaction when He presented the life and doctrine of *The* Logos, Jesus Christ.[6]

Throughout its development, however, Greek philosophy was largely systematic. It was also mostly rationalistic and —with the exception of cosmogonistic minorities such as the early Ionians—generally humanistic. Also, with the increasing systematization and specialization of Greek philos-

[6] John 1:1.

ophy, the way was paved for the apostate absolutization of scientific or theoretical thought.

The detailed development of Greek philosophy, however, can perhaps best be studied by applying the Christian philosophical criteria of theontology through eschatology to each thinker, wherever merited.

3. *The Ionian materialists*

The first school of Greek philosophy was the school of the Ionian materialists. They were pre-eminently monistic ontologists, regarded all living beings as having evolved from lifeless being (hulozoism), and even attempted to reduce all being to one materialistic essence in which the Greek matter motive dominated the Greek form motive. Thales of Miletus (about 600 B.C.) sought this materialistic essence in eternal water, arguing that air was merely evaporated water and that earth was merely hardened water. His pupil Anaximander of Miletus (575 B.C), however, sought the essence of all things in a boundless energy called "apeiron," whereas Anaximenes of Miletus (550) sought the essence in eternal air, and Heraclitos of Ephesus (500) in eternal and uncreated material fire, of which the human soul is just a temporary form (cf. the ancient Mycenaean matter motive).

Of course, there were also other differences between these thinkers. E.g., Thales and Heraclitos were both universalists (who absolutized universals and minimized particulars or individuals) and subjectivists (who sought the cosmic laws in the things subjected to those laws rather than outside and above those things). Anaximenes, however, was a partial universalist (who distinguished a human microcosm as well as a cosmic macrocosm); and Anaximander was in fact an objectivist (who sought the cosmic laws objectively outside the things subjected to those laws).

Again, Heraclitos taught the eternal flux of all things,

and he also taught that the processes of being and of knowing are both contradictory—on account of an internal logico-dialectical tension. This Heraclitian Logos doctrine is of particular interest to Christian philosophy.[7] Only change is permanent, and the "Logos" is the law of unchanging change. The "Logos" or Thought-Word, he believed, lies at the root of the ontic eternal flux, and reveals itself in the flux—and epistemologically, the human thinker must see to it that his "logos" or thought-word is attuned to the ontic "Logos," if he too would truly know; and this knowledge would be more reliable if he participates in socio-political life.

4. *Pythagoras and the Eleatics*

Pythagoras of Kroton, a Greek colony near Elea in southern Italy (550 B.C.), is best known for the discovery of the geometrical rule attributed to him, viz., that the square of the hypotenuse of a right-angled triangle is equal to the sum of the squares of the other two sides. Indeed, he may in fact be described as an objective mathematicist, for he attempted to reduce all being to objective mathematics; e.g., he typified masculinity in the figure two, femininity in the figure three, and marriage in the figure five $(=2+3)$. He also mathematicized music by studying the relation between the various lengths of the strings of musical instruments and the various sounds emitted when the various strings were vibrated.

In Pythagoras, therefore, the Greek form motive dominates the Greek matter motive. And this is also seen in his dualistic cosmology and anthropology: the heavenly divinity, which itself possesses a (limited!) harmony or form, eliminates the disharmony of the lower (material!) essence by ordering it into a mathematical form, by creatively changing the chaos into a cosmos or orderly uni-

[7] Col. 1:15f; John 1:1f.

verse; and the all-important and immortal soul of man, leaving its earthly prison of the human body after death, transmigrates over and over again from one body to another, even into the bodies of animals (to which men are therefore also akin), hoping ultimately to be free from the prison of the body altogether and to unify with the heavenly divinity of harmonious form. Cf. Plato! (For the Christian-philosophical viewpoint, on the relationship between the human body and soul, see the anthropological sections of chapter II, sections 2 and 5, above.)

Xenophanes of Elea, a contemporary of Pythagoras, "theistically?!" insisted that there was only one Ultimate Reality, "One god, the greatest among gods and men," who "abideth ever in the same place," and who was omnipresent and omniscient. However, he seems to have been a pantheist, for Aristotle later remarked that Xenophanes, "referring to the whole world, said the One was god." Xenophanes did, nevertheless, acutely observe that the conception of the true God was not the same as that of the different nations who falsely conceived of Him in their own racial image—the blue-eyed red-haired Thracians had their blue-eyed red-haired Thracian god on the one hand, and the snub-nosed black-skinned Africans had their snub-nosed black-skinned African god on the other. The true God of all men, Xenophanes correctly reasoned, must therefore be quite different.

Parmenides of Elea (about 500 B.C.), in addition to distinguishing between the divine and the cosmic and advocating the primacy of the former, also stood firmly opposed to the eternal flux or "perpetual movement" doctrine of Heraclitos. So firmly opposed was he to the Ionians, that he tended to deny all real flux—all "observed" movement was only illusory! It was the task of the goddess of Law and Order to prevent the becoming and passing away of being. The unchanging world was a spherical substantial form devoid of empty space. In epistemology, this led him to mistrust the senses (which seemed to represent things as being in motion) and to defend the unalterable truth of true thought by identifying it with true being. This, however, only resulted in a stagnant idealism—the opposite heresy to the fluid materialism of Heraclitos. For according to Parmenides, there was no real matter-in-motion. All that really existed was pure changeless form—an absolutization of the form motive! Cf. Plato! (Of course, from the Christian point of view, only the Triune God and His attributes [some of which are communicable to His creatures] are unchanging—but even within the unchanging Godhead, there is a non-static perpetual activity. For God is neither form nor matter—He neither changes nor stagnates—He is the *living* God—He *is*! And He is the independent God Who created both dependent matter and dependent form,[8] and Who independently sustains them both by His own almighty power.)

Zeno of Elea (not to be confused with the later Zeno of Citium [the Stoic]—who flourished more than a century later) was a pupil of Parmenides. Zeno attempted to show the absurd paradoxes which resulted from holding the opposite "all is flux" position. Change or motion is merely apparent: a flying arrow, he held, is at rest at each point of its path, and if it is in rest, it cannot be in motion! Cf. his "tortoise-beat-hare" problem. The absurdity here, of course, is Zeno's monistic subsumption of the kinematic sphere (of relatively sphere-sovereign motion) under the pre-kinematic spatial sphere.

5. *Empedocles, Anaxagoras, and the Atomists*

Empedocles of Agrigentum or Acragas in Sicily (about 450 B.C.) genially tried to reconcile the various versions of the matter motive of the different Ionian philosophers and

[8] Cf. Gen. 1:1-3 and 2:5-7.

materialists with one another, as well as with the form motive of Parmenides and the Eleatics. There are four basic material elements, he taught — fire (cf. Heraclitos), water (cf. Thales), earth, and air (cf. Anaximenes); but on the other hand, these four elements are mutually irreducible and constant, and there is a divine fire which has the primacy over against all else (cf. the Eleatics). All that exists, consists of a mixture of some or all of the four elements in varying amounts. They are drawn together by love, and separated by hate. Temporal history is part of the entire evolutionary process, and this process is epistemologically reflected in an image emanating from the observed object towards the observing subject who personally apprehends it.

Such a neat synthesis of the form and matter motives, however, was merely apparent. Even Empedocles' contemporary Anaxagoras of Clazomenae (in Ionia) multiplied the four elements into an indefinite (and essentially form-less) number of eternal "seeds," while increasing the dialectical tension within the dualistic Empedoclean synthesis by monistically reducing love and hate to equally eternal "form"—the *Nous* or panpsychic Mind. Hence, in addition to the macrocosmic and all-moving Mind, he posited a microcosm of innumerable motionless material "seeds"—which could only be moved by the Prime Mover (cf. Aristotle!), the immaterial Nous, Which was also the source of all true knowledge—intuitive knowledge, as opposed to mere sensational observation.

In Leucippus of Miletus (about 440 B.C.), the matter motive regained its primacy. Although a pupil of Parmenides, he rejected the latter's monism in favor of a plurality of basic irreducible realities which he termed "atoms" [= indivisible things; from: "a" (not) and "temnō" (I cut)]. These were the basic (and "divine") units of *all* reality (and even of the Mind). They were of irregular sizes and shapes, and they were moved around in an un-real empty space by "reasonable cause and necessity."

This view of Leucippus (and that of Democritus, below) can easily be recognized as the prototype of the theory which dominated atomic physics until the end of the nineteenth century A.D. Leucippus' views were perfected by the materialist Democritus of Abdera in Thrace (420 B.C.), a contemporary of Socrates. As a result of intercourse between solid matter and empty space, there was an initial "movement" which shook the originally mutually coherent atoms apart from one another into invisible myriads of tiny atomic particles of matter, doomed to move perpetually through the endless void, and only accidentally combined into various densities as visible objects by the *Anangkē*. And if Democritus' materialistic ontology was inconsistent, then so was his epistemology: empirical or experiential knowledge obtained by sensing "peeled off" atoms emitted from observed objects is inadequate, for such atoms can be damaged during their flight from the object to the observer; real knowledge, although it only relates to the (almighty!) atoms, is only obtained by the human mind, which is itself constructed of perfectly round atoms.

6. *Pre-Socratics in general*

We have now seen the failure of Pre-Socratic Greek ontology to arrive at a satisfactory theontological and/or existontological solution, in spite of many attempted monistic syntheses. The Ionian materialists Thales, Anaximander, and Anaximenes started the development of Greek philosophy by absolutizing the matter motive—only to have it synthesized with the form-dialectic of the contradictory Heraclitian "Logos" doctrine. Pythagoras and the Eleatic "theists" Xenophanes, Parmenides and Zeno stressed the primacy of the form motive—which in its turn, was later incorporated into the apparent form-matter syntheses of Empedocles and Anaxagoras. Yet even such syntheses were short-lived—Leucippus and Democritus again re-asserted the primacy of matter.

Democritus' matter, however, carried within it the seeds of its own destruction—ontologically, his material primacy was only to be challenged yet again by his non-immanent non-material "movement" which set matter in motion and divided it into atoms; and epistemologically, even the trustworthiness of materio-sensory impressions had to be abandoned in favor of the epistemological primacy of the mind! The matter-god and the form-god had both failed.

The fertile Greek mind had therefore failed to develop a true ontology and cosmogony by operating with the form-matter motive. Expectantly, Greek philosophy now entered its Golden Age and focused its attention particularly on the question of epistemology.

7. *The Epistemists*

By "epistemists" is here meant those Greek schools which epistemistically absolutized epistemology, irrespective of whether that epistemology was relatively true or radically false. The word is therefore used here as a blanket expression to include the sophists and the skeptics and the cynics.

Protagoras of Abdera (450 B.C.) was the oldest (and one of the most honorable) of the sophists (cf. Greek: "sophizō" = to make wise)—a school of journeying teachers which had come into being to give paid lectures to the wealthy new class of democratic citizens especially in Athens. Accordingly, Protagoras specialized in teaching wealthy young citizens (including several who later became disciples of Socrates) humanistic and pragmatic civic virtues—as opposed to absolute truth. Not a god—as in all previous Greek philosophy—but "man is the measure of all things," he believed. There are no universals, he nominalistically declared. Laws are useful, but they do not derive from a god (as previously believed) but from a pragmatic social contact between individual men. Even truth is relative: indeed, there is really no such thing as absolute truth, for there are always two sides to every argument, everyone is entitled to his own individual opinion, and truth is what works: "I know not whether the gods exist or not; the question is difficult and life is short." (Cf. James and especially Dewey!) All nature is pure matter—and only *man* can "form" it!

The skeptical element in sophism was taken much further by Protagoras' contemporary, the egoistic rhetorician Gorgias of Leontini in Sicily. Not only is absolute knowledge impossible, but even relatively true knowledge is unachievable. One can be sure only that it is uncertain whether anything really exists, for there is a gap between the thing-in-itself and the thing-for-me (cf. Kant!), and another gap between my knowledge and my ability to express that knowledge in language, and a further gap between my language and another's understanding of my language! The seeds of empirico-epistemological uncertainty present in Parmenides and Democritus now came to fruition!

A century later, this agnostic trend in sophism had degenerated into full-blooded skepticism: the denial of the objective existence of truth. For Pyrrho of Elis (330 B.C.), the senses are untrustworthy (cf. Parmenides), all knowledge is uncertain, there is no criterion for judging the truth, and one should therefore not take life too seriously. And for Carneades of Athens, a further century later, the most one can achieve is probabilism—a probable knowledge of things; even the gods are mortal, and all dogmatism even in the fields of theology and ethics was strenuously opposed.

Clearly, all these thinkers had abandoned the primacy

of the form motive and had agnostically fallen under the domination of the matter motive.

It is not to be thought, however, that the sophists' agnosticism and indifference to truth went unchallenged. One of Gorgias' own disciples, Antisthenes, abandoned him, and started the cynic philosophy (named after the "Cynosarges" or Dog's Tomb, the building in which the school gathered). He emphasized ethical virtue as the chief aim in life. This should be achieved by hard work and learning and independence of irrelevant criteria such as civilization, customs, and social status. The simpler one's life, the easier it is to attain true happiness. His pupil Diogenes of Sinope and later of Athens (380 B.C.) carried this so far that he even went to live in a barrel and regarded pain and hunger as useful means of acquiring virtuous self-control; he defied convention, became indifferent to humanity, and lived "naturally"—like an animal!

8. *Socrates*

The first really vigorous challenge to the epistemological agnosticism of the sophists, however, came from Socrates of Athens (469–399 B.C.). In Socrates, as later in Kant, a "Copernican Revolution" took place—rather than assume the inherent ability of his own thought to yield him correct information about the cosmos, as most of his predecessors had done, Socrates began with an examination of the unavoidable limitations of his own epistemological prowess (cf. Dooyeweerd). Socrates did not claim to be wise. He actually believed he knew very little. But in admitting his own epistemological limitations, Socrates thought he was wiser than those who were not wise enough to know that they only knew very little.

It is not to be assumed, however, that Socrates denied the possibility of real knowledge: he merely wished to eliminate semantic problems and arrive at conceptual clarity. And this he did by positing a series of questions which enabled his addressee, by answering them, to gain a clear meaning of phrases such as "virtue," "good," "beautiful," etc. So this question-and-answer method, *dialegein*, the so-called "Socratic dialogue," was engaged in to promote understanding rather than sophistically to prove a debating point.

To define an idea, Socrates would collect all possible examples thereof, strip them of their non-essentials, and thus inductively arrive at the definition. Although Socrates in this sense may be said to have originated the inductive methods so fruitfully employed by later natural science, and although he remained true to (sophistic) anthropocentricity, he was firmly convinced of the absolute values and their basic unity; values such as truth, ethics, wisdom, knowledge, and virtue, the unchangeable and non-material form motive *kalokagathon* or "the beautiful and the good." This was the true *Nous* which teleologically and form-atively lay at the root of the cosmos and which man should reflect on theoretically, and which, once man had achieved the virtue of such correct knowledge, he would never desert, because the *daimonion* or the divine power or the *Nous* within the human soul will prevent enlightened man from doing evil.

With all praise to Socrates, however, the Christian philosopher must nevertheless observe that he underestimated the blinding and paralyzing power of sin; and that he apparently did not teach that the *Nous* inheres in a supracosmic God. Nevertheless, it must be conceded that Socrates was brave and honest, and had a profound insight into the exalted nature of human virtues.

9. *Plato*

According to the modern philosopher and mathematician A. N. Whitehead, the history of philosophy is nothing but a series of footnotes to Plato. The consistent Christian philosopher, on the other hand, would prefer to say that the whole of the history of philosophy should be footnoted under Adam and, more particularly, under the Second Adam Jesus Christ. Certainly, however, Plato of Athens (427–347 B.C.), the founder of the Academy, does unquestionably rank as one of the greatest philosophers of all time.

A pupil of Socrates, Plato lived at a time when an unenlightened democracy was threatening to destroy the good government of Athens. Unless a state is rooted in a religious foundation, and unless its rulers are philosopher-kings, he believed, such a state would perish (cf. his *Republic*).

Theontologically, God is the automotive or Self-Moving Principle of the universe, just as the human soul, i.e., the intellect, is the self-mover of man, the principle of life, the efficient cause of all which visibly exists. In Plato's final phase, however, God was identical with the soul, and was described as "that which moves by itself."

Ontologically, there is an invisible world of pure Ideas, *universals* such as Justice, Goodness, and Virtue, a supratemporal world of pure and perfect Form, containing the prototypes of our visible world and its reflected and secondarily-real *particulars* such as justice, goodness, and virtue. "It is through The Beautiful that beautiful things become beautiful for me."

Epistemologically and anthropologically, it is the immortal and eternal soul which enables man to know the world of eternal Form. The old Mycenaeans (who stressed the primacy of matter, of the body) believed that the soul simply faded away at death. But Plato, like Pythagoras, believed that the soul eternally pre-existed in the Form-world before it was incarcerated in its material prison (the human body), and that it returns back to that Form-world on death. All true human knowledge is therefore merely the soul's reminiscence of what it previously learned in the

Form-world—and this is what enables man to make universal concepts. The physical world and the physical human body help to remind the soul of the Form-world (which they faintly resemble), but, further than that, they are of very limited value. In fact, the body and its desires can even hamper the soul (i.e., for Plato, the intellect) from regaining its freedom. The soul and philosophy (the food of the soul) are all-important. For instance, ("secular") politics as such is not evil, but the perfect politician needs at least fifteen years advanced study in ("sacred") philosophy and mathematics, in addition to his three years ("secular") military training in politics.

Plato received much common grace. He believed in God, in absolute values, in the dual nature of man, and in personal immortality beyond the grave. As such he should be honored. But Plato's views were also stained by sin. As such, his God was not the Triune God of Scripture—nor indeed even a really *personal* Being; his values were abstract and he falsely assumed the existence of an essentially non-material "other-world" essentially *opposed* to this material world. Saddest of all, he unscripturally downgraded the value of *this* world, *this* life, and *this* body; and it has been views like this which—*via* Plato's pupil Aristotle, Aquinas, and even Protestant scholasticism—have so often paralyzed some Christians from living lives fully relevant to Christ *this* side of the grave.

10. *Aristotle*

Aristotle of Stagira and later of Athens (384–322 B.C), a pupil of Plato, founder of the Lyceum and teacher of Alexander the Great of Macedon, had a truly encyclopaedic mind, and expressed himself on philosophy, ethics, art, poetry, politics, literature, rhetoric, history, logic, psychology, biology, and physics. His influence on the Roman Catholic Church via Thomas Aquinas—and, via Rome, even on some only semi-Reformed Protestants—makes it very important for us to understand him correctly.

Theontologically, Aristotle regarded God as Pure Reason, as the impersonal Prime Mover which does not Itself move or do anything, being deistically removed from the cosmos.

Cosmologically, Aristotle held that the (material) universe is co-eternal with God, and is hierarchically arranged with pure matter on the lowest level (which matter evolves into plants, animals, and man) and with the universal rational spirit, the heavenly bodies (and the deity) at the top. And matter, plants, animals, and man are all distinguished into a lower qualityless "part" consisting of matter, and a higher essential part consisting of "form," which latter (*per contra* Plato) is only distinguishable from and never separated from the matter and never referred back to a different Form-world.

Anthropologically, Aristotle correctly rejected the Platonic pre-existence of the soul, and rejected the idea of the soul's so-called "compartments" (will, intellect, emotions, etc.) in favor of the soul's "abilities." Although rejecting Plato's dual*ism* between body and soul and the idea that the body is inferior to and the prison of the soul, Aristotle nevertheless correctly insisted on the dual*ity* of the body and the soul, while simultaneously trying to teach the radical unity of body and soul. But Aristotle failed to achieve such a unity—not because he correctly saw that the soul and the body were two distinct entities, but because he incorrectly ultimately assumed that the soul was of so very much greater importance than the body in that the body is merely the human potentiality, the *material* sub-stratum, which follows after and needs to be perfected by the soul as the human actuality and the *form*-al superstratum, and is teleologically intended thus to be perfected.

Eschatologically, Aristotle did not teach the immortality of the soul, and still less of the body. But as a Greek, he just could not face the awful consequences of the annihilation of personality, and especially of the intellect. So in his *De anima* (Concerning the soul) he concluded that *part* of the soul, the *nous* or intellect, is immortal—and deified it. But hereby Aristotle denied not merely the previously claimed unity of soul and body, but even the previously claimed unity of the soul itself.

Politically, it is only in the state that man reaches his complete form. All other societal spheres (family, school, temple, etc.) are subjected to the state, which should dominate all of life. Aristotle taught his pupil Alexander the Great well! Alexander the Great's totalitarian world dictatorship effectively strangled all other non-governmental societal spheres; culture pined, and Greek philosophy declined.

From the Christian-philosophic point of view, Aristotle in some respects received even more common grace than did Plato, especially in formulating the durable so-called four laws of logic. Cosmologically, he correctly rejected the Platonic Form-world and taught that this our (visible) universe is the only one—this present universe, in which Aristotle's idea of the upward-bound progression from matter through man is in remarkable agreement with Genesis.[9] And anthropologically, Aristotle was also correct in rejecting the Platonic ideas of the pre-existence of the soul and the body as the soul's prison; correct in affirming the duality yet radical unity of soul and body, and in affirming the immortality of the soul's intellect.

But Aristotle was wrong in thinking of God deistically as a *Deus otiosus* or lazy God and also as impersonal Reason; wrong in his view of the eternity of the universe and its evolution; wrong in his hierarchical subjection of man to the universal rational Spirit (*sic!*) and to the heavenly bodies; wrong in his view that the body follows after the soul

[9] Gen. 1.

87

or is merely a potentiality (*per contra* Gen. 2:7); wrong that the body is relatively unimportant and is annihilatable; wrong that the soul (except for the *nous*) is not immortal; wrong that the *nous* can be separated from the rest of the soul; perhaps also wrong that the *nous* is the prime aspect of the soul (as over against the will, the emotions, etc.); and certainly wrong that the state should control all other societal spheres.

Many of these wrongful views have been taken over via Aquinas into Catholicism and sometimes even into Protestantism, with catastrophic effects.

11. *The Hedonists*

Hedonism or the idea of pleasure in moderation as the highest good had already been advocated by the materialist Democritus (q.v.), but it was especially Aristippus of Cyrene (435–366 B.C.), an off-beat disciple of Socrates and founder of the Cyrenaic school, who promoted this view. He denied all social responsibility and played down the value of reason and glorified the freedom of the individual—especially his freedom from pain and his freedom to enjoy every variety of sensuous pleasure (which latter, however, should be in moderation, lest it turn to pain).

Epicurus of Samos and later of Athens (341–270) B.C.) was the founder of the Epicurean school (cf. Acts 17:18). Even the (deistic) gods are material, he believed, and the real world, the material one, is composed of indivisible atoms (cf. Democritus) from which evolved the universe, plants, animals, and man (cf. Aristotle). There is no such thing as human immortality, for death annihilates human personality, and the religious fear of death is one of the main sources of psychic disorders. Accordingly, one must make the best of *this* life—too-this-worldliness! Individual happiness and pleasure—especially intellectual pleasure (*per contra* Aristippus)—is all that counts, and social and political involvement is highly undesirable.

Lucretius of Rome (96–55 B.C.), an impassioned hedonist who finally went insane, provided one of the chief accounts of Epicurean philosophy in his work *On the Nature of Things.* Here he taught a consequential materialism of the gods, the universe, and even of the (mortal) soul. In Lucretius, the pendulum largely swung back from cultural philosophy to natural philosophy (cf. Democritus).

In the light of the above materialistico-evolutionistic and hedonistico-individualistic views of the Epicureans, the Apostle Paul's sermon on Mars' Hill[10] takes on new meaning. One cannot easily overestimate the power of this heresy, for later thinkers to be influenced by hedonism include philosophers like Condillac, Helvetius, Bentham, Mill, Sidgwick, etc.

12. *The stoics*

Together with the Epicureans, the stoics (named after the "Stoa," a portico in Athens where the school met) became among the most influential of the Post-Aristotelian Hellenistic philosophers, cf. Acts 17:18, and even developed their own system of logic. They arose after the death of Aristotle, against a background of increasing imperialism and world government. Repudiating Epicurean hedonism and individualism, they, like the cynics, rather stressed an austere personal indifferentism, contempt of external evils, and the necessity of leading an unsophisticated and natural life; but they differed from the cynics in advocating a humanitarian cosmopolitanism. Although pagan, stoicism widely influenced the Mediaeval Church, the Renaissance thinkers, Shakespeare, Spinoza, Kant, Rousseau, Emerson, etc.

Zeno of Citium in Cyprus (335–265 B.C.) held that the

[10] Acts 17:18-32.

world is pantheistically animated by the World-Soul or Absolute Reason or the impersonal Logos, which fatalistically governs all that comes to pass (cf. Heraclitos). The world develops through cycles, from fire through the four elements (cf. Empedocles) and through matter, plants, animals, and man (cf. Aristotle). The soul or logos of man (collectively) is akin to the World-Soul or Logos (cf. Heraclitos), and human virtue is to be seen as a passionless rational agreement with all other men (irrespective of their race or nationality); and the natural order ultimately returns to fire at the end of the cosmogenic cycle when all human personality is conflagrated.

Cleanthes (310–232 B.C.), formerly a porter, succeeded Zeno as head of the stoical school. Indulging in heavy manual labor even in old age, he wrote many poems, including his "Hymn to Zeus," from which the Apostle Paul quoted.[11] He was succeeded by Chrysippus (280–207 B.C.), a systematician, logician, and writer of seven hundred books, who regarded the faculty of being able to make reasonable judgments (that is, judgments in accordance with nature or Absolute Reason) as the distinguishing mark between man and the animals.

Prominent Roman stoics were: Seneca (4 B.C. – A.D. 65), a jurist, ethicist, psychologist, and natural scientist who greatly influenced Thomas à Kempis, Montaigne, Rabelais, Bacon, Shakespeare, Milton, Wordsworth, and Emerson; Epictetus (A.D. 60–110) and his disciple Arrian, who influenced Hadrian, Marcus Aurelius, Montaigne, and Kant, who taught that reason ruled the world and is identical with God, and who regarded Christians as courageous but unreasonable; and Emperor Marcus Antoninus Aurelius (A.D. 121–180), who ascetically ruled his empire with rationality and consideration, and who was even praised by his much-maligned Christian subjects.

[11] Acts 17:28 (q.v.).

In the light of the stoical beliefs of pantheism, logical rationality, equality of the sexes, abolition of slavery, kindness to enemies, personal asceticism and cosmopolitan humanitarianism, Paul's sermon on Mars' Hill[12] is seen as the masterly and scholarly address it really is—especially when one remembers that he was then addressing the pleasure-seeking and individualistic Epicureans and the pleasure-hating and anti-individualistic stoics at the same time and in the same words!

13. *Syncretistic non-Christian philosophers*

Amongst those who tried to combine Plato and/or Aristotle with their own views, were Pliny and the two Plutarchs.

Gaius Plinius Secundus or the Elder Pliny (A.D. 23–79), soldier, sailor, orator, grammarian, lawyer, historian, astronomer, geographer, zoologist, botanist, anthropologist, humanist, and neo-Aristotelian philosopher, developed his own creed of pantheism and rejected the immortality of the soul. A man of encyclopaedic, vast knowledge and intense curiosity, he characteristically met his death by suffocation when curiosity drove him to observe the volcanic eruption of Vesuvius too closely. Plutarch of Chaeronea (A.D. 50–120), biographer, moralist, educationalist, naturalist, archaeologist, religionist, and neo-Platonistic philosopher, had much influence on the early Church Fathers and the Protestant Reformers Zwingli and Melanchthon. And Plutarch of Athens (A.D. 350–430), who sought to reconcile Plato and Aristotle by recommending the study of the last first, commented on the latters "Psychology" that souls do not perish when sensation ceases.

More complicated syncretisms are encountered in thinkers like Cicero, Philo, and Plotinus. Cicero, the mighty orator, lawyer, and philosopher of ancient Rome, tried to combine

[12] Acts 17:18-34.

the best of Plato, Aristotle, skepticism, and stoicism, and taught the dignity of man, the freedom of the will, the virtue of duty and the immortality of the soul. He considerably influenced the Early Church Fathers, Erasmus, Copernicus, Voltaire, and Jefferson; and John Adams, the second President of the United States, claimed that "all the epochs of world history combined were unable to produce statesman or philosopher as great as Cicero."

Philo of Alexandria (25 B.C. – A.D. 50), a Jew, tried to synthesize Greek philosophy (especially Platonism and stoicism) with the Old Testament, arguing that the former must have been derived from the latter. In Philo we see an interesting combination of common revelation, common grace, and special revelation—but no special grace! God could not defile Himself by touching unclean matter (cf. Plato), so He caused energies to emanate from Himself (into Platonic ideas, alias Biblical angels!), and which unite to form a Logos (cf. stoics), a second God, the Idea of ideas and the Archangel of all angels, the first-born Son of God, and the creative Word,[13] who forms all things out of chaotic matter, including man with his immortal spiritual soul (Platonically!) imprisoned in his evil material body, which soul can, however, identify itself with the spiritual essence of deity by mortifying all sensual desires and by intellectual cleansing. Philo's influence on Catholic scholasticism and Post-Renaissance humanism (e.g., Descartes and Spinoza) has been tremendous. Christians, beware!

More involved still was the thought of the setting sun of paganism, Plotinus of Rome (A.D. 205–270), who combined the mystique of India with the philosophy of Plato to create such a lofty concept of God that even the great Augustine dangerously declared that in order to become a Christian, Plotinus would have to change "only a few words." God, said Plotinus, is radically One, so exalted that He is only

[13] Cf. Gen. 1 and Prov. 8.

negatively knowable, yet so resplendant in glory that the universe could not but come into being as an overflowing of His superabundant reality; which overflowing or emanation of the universe, having taken place in three axiologically deteriorating stages (Spirit, soul, and matter; cf. the trinity!), axiologically ameliorates as it flows back to God from Whom it proceeded.

14. *Summary*

In this synopsis of Ancient Greek Philosophy (and of the further development thereof in Rome and elsewhere), it has been seen that the whole unfolding thereof has been dominated by the dialectical tension found in the form-matter motive at its root.

Amongst the Ionians, the matter motive was supreme, only to be relegated under the primacy of the form motive by Parmenides and the Eleatics. Empedocles and Anaxagoras seemed to achieve a synthesis between the two motives, but this was soon destroyed when the atomists and the sophists reasserted the primacy of matter—only to be once more rejected under the hegemony of the form motive as squarely established by the great Socrates, Plato, and Aristotle.

In Post-Aristotelian times, however, the position again fluctuated. The hedonists and the Epicureans re-asserted the primacy of matter—only to be challenged by the form-conscious stoics. And the final unsatisfactory syncretisms of philosophies like those of Cicero, Philo, and Plotinus only served to underline the inability of the form-matter motive as such to present a true understanding of the cosmic order.

The form-matter motive had proved to be incorrect. It had run its course. A new motive was called for. And the correct answer was to be given by God Himself when He stated the creation-fall-recreation motive anew in the earthly life, death, and resurrection of Jesus Christ.

Chapter V

EARLY CHRISTIAN PHILOSOPHY

The Thinkers of the Ancient Church

1. *Survey*

In the previous pages we have seen how God *created* the world "very good"; [1] but that when man *fell* into sin, the whole creation was cursed,[2] even though God Himself immediately promised to redeem or *re-create* it in His own good re-(d)emptive time.[2] And we also saw that, after the fall, neither Eastern philosophy with its dialectical religious basic motive of "too-this-worldliness"-"too-other-worldliness" nor Greek philosophy with its dialectical religious basic motive of form and matter, did justice to these three religio-philosophical basic motives of creation, fall, and re-creation. Only in the uninfluential Hebrew philosophy were these ideas preserved. And their universal promulgation was severely restricted until the earthly incarnation of the great Creator Himself Who would re-create His fallen creation and by His outpoured Spirit proclaim this recreation through the testimony of the early Church and the writings of its sanctified thinkers.

In this chapter, then, we will successively deal with the Christian-philosophical importance of Jesus Christ, the Holy Spirit, the Apostles, the Apostolic Fathers, the Christian Apologists, the Early Gnostics, the Anti-Gnostic Fathers,

[1] Gen. 1:31.
[2] Gen. 3:15f.

the Alexandrine Fathers, various early enemies of Christianity, the Christological controversies, and Augustine.

2. *Jesus Christ*[3]

Jesus Christ is the Lord of history and of time—in Him B.C. became A.D.: ". . . when the fullness of the time was come, God sent forth His Son."[4] The Logos or God the Son was sent forth as the Son of God and as the Son of man— two natures united in one Person, the God-man Christ Jesus.[5] As the Son of God, He is the Second Person of the Holy Trinity; as the Son of man, He is the Son of Adam, the Second Adam.

As the Son of God,[6] He is from everlasting unto everlasting—He *is*. As such, he is theontologically One with the Father.[7] Existontologically, He is the Logos—the Ground of all cosmic being.[8] Cosmogonically, all things were created by Him; and cosmologically, by Him all things consist.[9] Anthropologically, He gives life to all men,[10] and epistemologically (cf. the idea of common revelation), He enlightens every man that cometh into the world.[11] Federologically, He eternally contracted with the Father to go and save the elect in time.[12] Hamartiologically, He was Himself made the perfect sin-offering for His elect;[13] soteriologically, He saves them;[14] and eschatologically, He shall perfect all things.[15] And philosophically, in Him the Supreme Philosopher are hid(den) *all* the treasures of wisdom and knowledge[16]—the very antithesis of false philosophy, which is *not* according to Christ.[17]

[3] First read again chapter I, sections 7 and 20; and chapter II, sections 2 and 5.

[4] Gal. 4:4.
[5] Luke 3:23,38.
[6] John 3:16.
[7] John 10:30 cf. 1:1.
[8] Col. 1:15.
[9] Col. 1:16-17.
[10] John 1:4.

[11] John 1:9 cf. II Cor. 4:6.
[12] John 17:4-6.
[13] II Cor. 5:21.
[14] Matt. 1:21-23.
[15] I Cor. 15:22-28.
[16] Col. 2:3.
[17] Col. 2:8-9.

But He was not only the Son of God. He was also the Son of man,[18] the Son of Adam,[19] the Second Adam.[20] As such, He had a beginning in time, when He was born of a human virgin mother about 4 B.C. And He died a human death in time on the cross of Calvary, about A.D. 29—even though His once created humanity had everlasting continued existence and was invested with everlasting life at His resurrection from the dead three days later. As the Son of man or Second Adam, He believed: theontologically, that God is; [21] existontologically, that the universe really exists, and exists in God; [22] cosmogonically, that God created and sustains the universe; [23] cosmologically, that the universe has a God-given pluriform structure; [24] anthropologically, that man consists of body and soul[25] and that the entire human race descended from Adam and Eve; [26] federologically, that God had made a covenant of works with Him,[27] the benefits of which He would confer on all those who believed in Him; [28] hamartiologically and soteriologically, that He was the Lamb of God that taketh away the sins of the world; [29] and eschatologically, that He finished the covenantal work which God gave Him to do[30] and then entered into His glory.[31]

As Second Adam, however, Christ did not start to keep the covenant of works from the same point at which the first Adam started *before* the latter's fall into sin; but Christ started to keep the covenant of works from the point which Adam reached *after* his fall into sin. That is to say, Christ the Second Adam did not start to keep the covenant of works as *Adam supralapsarius*, but as *Adam infralapsarius*—yet Himself without sin. For the Son of man did

[18] Matt. 16:13.
[19] Luke 3:23,38.
[20] I Cor. 15:22,45-47.
[21] Mark 10:18.
[22] Matt. 6:9.
[23] John 5:17.
[24] Matt. 6:26f.

[25] Matt. 10:28.
[26] Matt. 19:4f.
[27] Isa. 42:1-7; 61:1-2 cf. Luke 4:16-21.
[28] John 17:6-22; Matt. 26:27-29.
[29] John 1:29.
[30] John 17:4 and 19:31.
[31] Luke 24:26.

not step into the shoes of the unfallen Adam, but of the fallen Adam. Although personally without sin,[32] the Son of man (unlike the unfallen Adam) nevertheless came in the likeness of sinful flesh,[33] partook of flesh and blood as the Seed of Abraham and the Seed of the woman, and was tempted in all points like as we are.[34] By His *passive* obedience, the Second Adam bore the death punishment for the sin of Adam and his descendants who also transgressed the covenant of works.[35]

But Christ the Second Adam not merely restored man from *Adam infralapsarius* to—at least in principle—*Adam supralapsarius*. Having done that, by His *active* obedience as federal Head of the entire elect human race, He further proceeded to keep the covenant of works perfectly and Himself thereby became *Adam ultralapsarius* in order to earn eternal life for His own descendants, viz., the fallen Adam and his elect descendants.[36] And so Christ has made each of His descendants—at least in principle—an *Adam ultralapsarius*. And this Christ did by perfectly keeping God's moral law and perfectly executing the cultural mandate of the covenant of works when He subdued the earth and the sea and the sky.[37] So now, as the Second Adam, Christ has Himself been made "perfect through sufferings," [38] for, "though He were a Son, yet learned He *obedience* by the things which He suffered; and, *being made perfect*, He *became* the Author of salvation unto all them that *obey*

[32] Heb. 4:15.
[33] Rom. 8:3.
[34] Heb. 2:14-18 and 4:15.
[35] Hos. 6:7 marg.; Gen. 1:26-28; 2:15-17; 3:15-17; 3:14-19; John 1:29; 10:11-18; 12:23-33; 17:4; 19:30.
[36] Hos. 6:7 marg.; Gen. 2:9,15; 3:15,20-22 cf. Rev. 1:13,17-18; 2:7; 22:2; Isa. 53:10; John 5:21,24; 6:28-29,38-40,51; 10:37-38; 11:23-26; 13:36; 14:2-3; 15:24; etc.
[37] Gen. 1:26-28; 9:1-6; Ps. 8 cf. Heb. 2; and cf. Matt. 8:23f; 21:18f; 27:45 cf. Mal. 4:2 and John 8:12; Mark 1:13; 6:45f; Luke 2:13-15 and 24:51; John 11:38f; 21:3-11; Acts 1:9.
[38] Heb. 2:10.

Him.[39] So Christ as the Second Adam has now, through His resurrection, entered "into His glory," the glory of everlasting human life.[40] And so, in Christ the Second Adam, infralapsarian man is not merely restored to supralapsarian man, but principially perfected unto ultralapsarian man, into what Adam never became but would ultimately have become had he never sinned at all and had he obediently executed the covenant of works and its cultural mandate.[41]

But after the execution of the Adamic covenant of works on Cavalry's cross, the Risen Christ as the triumphant Second Adam ordered His followers, His descendants, to execute the covenant further. His descendants. For He bore them in His wounds, brought them forth from His bleeding body in their moment of birth and His moment of death. In that moment "He saw His seed," He foresaw all His children. He saw all the travail, the birth-pangs of His soul, and brought about the birth, the rebirth, of His descendants— who were born from above, born of God, born in and from the body of God the Son.[42] As the Second Adam, He commands His regenerated descendants: "Go ye into all the world, and preach the gospel to every creature!"[43] To declare . . . *all* the counsel of God![44] "Go ye therefore, and teach all nations, baptizing them in the name of the Father, and of the Son, and of the Holy Ghost: teaching them to observe *all* things *whatsoever* I have commanded you"[45]— *all* things, *including* those things He as the eternal *Word* of God had *said* to the parents of the human race as the fed-

[39] Heb. 5:8-9.
[40] Cf. Luke 24:56; John 17:4-5; Acts 2:27-28; 7:55-56; 13:32-34; Heb. 2:14-15; *4:3-14* (N.B.!) ; 10:12-16; 11:13-19,24-26,39-40 cf. 12:1-2, 22-24; 13:14,20-21.
[41] Gen. 1:26-28; 3:22; Ps. 8 cf. Heb. 2; Rev. 1:13; 2:7; 5:12; 22:2.
[42] Isa. 53:10-11.
[43] Mark 16:16.
[44] Cf. Acts 20:27.
[45] Matt. 28:19-20.

eral heads of their children when "God *said* unto them, 'Be fruitful, and multiply, and replenish the earth, and subdue it: and have dominion over the fish of the sea, and over the fowl of the air, and over every living thing that moveth upon the earth!' " [46]

In the ascended Christ, the Second Adam has been manifested to His descendants. The Lord of culture has been "made manifest to His saints." [47] Christians are still in practice imperfect sinners. But notwithstanding this, blessedly impelled by the mighty power of the indwelling Spirit of the sinless Christ, they must now go forth with the gospel in *all* its fullness and subdue the earth. Through them, the covenant-keeping descendants of the Second Adam, "God would make known amongst the Gentiles (or the heathen nations) what is the riches of the glory of this mystery, which is: "Christ in you," the Hope of glory!" [48] And Christ must be witnessed to, and Christians must continually be "warning every man in all wisdom." [49] Warning every man that Christ the only Savior of hell-deserving sinners is also the God of culture, the Wisdom of God, the Second Adam, the Lord of glory, the Supreme Philosopher.[50]

Christ must be witnessed to. But Christians cannot confine their witnessing to the vitally important souls of men. For Christ saves not merely the soul of man; He saves the *whole* man—soul *and* body *and* mind. Again, Christ is not just the Savior of *man*—He is also Savior of the world, and all its fullness. He is not only the human Christ—not merely the Church's Christ—He is also the cosmic Christ, the divine Lord of all the *universe!* [51]

[46] Gen. 1:26-28; cf. Ps. 8; Heb. 2:6-8b,9-11; 10:12-16; I Cor. 15:22-28, 45-49,58; Rev. 14:13; 22:1-5.
[47] Col. 1:26-28.
[48] Col. 1:26-28.
[49] Col. 1:26-28.
[50] I Cor. 2:8.
[51] Eph. 1:10,20-23; Col. 1:20.

Lord of all the universe! This must be the scope of the Christian's testimony in the world of culture. Not merely "youth for Christ," but also "art for Christ," "politics for Christ," "philosophy for Christ," and "science for Christ." [52] The culturally minded Christian is called by God to develop a Christian art and a Christian politics, a Christian philosophy and a Christian educational system. The Christian who confines his religion to soul-winning and church attendance, *vital* though they are, is in fact confining the full scope of the blood of the cross, which was shed to reconcile all things, "whether they be things in earth, or things in heaven." [53] For "at the name of Jesus, every knee should bow, of things in heaven, and things on earth, and things under the earth. And every tongue should confess that Jesus Christ is Lord, to the glory of God the Father." [54]

3. *The Holy Spirit*

After Jesus Christ the Son of God and the Second Adam had re-created His fallen creation in principle, He sent His Holy Spirit Who, *inter alia*, inscribes this creation-fall-recreation religious basic motive on the hearts of the believers, on the basis of which Christian theology and Christian philosophy can unfold during the following centuries.

Theontologically, God the Supreme Philosopher is Spirit,[55] and the divine philosophical Spirit both "searcheth the . . . deep things of God" and (existontologically) *"all* things, yea." [56] Cosmogonically, the Spirit moved upon the face of the primordial waters; [57] and cosmologically, He garnishes the heavens and animates all living creatures.[58]

Especially anthropologically and epistemologically, how-

---

[52] Cf. John 14:12.
[53] Col. 1:20.
[54] Phil. 2:10-11.
[55] John 4:24.

[56] I Cor. 2:10.
[57] Gen. 1:2; Ps. 33:6.
[58] Job 26:13; 34:14-15 cf. 33:4.

ever, it is most important to understand the various philosophical operations of the Spirit, which operations may perhaps be characterized (respectively) as: supralapsarian, infralapsarian, and ultralapsarian.

The *opus hominibus supralapsarium* of the Spirit was to create man and enlighten him.[59] The *opus hominibus infralapsarium* of the Spirit was and is to seek fallen man, strive with him, to enlighten all men unto knowledge and wisdom, and to keep them alive.[60] And the *opus hominibus ultralapsarium* of the Spirit is His special work in the elect alone. It is this last operation with which we are now to be concerned.

Now the Spirit again works in at least three ways in the hearts of His elect. Firstly, He regenerates *all* the elect, and progressively sanctifies and enlightens each one of them for their own salvation and to His glory.[61] Secondly, He inspires only *certain* of the elect to write the books of the Bible.[62] And thirdly, He calls and equips *each* one of the elect to do a special work for Him vocationally—which spiritual call and equipping[63] is not only to a whole variety of different kinds of most important and God-honoring vocations in the institutional Church,[64] but also to a whole variety of different kinds of God-honoring vocations outside the Church as an institute, such as: married and unmarried,[65] husbands and wives,[66] slaves and freemen,[67] Jews and Gentiles,[68] statesmen, soldiers, and tax-collectors,[69] magis-

[59] Gen. 1:26-28; 2:7-19; Job 33:4.
[60] Gen. 3:8; 6:3; Job 32:8; Jas. 1:5.
[61] John 3:3f; Rom. 8:1f; I John 2:20,27; 4:2f.
[62] II Tim. 3:16; II Pet. 1:21.
[63] II Cor. 3:1-6.
[64] Cf. I Cor. 12:4,13,28-30; Eph. 4:4,8,11f; Acts 6:1-4; 20:17,28; Rom. 12:3-8; I Tim. 3:1-13; 5:17-19.
[65] I Cor. 7:7,24,27f.
[66] I Cor. 7:15-17,20.
[67] I Cor. 7:20-24.
[68] I Cor. 7:17-20.
[69] Ex. 3:4,10; Luke 3:12-14.

trates and lawyers,[70] kings and farmers,[71] artists and philosophers,[72] etc. As regards the vocation of the Christian philosopher, see further chapter I, sections 7-9 above; and it must be remembered that the Spirit Who instructed man to dominate the earth and the sea and the sky[73] which He had made,[74] is the same Holy Spirit Who shook the early Christian assembly and enabled it to speak the Word of God with all boldness.[75]

4. The Apostles

Jesus Christ and His Holy Spirit do not, of course, call every Christian to be a philosopher, nor even call every called philosopher to be only a philosopher; but even amidst the urgent needs of the New Testament Church, They did give much philosophical insight to the Apostles Paul and John in particular.

As regards Paul (?–A.D. 64), it must be remembered that he was an extremely learned man,[76] raised in the university town of Tarsus, and thoroughly acquainted with the influential philosophies of the stoics and the Epicureans and other philosophists, and with the Christian philosophical refutation thereof.[77] Doubtless he was also well acquainted with Greek philosophy and literature in general.[78]

Theontologically and existontologically, Paul was thoroughly Trinicentric,[79] and cosmologically, he upheld the principles of cosmic variety.[80] Anthropologically, he strongly

[70] Ex. 18:13-26; Rom. 13; Tit. 3:13.
[71] I Sam. 16; Gen. 2:15.
[72] Ex. 31:1f; Eccl. 1:13; 3:10-14, etc.
[73] Gen. 1:28.
[74] Gen. 1:1-2; Ps. 33:6f.
[75] Acts 4:24-31.
[76] Acts 22:3; 26:4-5,24.
[77] Cf. Acts 17:16-34; I Cor. 1:17 - 2:16; and cf. chapter IV, sections 11-12 above.
[78] Acts 17:28; I Cor. 15:32-33; Tit. 1:12f.
[79] Acts 17:28; Rom. 1:1-4; 11:36; II Cor. 13:13; Eph. 1; Col. 1.
[80] I Cor. 15:39-41 cf. 12:27-30.

believed in the covenantal headship of Adam.[81] Epistemologically, he taught that God revealed Himself to men in nature, history, and conscience,[82] and in Christ.[83] Hamartiologically, he warned against being spoiled by vain deceit and philosophy and science falsely so-called—falsely called philosophy because, unlike True Philosophy, it was not "after Christ."[84] Soteriologically, the recreative work of Christ is of cosmic scope,[85] he believed, and eschatologically, the recreation of the cosmos will take place in a clear-cut and orderly fashion.[86]

The Apostle John (?–A.D. 96) seems to have been inspired by the Holy Spirit particularly to counteract the speculative Logos doctrine of Greek philosophy, and, in the light of God's special revelation, to correct sinful man's imperfect understanding of God's common revelation (cf. Heraclitos, the stoics and Philo in chapter IV, sections 3, 12, and 13 above).

Theontologically, John was at pains to point out that the Logos is very God of very God and ontically congruent with the ground of all cosmic being.[87] Cosmogonically, all things without any exception were created and are sustained by the Logos;[88] and cosmologically, the cosmos in all its different parts are His by creation and by recreation.[89] Anthropologically, the Logos Himself became man and dwelt amongst men,[90] epistemologically revealing the very Ground of the universe to men in general and to His beholders in particular.[91] Soteriologically, there is salvation only through

[81] Rom. 5:12f; I Cor. 15:21f.
[82] Acts 14:15-17; Rom. 1-2.
[83] I Cor. 15; Col. 2; Eph. 4; Tit. 2:11.
[84] Col. 2:8; I Tim. 6:20.
[85] Eph. 1:10-23; Col. 1:13-20.
[86] I Cor. 15:22-28; I Thess. 4:13-17; Rom. 8:19f.
[87] John 1:1.
[88] John 1:3; 5:17.
[89] Rev. 1:4-8; 4:1 - 5:14.
[90] John 1:14.
[91] John 1:4f,9f; 14:6-9; I John 1:1-4.

faith in the Logos,[92] Who taketh away the sins of the world,[93] and Who eschatologically redeems the entire cosmos.[94] In John's inspired opinion, the Logos Who became flesh was the Great Philosopher of mankind, the greatest soul the world had ever known, for, apart from doing the things recorded by John,[95] the Logos also did so "many other things . . . , which, if they should be written every one, I suppose that even the world itself could not contain the books that should be written." [96]

The inspired Apostles Paul and John, then, rejected the false and dialectical "too-*this*-worldly"-"too-*other*-worldly" religious basic motive of Eastern philosophy as well as the equally false and dialectical "form-matter" motive of Greek thought. Instead, they advocated a profoundly Christian life and world view rooted in the biblical religious basic motive of Trinicentric creation, fall, and recreation.

5. *The Apostolic Fathers*

The Apostolic Fathers were those early Christian thinkers who, although they had not known Jesus Christ personally while He was on earth, had nevertheless known the Apostles personally.

Clement of Rome (?–A.D. 96), apparently one of Paul's helpers,[97] enjoined the Christians to be peaceable and loving and humble. Ignatius of Antioch (?–A.D. 111) and Polycarp of Smyrna (A.D. 69–155), friends of the Apostle John, pleaded for the unity of the Christian community and against heretical preachers, and were martyred in the Colosseum at Rome; whereas Papias of Hierapolis, a friend of Polycarp, wrote an exposition of the Words of the Lord which was widely quoted by later Christians.

[92] John 14:6; I John 2:23.
[93] John 1:29.
[94] John 14-16; Rev. 5-6; 18-22.
[95] John 20:30.
[96] John 21:25.
[97] Cf. Phil. 4:3.

104

6. The Christian Apologists

From about A.D. 140 onwards, a number of writings appeared which sought to defend Christianity against attacks from non-Christians, such as Marcianus Aristides' theontological and cosmological *Apology* or Defense of the Christian Faith submitted to Emperor Antonius Pius.

More important are the works of Flavius Justinus the Martyr (about A.D. 100–164). In his *Dialogue with Trypho* the Jew, he maintained that philosophy is an excellent divine gift intended to lead man to his Maker. Discussing the inadequate philosophies of Heraclitos, Pythagoras, and the stoics, he nevertheless correctly pointed to the common-revelatory significance of the Logos doctrine in ancient Greek thought—even though he underestimated the perverting role of sin therein. Still, he was not free from Platonic influence, especially in his two Apologies, and the syncretistic influence of Philo can also be detected, especially in his Logos doctrine.

Other Christian Apologists who used philosophy to defend their views were Athenagoras and Theophilus of Antioch (both about A.D. 180).

7. Early Gnostics

A powerful non-Christian philosophico-religious movement which early threatened the very existence of the Church, was heathen Gnosticism. There were many varieties, but most of them agreed that the present material world is evil (cf. Oriental "too-other-worldliness" and Platonic anti-material "form-ness") and was not created by the Almighty God but by a lower god or "demiurg," with numerous other lower spirits or "aeons" ultimately connecting the demiurg to the world. The highest and good God is even above the demiurg, and He, pure Spirit, is absolutely divorced from this evil and material world.

The Apostles John and Paul appear to be attacking

kinds of Gnosticism in some of their writings,[98] and God has thus been pleased to warn His Church of all ages thereagainst. Certainly the creation-denying role of Gnosticism in infecting the pure creation-fall-recreation religious basic motive of true Christian theology and true Christian philosophy with the false form-matter religious basic motive of pagan Greek philosophy and the "too-this-worldly"-"too-other-worldly" religious basic motive of ancient Eastern philosophy, can hardly be underestimated. For its effects can to some extent be seen in the syncretistic nature-grace motive of Romanism and in some only semi-Reformed brands of Protestantism such as Pietism.

One of the most famous, elaborate and extreme forms of Gnosticism is the system of the heathen Valentine. Other influential figures were Saturnine (or Saturnol), Basilides, and the Ophites or "snake-brethren."

Saturnine, a pupil of Simon Magus[99] and Menander (who advocated the combination of the Persian dualism of Zoroaster with the Babylonian tradition of the Manda-aeon or divine power), dated from around A.D. 125. Saturnine believed the Father created all kinds of angels—seven of them being supposed to have created the earth. There are two kinds of men: the good group which inherits the so-called vital sparks from the higher world, and the bad group which does not and which serves matter. Christ is the unborn and incorporeal Son of God—He fought against demons, the bad group of men, and even against the God of the Jews. It is by asceticism that the vital sparks (of the spirit) are to be redeemed from matter.

Basilides, a Syrian of Alexandria, taught that there are two realms: a realm of light and a realm of darkness or matter. From the depths of the realm of light or the unborn God, there emanated a number of powers, including

[98] John 1, I John 4 and Col. 2.
[99] Cf. Acts 8.

106

the Logos and the angels. The angels then created the first heaven, and, out of that, other angels created a second heaven, and so on up to three hundred and sixty-five heavens (cf. the number of days in the solar year), the last heaven being the one observed by man and controlled by the seven spirits of the planets with the God of the Jews at the head. Now this latter heaven borders on matter, on the realm of darkness, which grasps the light particles of heaven and imprisons them.

Now the lord and the angels of this latter heaven created the visible earth and its peoples out of a mixture of light and darkness, and divided the nations amongst the spirits of the planets. But when jealousy arose amongst the leaders of the latter heaven which led to perpetual wars in heaven and on earth, the unborn and unknown God sent His first-born son, the *nous*, to earth as Christ, to preach to men the *gnosis* or true knowledge whereby man may ultimately be redeemed *from his body*! The *nous* cannot suffer, so that the crucifixion had no significance for the gnostics; Christ merely had a pseudo-body while on earth, but even that was not crucified—for, unbeknown to the Jews, they crucified Simon of Cyrene instead of Christ.

Valentine sought to unite all knowledge in a Hellenistic religio-philosophical synthesis. God, he believed, is *Buthos* or Depth and *Autopater* or Self-Father. From God there emanated in pairs: *Siche* or Silence (as feminine principle), from whose intercourse with *Buthos nous* or mind (masculine) and *aletheia* or truth (feminine) proceeded; and also *Logos* or thought (masculine) and *zoe* or life (feminine), as well as the so-called pairs of aeons or secondary divine beings.

Now one of these aeons was *sophia* or wisdom, who was unfaithful to her husband and desired *Autopater* for her mate. Consequently, she fell into matter (which was co-eternal with God). From the spiritual elements present in her, she bore Christ, Who climbed up to the spiritual world where He essentially belonged. But she also bore (from the material elements!) the *demiurgos* or world-maker, and also the devil. Both the Holy Spirit (which proceeded from the Church) and Jesus were given for salvation, in that they cause the divine light to come down into the soul of man: as soon as a soul sees the light, he is saved, for then he sees God. Not everyone can see this light, for there are three kinds of men: those who possess the true *gnosis* are the *pneumatic* or spiritual ones, who are pantheistically and completely absorbed into the deity; the *psychic* or emotional ones are the ordinary members of the church as a whole who do not possess the pneumatic seed of life and who receive a lower salvation; and the *somatic* or corporeal ones are destroyed by fire together with the matter.

The Ophites (from the Greek "ōphis" = a snake) or "snake-brethren"—together with similar groups such as the Nachasenes (from the Hebrew "nāchās" = a serpent), the Perates and the Cainites, were very active oriental Gnostics. The Perates taught that Eve was liberated from the Old Testament God by the Son (of God) Who appeared to her in the form of a serpent. The Cainites glorified Cain as the one who led the fight against the God of the Jews; and they glorified Judas Iscariot as the hero who achieved the triumph of getting the Jewish Messiah to be crucified.

Saddest of all, however, were the victims which Gnosticism claimed not outside but inside the Church. Marcion of Sinope, for example (about A.D. 140), apostasized from Christianity and became an agnostic. The Old Testament was false and its Jewish god who made the world, he held, was only an inferior demiurg. It is the New Testament God, Who revealed Himself in Christ, Who is the true God. He, the God of love, was cruelly nailed to the cross by the Old Testament god of wrath. Rejecting even all the New Testament books except those of Paul, he was excommunicated from the Christian Church, after which he established his own "church" which exalted asceticism and celibacy and which advocated repeated baptisms.

Another sad case was that of Tatian, originally a pupil of Flavius Justinus! Originally he strongly opposed Greek philosophy and adhered to a profoundly Biblical outlook, especially in the area of theontology and cosmogony. However, even at that time he almost totally rejected common revelation and common grace, and advocated a vigorous asceticism. This imbalance ultimately toppled him when he renounced Christianity for Valentinianism and subsequently started his own sect.

Tatian later advocated teetotalism and celibacy and opposed cosmetics and philosophy as works of the devil.

8. *The Anti-Gnostic Fathers*

Irenaeus of Lyons (A.D. 130–202), an acquaintance of Polycarp, emphasized the old Johannine cosmogonical Logos doctrine[100] and the idea of exnihilation, in his attack against the false demiurgy of the Gnostics; and in his idea of recapitulation, he emphasized the federal headship of the incarnated Second Adam, in his attack against the false re-incarnationism of the Gnostics (cf. Plato). And Irenaeus' pupil Hippolytus (about A.D. 200) accused the Greek philosophers of glorifying creation while being ignorant of the Creator.[101]

Perhaps the greatest of the Anti-Gnostic Fathers, however, was Tertullian of Carthage (A.D. 160–230). A lawyer converted to Christianity at the age of forty, Tertullian was the creator of standard theological terms like "trinity," "Person(s)," and "substance." Extremely opposed to the Gnostic philosophy that matter is evil, Tertullian reacted so violently that he: (a) taught that the human soul and

[100] John 1:1f; I John 1, etc.
[101] Cf. Rom. 1:25.

109

even God is material, and (b) rejected philosophy as such. This, coupled with Tertullian's extreme asceticism, tended to make him an unbalanced personality, as evidenced by his irrational statement: "I believe because it is impossible." (Cf. the Post-Kantian and especially the Post-Kierkegaardian Christian existentialists!) Confining his Christianity to Church activities, he started attacking other Christians who held political office under the Roman emperors. He also condemned Christian artists and even military service and second marriages. Not surprisingly, he ultimately quit the true Church and joined a proto-Pentecostal-type spiritualistic sect known as the Montanists. However, his countryman Cyprian of Carthage (200–258), although ascetic, did not go to the extreme of leaving the Church.

9. *The Alexandrine Fathers*

If Tatian and Tertullian had proved that a radically antiphilosophical attitude can lead a Christian into schismatic heresy, the Alexandrian Titius Flavius Clemens and his pupil Origen were to demonstrate the great danger of a syncretistic philosophical attitude "not after Christ." [102]

Titius Flavius Clemens or Clement of Alexandria (A.D. 150–216), after imbibing much Greek and Oriental philosophy and Gnosticism, was converted to Christianity. Attempting to synthesize Greek philosophy with Christian thought as Philo had done with Jewish thought, he erroneously regarded Christianity as basically a system of philosophy and deification of man to which one can graduate from Greek philosophy (where the divine Logos had enlightened heathen like Plato, the greatest of all philosophers).

Theontologically, Clement maintained that it can only be known what God is not (cf. the neo-Platonist Plotinus), and not what He is, although He, and not a demiurg, created

[102] Col. 2:8.

the world, and created it through His subordinate Logos immanent in Him and proceeding from Him. Anthropologically, man was originally created ethically neutral and with two souls (a carnal and a rational one) and a body. Hamartiologically, it was the sex act which caused the fall; original sin he denied, and man's will is still free. Soteriologically, one is saved by knowing of the exemplary life of Christ, and eschatologically he believed in the purging of the wicked after death in a spiritual fire (cf. Purgatory) and in the ultimate resurrection of the body (against the Gnostics).

Origen (185–253), the phenomenal writer of about six thousand books, carried these theories much further. Theontologically, his views of the Son and the Spirit were influenced by Philonic emanationism—the Son is a "Second God" lower than the Father, and the Spirit is in turn subordinated to the Son. Existontologically, he upheld the eternity of "created"(?!) reality alongside of God. Cosmogonically, he believed in an infinite succession of different worlds, and anthropologically he asserted the pre-existence of the soul and its eschatological elevation (together with the *apokatastasis* or universal restoration of even the devil and his angels) to union with God—only to go through an infinite succession of cosmogonies thereafter!

10. *Various early enemies of Christianity*

Apart from the Gnostics (section 7, above), early Christian thought also had many bitter and direct enemies amongst the heathen philosophies who made a specialty of attacking Christianity.

Lucian of Samosata (A.D. 125–200) regarded Jesus as a sophist who had been crucified in Palestine, and he regarded Christians as simple people who allowed themselves to be deceived. Celsus, a Platonically influenced Epicurean, however, was much more antagonistic: Christ was represented as the adulterous son of Mary and a Roman soldier; miracles were deceitful; God was just as unconcerned about people as He was about apes and flies; Jesus Himself was regarded as the greatest deceiver Who learned His magical tricks while in Egypt, and His resurrection from the dead was the "biggest lie."

Mani of Ctesiphon (A.D. 215–276) traveled widely, even as far as India and China, and constructed a synthesis between Western thought and even such elements as Zoroastrianism and Buddhism. The universe is the theater of a great struggle between the light and the darkness, which was unleashed when man first appeared. Buddha, Zoroaster, and Jesus represent pinnacles of light which tower above the material darkness all about (cf. Plato and gnosticism). Redemption is through ascetic self-effort to withdraw from contact with evil matter. Manichaeanistic tendencies are found in Lactantius (260–340) and, prior to his conversion to Christianity, in Augustine (see section 12, below).

Porphyry of Tyre (233–304) not only edited the writings of his teacher Plotinus (see chapter IV, section 13, above), but he also ascetically revised neo-Platonism and rationalistically opposed all magic and belief in devils. His book *Against the Christians* was an influential attack on Christianity.

Jamblichus of Syria (270–330), a pupil of Porphyry, constructed a polytheistic philosophy with a whole gamut of gods, demons, angels, and heroes. Amongst non-Christians, he has been hailed as an equal to Plato and the "Savior of Greece" and the "Healer of souls" right down to the nineteenth century. In Jamblichus one sees the complete chaos of the synthetic philosophies of the ancient world.

11. *The Christological controversies*

It has been seen above that Philo regarded the Logos as a mere emanation from God, and that the Gnostics constantly emphasized the difference between the good God and the lesser god or demiurg who created the world. Against this background, there was a constant tendency amongst the early Christians to water down the Johannine doctrine that the Word was God.[103] What was ultimately at stake here is not merely Christian theology or Christian philosophy, but even the Christian religion itself—for as God alone should be worshiped, Christians would be polytheists in worshiping Christ, if Christ were not very God of very God. If Christ be not God, He should not be worshiped—but in that case there would be no real Mediator between God and man; and with no Mediator there would also be no connection between (a deistic!) Creator and (an ontically and epistemologically barren!) creation—i.e., there would be no possibility of a living philosophy.

Around 230, the heretic Sabellius of Lybia, although stressing the oneness of the Trinity, denied the threeness—Father, Son, and Spirit are just three different names or modes of the one and the same divine Person; one may just as well say that the Father died on the cross.

From about 300 onwards, Arius of Alexandria, following Origen's ideas to their logical conclusion, advocated the opposite heresy to Sabellius—Arius stressed the threeness but denied the oneness of the Trinity: the Father, Son, and Spirit are three distinct entities, but only the Father is God. The Son is like God (*homoiousias*), but not identical to God (*homoousias*); for the Son is the first of all creatures (and thus like Aristotle's universal rational spirit between God and the cosmos).

Arius' chief opponent was the orthodox and godly Athanasius of Alexandria (298–373), who held to the absolute equality of the Father and the Son.[104] However, Eusebius of Caesarea (260–340) sought to preserve the unity of the Christian Church by compromising the teaching. A great Christian historian, yet unfortunately strongly influenced by (neo-)Platonism, he proposed that all Christians accept

[103] Cf. John 1:1f.

the Origenistic formulation (see section 9, above) of a moderate subordinationism.

Fortunately for Christianity, however, Athanasius carried the day. The General Council of *Nicea* in 325 confessed that the Son was "God of God, Light of Light, true God of true God, begotten not created, of the same essence as the Father, and through Whom all things were made," and that "the Holy Ghost (was) the Lord and Giver of life." And the later Athanasian creed affirmed that "it is necessary to eternal salvation . . . [to] believe and confess that our Lord Jesus Christ is both God and man."

Gregory of Nyssa (335–395) solidified trinitarianism— even though his neo-Platonic background prevented him from arriving at a pure trinicentrism. Although advocating ultimate *apokatastasis* and mystical asceticism as the way to the deification of the soul, he correctly taught that the Son was eternally begotten and of the same essence as the Father and that these were distinct Persons within the one essence of God—even though Gregory regarded the three Persons as the independentized three relations between Creator and creation, viz., cause, means, and purpose (cf. Aristotle). Ambrose of Milan (340–397), a great Christian ethicist, also strongly opposed Arianism.

Later, Nestorius of Germanica and Eutyches of Constantinople gave further evidence of the danger of trying to synthesize Greek and Christian philosophical motives. In about 428, Nestorius — dualistically and spiritualistically separating soul and body antithetically from one another as good and evil—taught that there were two persons in Christ, a spiritual divine person and a "natural" human person, which, of course, distinctly denied the unity of Christ's personality. Anxious to remedy this, Eutyches reacted too far the other way by rationistically trying to preserve the unity of Christ's person by confusing His two natures. But this meant He was neither God nor man, but a hybrid mon-

114

ster, who could exercise neither the divine prerogative of forgiving sin nor the human duty of keeping the Adamic covenant of works. When this was realized, the Council of Chalcedon in 551 rejected both these heresies and emphasized that the divine and human natures of Christ were "unmixed and unaltered, undivided and unseparated."

12. *Augustine*

Without the slightest doubt, Augustine was the greatest Christian philosopher (and also the greatest Christian theologian) of the early Christian centuries—and possibly of all time. Born in Carthage in 354, he received a thorough education in the Latin and Greek classics, and then sought rest for his passionate soul first in Manichaeanism and then in neo-Platonism (and especially in that of Plotinus). But his soul found no rest, until it later came to rest in Christ, as a result of hearing the preaching of Ambrose of Milan.

Theontologically, Augustine wrote fifteen volumes on the Trinity, and asserted that God is the highest truth, good, and beauty, the Ground of all being and Form, essentially distinct from all other (created) being. Cosmogonically, this present creation is the only creation, exnihilated with and in time to the glory of God. Cosmologically, all that God created is "very good" and triunely reflects His Trinity, and is sustained in its dependent being by God's continual Providence—matter is good! (*per contra*, the Gnostics!)

Anthropologically, Augustine denied the pre-existence of the soul, although he regarded it as the highest of all creatures and as triune (memory, understanding, and will); it thus reflects the Trinity. However, the body is in no sense the prison of the soul (*per contra*, Plato). Man was created according to the image of God, completely harmoniously, possessed of great intuitive wisdom, not subject to laborious exhaustion, and as lord of the animals, etc. The body, as distinct from the utterly immortal soul, was created mortal, but could become immortal if Adam did not fall. Although Augustine regarded reason as the most important spiritual gift, he did not subordinate the will thereto—nor *vice-versa*.

Hamartiologically, Augustine believed that evil had no eternal or substantial essence (*per contra*, Mani), and was merely a radical diminution of virtue— a *privatio boni actuosa*. It had cosmic proportions, damned the entire human race in Adam's original sin, whence it is transmitted to every descendant of Adam by natural generation. Soteriologically, he regarded supralapsarian grace as an *adjutorium quo fit* or a help whereby one can (achieve eternal life), and infralapsarian saving grace as a *sine qua non* utterly necessary for salvation.

Epistemologically, Augustine clearly saw the pre-scientific and religious nature of all knowledge: he believed in order that he might understand, not *vice-versa* (*per contra*, rationalism!), and it was necessary to believe the Holy Scriptures in order to arrive at truth. All science should be Christian, and Christian philosophy, for example, should be developed as a handmaiden for Christian theology.

Philosophico-historically, the entire course of world history is the unfolding of the mighty struggle between the forces of good and the forces of evil, between the City of God and the Secular City. The State and the City of Babylon are not identical, but the Church is superior to the State.

Psychologically, his self-analysis yielded useful results and anticipated modern theories, and, especially after his controversy with the heretic Pelagius of Britain (360–420), he taught the total soteriological inability of the depraved human will. And eschatologically, he taught the resurrection of the flesh and the eternal punishment of the wicked in a place of physical fire.

In his work called the *Trinity*, Augustine developed his theontology; in his *Commentary on Genesis* and in his *On the Orders*, he expounded his cosmogony and cosmology;

in his *On the Immortality of the Soul* and his *Confessions*, psychology; in his *City of God*, his philosophy of history, and in his *Against the Academicians*, his epistemology. Augustine's influence on Luther, Calvin, Pascal, Descartes, and Leibniz was tremendous. However, a remnant of neo-Platonism is seen in his thought in his apparent elevation of the spiritual above the material: the soul is vastly superior to the body, the Church to the State, faith to reason, "spiritual" matters to cultural pursuits, theology to natural science and even to philosophical science—philosophy was, in fact, merely the handmaid of theology, rather than a fully fledged, relatively independent, sphere-sovereign sister-science governed by pre-theological and independent and pre-scientific and God-given faith in the Lord and in His infallible Word. Augustine's misapprehension was destined to encourage the later development of (1) the Romish nature-grace religious basic motive which radically subjected the material to the "spiritual," and (2) as a reaction thereagainst, the humanistic science-freedom motive which radically subjected the "spiritual" to the material—instead of encouraging the radical subjection of both the material and the spiritual to God and to His Word. (See: chapter I, section 20, above.)

Yet notwithstanding all this, Augustine's philosophy is still basically molded according to the Biblical religious basic motive of creation-fall-recreation—if his philosophy did have some non-Christian elements in it, it was certainly not his intention; *per contra*, Origen and Aquinas! And Augustine's later true successors, the Reformers in general and Calvin in particular, would intentionally try to remove those non-Christian elements and develop an exclusively Biblical life and world view.

13. *Summary*

The apostate "too-this-worldly"-"too-other-worldly" and

117

form-matter religious basic motives of Oriental and Greek thought respectively, were challenged by the true creation-fall-recreation religious basic motive of Christian philosophy in the life and teaching of Jesus Christ the Second Adam and His Holy Spirit as also infallibly manifested in the writings of the inspired Apostles such as Paul and John.

This testimony was continued by the Apostolic Fathers, but it was particularly the Apologists who consciously began to develop a real Christian philosophy, or at least the embryonic stages thereof. The anti-Christian attacks of the heathen Gnostic philosophers and other enemies of the gospel forced the Anti-Gnostic Fathers and especially the Alexandrine Fathers to develop a Christian philosophy to equip God's people with their own life and world view— even though these attempts contained many imperfections and sometimes indeed neo-Platonic heathen influence. But after the Christological controversies had finally hammered out the doctrines of the eternal deity of Christ the Logos and the ontological Trinity of God to the satisfaction of the Christians, Christian philosophy reached its greatest statement in the early Christian era in the writings of Augustine of Hippo, who would long dominate Christian thought and its subsequent development in succeeding centuries, and whom many still consider to be the greatest Christian philosopher of all time.

Chapter VI

MEDIAEVAL WESTERN PHILOSOPHY

Stagnation and Synthesis

1. Survey

After the death of Augustine (A.D. 430), in whom early
Christian philosophy reached its climax, a slow retrogression set in, ultimately resulting in the humanistic Renaissance; and this deplorable trend was only checked by the
the Protestant Reformation and its rediscovery of the true
and Christian basis of theoretical thought.

The reasons for this slow retrogression and for Christianity's inability to continue with the forceful Augustinian
Christianization of the whole of life, were both external
and internal.

Externally, the fall of Rome and Odoacer's barbarian
invasion from the north in 476 greatly weakened the forces
of Christianity (which were already undermined by internal
factors), and pious believers left the cities now occupied by
the barbarians and fled to the rural areas where they established monastic communities. Again, the rise of Islam
and Islamic thought and, less importantly, the resurgence
of Jewish thought, both of them hostile to Christianity (and
both of which influenced the rise of later scholasticism)
tended to check the spread of the true Christian outlook.

Internal factors, however, were even more instrumental
in the stagnation of Christianity and the advent of the

119

Dark Ages. Firstly, there was the continuing influence of latent neo-Platonism which even the great Augustine had not entirely overcome. Secondly, there was the increasing Romanization of Christianity on account of its centering around the imperial city of Rome, with all its pagan influences. And thirdly, there was the growth of monastic communities after the fall of Rome; and the increasingly unnatural lives of such communities, coupled with the resurgence of Platonism and Aristotelianism from the tenth century onwards, divorced the world of nature from the world of grace and led to scholasticism on the one hand and to mysticism on the other, both of them governed by the apostate religious basic motive of nature-grace.

In this chapter on mediaeval philosophy, we will successively deal with Islamic philosophy, Jewish philosophy, orthodox Christian philosophy, pseudo-Christian philosophy, Thomism, voluntarism, and mysticism.

2. *Islamic philosophy*

A world event of major significance took place with the birth of the religion of Islam. After establishing itself in Arabia, its views were forcibly propagated elsewhere too, so that by the time Charles Martel finally checked it in 732 at the Battle of Tours, it was dominant from Spain through North Africa to Afghanistan. Then Islam gradually mellowed; its scholars absorbed some neo-Platonism and especially neo-Aristotelianism and even became the chief bearers of Hellenistic philosophy during the dark ages; and ultimately they even influenced the Christian scholastics themselves.

Mohammed (570–632) was the great founder of the religion of Islam. Influenced by Judaism, Christianity, Arabian heathenism, Gnosticism, and Babylonian thought, he established a rigid new life and world view. Theontologically, he repudiated both polytheism and the Trinity in favor of a strict monotheism (or rather: deism); cosmologically, he believed that the world is continually recreated and upheld by the sovereign power of Allah; anthropologically, he largely embraced the Biblical account as to the origin, essence, and destiny of man; epistemologically, he repudiated and viewed the Bible as a corrupted account of divine revelation, regarding his own pronouncements, which were later compiled into what is now the *Koran*, as the only infallible and inspired rule of faith; Christologically, he regarded Christ as a virgin-born miracle-performing prophet second in importance only to himself, repudiating His deity and saviorhood yet insisting on His second coming; soteriologically, he advocated salvation by works such as credal recitation, prayers, almsgiving, asceticism, and pilgrimage; and eschatologically, he placed great emphasis on the horrors of the Day of Judgment and the sensuous pleasures of Paradise.

After a period of political and religious consolidation, Islamic philosophy began to develop, the first great Arabic thinker being Al-Kindi of Baghdad (800–870), a highly educated man of encyclopaedic knowledge. Combining his Islamic ideas with neo-Platonism, neo-Aristotelianism, and neo-Pythagoreanism, he was the first man to apply mathematics to physics and to medicine, and he also wrote on music and psychology. Philosophically, he represented God as the *Nous* or intelligent cause of the cosmos, Who, by communicating Himself through many emanations, liberates and immortalizes man.

Even more under the influence of Greek thought was Al-Farabi of Damascus (870–950). Metaphysically, he followed neo-Platonic or Plotinian emanationism, but in logic he was "The Second Aristotle" and used the Stagirite's laws of thought to schematize Islamic doctrine. Rather syncretistic in his views of God, time, and space, he was also an authority on music and on the intellectuality, unity, and substantiality of the human soul. Although basically a mysticistic idealist, his works were nevertheless very instrumental in promoting the views of Aristotle amongst the Arabs.

The mysticistic trend towards pantheism—perhaps as a reaction against the stark deism of Islamic orthodoxy—is further developed in the thought of Avicenna of Bokhara (980–1037), the real founder of Islamic scholasticism. A celebrated physician, he was also an accomplished logician, metaphysician, mathematician, and physicist. A student of the writings of Al-Farabi, he tried to synthesize Islam, neo-Platonism, and Aristotle. God and the world are co-eternal (cf. Aristotle); reality emanates from God into negative matter (cf. Plotinus); and he anticipated Thomas Aquinas in teaching that universals exist *ante res* (or before particular things, in the mind of God), *in rebus* (or imminently in each particular) and *post res* (or as an epistemological abstraction after inductive observation of the particulars).

A rather more orthodox Islamic voice was heard from Al-Ghazzali of Baghdad (1059–1111), who renounced the heretical philosophy of Avicenna in his book *Destruction of the Philosophers*, in which he anti-emanationistically asserted God's universal causality and His eternal pre-existence prior to the essentially non-co-eternal temporal world. Yet he nevertheless placed neo-Platonic mysticism at the disposal of his theological Sufism or Islamic mysticism.

However, Averroës of Cordova (1126–1198), a student of medicine, politics, astronomy, and jurisprudence, and the greatest Westernized Moslem scholar, was a convinced Aristotelian who assailed the anti-philosophical Al-Ghazzali in his book *Destruction of the Destruction of the Philosophers*. This book, translated from Arabic into Latin, profoundly influenced Christian philosophers for the next two hundred years. Averroës asserted the eternal existence of the world, denied personal immortality, and taught that the same proposition may be theologically true yet philosophically untrue, and the other way around. Like Clemens Alexandrinus, he believed that religion is adequate for the common man but that the full truth is found only in philosophy. Not surprisingly, he was violently attacked by orthodox Moslems and later by Thomas Aquinas, and his havoc-causing views were condemned by the Christian Church in 1277. Clearly, anyone who elevated philosophy above theology was anathema to the scholastics who themselves elevated theology above philosophy!

3. Jewish philosophy

After the rejection of the Second Adam and Messiah Jesus Christ, the Jewish nation as a whole not only shut its eyes to the additional divine revelation of the New Testament, but also departed more and more from the true meaning of the Old Testament, particularly by multiplication of the vain traditions of men (Matt. 15:9) which thenceforth increasingly dominated Jewish life.

These legalistic human traditions, later codified in the Talmud or "(Book of) Research," probably commenced as far back as the Exile (597 B.C.), but acquired a much accelerated impetus after the Roman destruction of the reconstructed temple in A.D. 70 and the dispersion of the Jewish remnant amongst the Gentiles. For the first two hundred years of the Christian era, Jewish rabbis developed opinions on marital, social, and other matters, and in the third century these opinions were codified in a book known as the Mishnah or "Repetition," which was in turn supplemented during the next three centuries by copious discussions thereof and commentaries thereon in a book known as the Gemara or "Learning." These two books together comprise what is now known as the Talmud.

123

The necessary reaction to the unavoidable formalism of the legalistic Talmud had to be forthcoming, and it took the form of the *Cabbalah*, a mysticistic body of Jewish literature which developed for over a thousand years from the mediaeval post-Talmudic era right down to the Chassidism of the modern Jewish philosopher Martin Buber. In Cabbalism, God manifests Himself in ten emanations (cf. Plotinianism) such as Wisdom, Reason, Knowledge, etc., whereby man, by dedicating himself thereto, can enter into a mystical union with God.

From the ninth century onwards, Jewish thought became more and more syncretistic. Saadia of Egypt (892–942), for example, a mathematician, philologist, and philosopher, believed that Judaism was reconcilable with the "truth" of Hellenism, Christianity, Manichaeanism, Zoroastrianism, and Hinduism. This "truth" was that faith is not opposed to reason, and that all who think otherwise are in error, be they Moslems, Jews, Christians, or heathen.

More in the true neo-Platonic mold was Gabirol of Malaga alias Avicebron or Avencebrol (1020–1070), whose book *The Fountain of Life* greatly influenced Franciscans like Alexander of Hales and Duns Scotus, although it was assailed by most of the Dominicans and especially by Thomas Aquinas. Gabirol taught the Platonic ideas of the pre-existence of the soul, the reminiscence theory of knowledge, the basic antagonism between form and matter, and the Plotinian idea of emanationism.

The great Jewish poet Judah Halevi (1080–1140) acutely observed that Judaism centers in the Jewish people as a whole and not in the personality of its founder, as do the religions of Christ and Mohammed. Although somewhat influenced by Platonism, and especially by the idea of God as the principle of form, he rejected Aristotle's view of the iron causal necessity of the nature of the deity as incompatible with the personality of God.

It is remarkable that Jews have regarded Moses Maimonides of Cordoba (1135–1204), an accomplished physician and rationalistic Aristotelian, as second in Jewish history only to Moses the Lawgiver. Foreshadowing the Christian scholastics in general and Thomas Aquinas in particular (who followed this trend), and believing in three sources of knowledge (experience, reason, and Scripture), Maimonides attempted to supplement Judaism with Aristotle and religion with reason. Cosmogonically, he believed that the world was only possibly eternal; and eschatologically, that only the souls of the just are immortal.

Levi ben Gershom or Gersonides (1288–1344), the greatest astronomer of his time, was also an authority on the Bible, the Talmud, ethics, logic, mathematics, metaphysics, physiology, and psychology. Not only did he rationalistically regard intellectuality as a condition of immortality, but he also insisted that natural science must be pursued independently of the Bible. As such he agreed with the scholastic and later humanistic separation of science and religion.

A bitter opponent of Christianity, Aristotelianism and neo-Platonism, was Hasdai Crescas of Barcelona (1340–1410), who had great influence on Spinoza. His principal work, however, *The Light of God*, defended Judaism against all other systems of thought and even against the syncretism of Maimonides and Gersonides.

Joseph Albo of Aragon (1380–1440) was a pupil of Crescas, and he shared his teacher's theological Judaism and opposition to philosophy and to Christianity. To him, the three principles of every religion are: God, revelation, and justice.

One of the last great figures at the end of the Mediaeval Ages and at the beginning of the Renaissance was the statesman and physician Judah Abravanel (1460–1530), who was also an authority on philosophy, mathematics, and astronomy. Moving from Portugal to Spain and thence to Italy, he lectured frequently and influenced many Renaissance figures, such as Pico della Mirandola. His chief work, *Dialogues About Love*, although somewhat pantheistic, is a great step forward in the history of aesthetics, and regards love as the very essence of cosmic being and physical beauty as ethically qualified.

4. *Orthodox Christian philosophy*

After the death of Augustine in 430 and Odoacer's overthrowal of the Western Roman Empire in 476, Europe entered its Dark Ages, and syncretism and Islam dominated the world of thought. During this period there were no really original Christian thinkers until the advent of Anselm some six hundred years later. There were, however, some Christian men of lesser stature, and we will here briefly touch on the views of a few such men.

Firstly, there is Isidore of Seville (560–636), a theological and philosophical encyclopaedist who compiled opinions of earlier Church Fathers. He adhered to a clear-cut distinction between the being of God and the lesser existence of the creation, and opposed all mysticism with the Bible as the authoritative Word of God.

Secondly, there is the Venerable Bede of Jarrow (672–735), an English theologian, grammarian, naturalist, and historian, whose compilatory work was so impressive that he is sometimes called the Father of English History.

Then there is John of Damascus (700–754), the writer of the standard theological textbook of the Eastern Church. Unfortunately, however, he regarded all the non-theological sciences, including philosophy, as nothing but handmaidens of theology, and his great love for Aristotelian logic and metaphysics probably merits him the title of the "Early Thomas Aquinas of the East."

An influential figure in the West was Alcuin of York (735–804), who taught the Emperor Charlemagne. Influenced by Augustine, Alcuin was an accomplished theologian, grammarian, logician, poet, and astronomer, and played a prominent role in refuting the Adoptionistic heresy that Christ was the Son of God according to His human nature by adoption only.

A very brave man who asserted the doctrine of God's sovereign grace amidst the deepening apostasy of the Church, was Gottschalk of Saxony (808–868). A great champion of the then obsolescent Augustinian theology, he strongly advocated God's absolute predestination of all things, and even of the reprobate to their eternal damnation. At the Synod of Mainz, however, the proto-Arminian enemies of God's free grace got the upper hand, and Gottschalk was whipped, imprisoned, and anathematized. Hereafter, the glorious truth of unconditional election was suppressed until God later raised up Anselm, Luther, and Calvin to reassert that salvation was from the Lord alone.

Another outspoken man was Peter Damian of Ravenna (1002–1072). An extreme ascetic, he denounced the sins of the clergy, opposed celibacy and simony, and even persuaded the German Emperor not to divorce his wife.

The last and greatest of the pre-scholastic mediaeval Christian thinkers was Anselm of Canterbury (1033–1109), a churchman, ascetic, politician, and philosopher, in whom Augustinianism again underwent a revival. In his *Why Did God Become Man?* he elaborated the central importance of the incarnation of Christ and His punitive substitutionary atonement and satisfaction for His people; in his *Concerning the Truth*, he developed the Augustinian view that one must first believe in order to understand, and that reason requires revelation as its basis; and in his *Monologue,* he propounded the still popular "ontological" proof for God's existence—which was, however, later refuted by

Aquinas and Kant, even though it still convinced Descartes and Leibniz.

5. *Pseudo-Christian philosophy*

Alongside of orthodox Christian philosophy was the philosophy of Christian heretics, the first of whom was Pelagius of Britain (360–420), the chief opponent of the great Augustine. Pelagius particularly attacked Augustine's doctrine of the transmissibility of original sin, of total depravity and of the bondage of the will. By teaching the soteriological ability of the fallen human will, Pelagius paved the way for Romish synergism and Arminian anthropocentrism.

Less obviously a danger to Christianity was the anti-Arian yet syncretistic Christian Aristotelian, Boëthius of Rome (475–524). While jailed by corrupt politicians for opposing their corruption, in addition to translating Aristotle's *Logic* and the writings of Cicero and Porphyry, and working on his own views of logic, arithmetic, and music, Boëthius also wrote his famous work on *The Consolations of Philosophy*, in which he elevated men above the blind forces of irrelevant fate. He subjected the three divine Persons to the divine Being as Pure Form, Which uses suffering to comfort man and philosophy to improve morality (cf. the stoics).

More conspicuously syncretistic were the late fifth or early sixth century anonymous writings falsely attributed to the Apostle Paul's convert Dionysius the Areopagite (cf. Acts 17:34). These writings, commonly referred to as those of Pseudo-Dionysius, combine Christianity and neo-Platonism by eschato-pantheistically teaching man's mystical deification and by inserting a whole series of mediators between God and man (such as seraphs, cherubs, and thrones in heaven; and sacraments, bishops, and monks on earth). Unfortunately, these ideas have had much influence upon later Christian art, literature, philosophy, and theology.

The heretical views of Pseudo-Dionysius were unfortunately translated from Greek into Latin (and thus spread
throughout the West) by John Scotus Eriugena of Ireland
(ca. 812–877). But he was also a philosopher in his own
right, and generally regarded as the first independent
thinker of the middle ages and the greatest thinker of the
ninth century. In his book *On the Division of Nature*, Eriugena pantheistico-emanationistically held that God and
creation are basically the same; so too are philosophy and
religion, which he approached from an overwhelmingly neo-
Platonic mysticistic viewpoint (yet with a thin Christian
veneer); for whenever revelation and reason clash, pref-
erence must always be given to the latter.

Perhaps most influential of all was his "realistic" opposition to the nominalistic assertion that only particular things
are real, by insisting on the even greater reality of abstract
and general ideas (cf. Plato), by insisting that the more
general things are, the more real they are, so that the most
general things are the most real (cf. Plotinus). This not
only means that God is the most real *because* He is the most
general, the Idea of all ideas (cf. Plato), but also that the
various different creatures possess different degrees of being according to their generality or particularity. And this
is a far cry from the Biblical teaching of God as the Source
of all Being and of the various different creatures as all participating in the same degree of created existence and all
equally utterly dependent on the Creative Being of the
Triune God alone.

This realistic emphasis on the priority of generalities
or universals to particulars, as taught by Eriugena and later
by Anselm, was sharply opposed by the anti-Platonistic
Aristotelian Roscelin of Tours (1050–1120), who, from a
nominalistic viewpoint, not surprisingly rejected the (abstract?!) idea of the Trin*ity* in favor of a more empiricistic
and less rational(istic?!) *Tri*theism—for to him, all uni-

versals were merely words, and so the unity of the Trinity was accordingly unreal.

His pupil Abelard of Paris (1079–1142), however, criticized him from a conceptualistic or semi-realistic viewpoint. Abelard was an intellectualistic rationalist who, like Eriugena, subjected faith to reason and identified theology and philosophy. Having tabulated the "contradictions" of the Bible and of the Church Fathers, championed free will as the basis of all ethics, and rejected the Anselmic doctrine of Christ's punitive atonement as a satisfaction for sin, he was particularly opposed by Bernard of Clairvaux, and his interpretation of the Trinity was twice ecclesiastically condemned as heretical.

6. *Scholastic philosophy*

Mediaeval philosophy with its neo-Platonic and Aristotelian elements smoothly drifted into scholasticism, which preoccupied itself especially with the relationships between theology and philosophy, faith and reason, and universals and particulars. It may be distinguished into early scholasticism up to 1200 (Eriugena, Anselm, Abelard, Bernard, and Lombard), middle scholasticism from 1200 to 1350 (Alexander of Hales, Bonaventure, Albert the Great, Thomas Aquinas, and Duns Scotus), and late scholasticism from 1350 to 1500 (voluntarists like Ockham and also mysticists like Eckhart). Having already dealt with most of the early scholastics, we will here deal chiefly with the middle scholastics (giving separate treatment to the great Thomas Aquinas) and then proceed to deal with the late scholastics.

The last of the early scholastics was Peter Lombard of Bologna (1100–1160), whose *Four Book of Sentences* became the chief theological textbook for many generations. Lombard believed that metaphysics should be proved from Scripture and defended by Christian reason, but he rationalistically considered true knowledge to be higher than faith, fragmentary though such knowledge necessarily must remain.

The first great thinker of the middle scholastic period and the first scholar to write a textbook after the removal of an ecclesiastical ban on the teaching of all of Aristotle's writings, was Alexander of Hales (1180–1245) who, in his work *The Summa* (or "Highlights") *of Universal Theology,* tried to synthesize Aristotle, Augustine, and the Arabian philosophers (cf. Avicenna). God is "pure activity" and without matter and form; and universals (cf. Avicenna) first exist *ante res* (cf. Plato) and only thereafter *in rebus* (cf. Aristotle).

Alexander had much influence on Bonaventure, Albert the Great, and Thomas Aquinas.

Alexander's student John of Fidanza or Bonaventure (1221–1274), a close friend of Thomas Aquinas, sought to combine Plato and Aristotle, yet largely subjected them both to Scripture and to the traditions of the Church, distinguishing between "supranatural" theology and "natural" philosophy (cf. the scholastic nature-grace motive!). Epistemologically, he somewhat empiricistically regarded the mind as originally a *tabula rasa* or blank tablet; yet not only is knowledge derived from human science, but some general ideas are also rationally derived and infused by God. The highest knowledge is mystical, and is effected by divine grace, which alone provides knowledge of the Trinity.

So encyclopaedic was the knowledge of Albert the Great of Bavaria (1193–1280), that he was believed to have almost superhuman knowledge and was rather descriptively called "The Universal Doctor." As a commentator on Aristotle, physicist, botanist, zoologist, logician, and (moderately realistic) philosopher, he was almost without peer in his day. Learning from Plato, Aristotle, the Arabs, and the Jews, he did not hesitate to disagree with any of them where he thought they were wrong. His own personal influence itself was massive, quite apart from his lasting influence on and through his even more famous and more influential student, Thomas Aquinas.

7. *Thomas Aquinas*

Thomas of Aquino (1225–1274) was the greatest of the scholastics and the most authoritative Roman Catholic scholar of all time. Canonized in 1323 and made a Doctor of the Church in 1567, Pope Leo XIII exalted his thought to the status of *the* official philosophy of the Roman Catholic Church in 1879f. Because his philosophy dominates the outlook of the huge Church of Rome and even of many semi-Reformed Protestants, and because there is a strong upsurge of influential neo-Thomism in philosophical circles today (cf. Maritain, Gilson, D'Arcy, Grabmann, De Wulf, Sassen, and Robbers), a rather detailed treatment is merited. For Thomas is as important in a Christian introduction to the history of philosophy as are Plato and Aristotle—if not more so.

As an accomplished scholar, apart from his commentaries on Aristotle, on the Christian Scriptures, on Böethius' treatises, and on Lombard's *Sentences*, Thomas also wrote his *Disputed Questions* and is especially famous for his encyclopaedic *Summa of Theology* and his *Summa against the Heathen*. It is particularly in the latter work that he unfolds his philosophical views.

The Hellenistic religious basic motive of form-matter (then widely prevalent), implying particularly in its Platonic yet even in its Aristotelian structure the primacy of the form motive above that of matter (cf. Plato and Aristotle, above), influenced Thomas and his predecessors to synthesize it with the Christian religious motive of creation-fall-recreation and thus to distinguish the "supranatural" world of "form" from the "inferior" and "natural" world of "matter" in terms of the new (and synthesized) religious motive of nature-supra-nature (or nature-grace).

Hellenistic thought had been synthesized with the Koran by Averroës and with Judaism by Maimonides. Now it was also to be synthesized with Christianity by Aquinas. Indeed, it was perhaps the belief that there was a need to find a widely acceptable basis for philosophical discussion between Platonistic and/or Aristotelian Moslems and Jews and Christians which drove the scholastics in general and Thomas in particular to develop this new religious motive, and to distinguish between "natural" theology and philosophy and their principle of "reason" on the one hand and "supranatural" theology and its principle of "faith" on the other. For although Christian faith was necessary in order to understand "supranatural" theology, it was believed that simple "reason" (common to Moslems, Jews, Christians, and all men) was sufficient in order to understand "natural" theology and philosophy.

According to the Bible, man *is* the image of God; but according to the scholastics and Aquinas, the image of God is just an extra "supranatural" gift which God gave to "natural" man. Before the fall, man did not need to possess supranatural grace in order to be a man as such, according to Aquinas, but he possessed it as a gracious and extra gift superadded to his already essentially human nature. However, when man fell into sin, according to Aquinas he lost "supranatural" or saving grace (which is restored in baptism), but he maintained his reason almost entirely intact by virtue of continuing "natural" grace; and it is on this common basis of natural grace that Christians could reason with unbelievers at the level of philosophy and "natural" theology—the only level at which it was believed such a "dialogue" could take place, seeing that unbelievers do not accept the authority of God's "supranatural" revelation in Scripture. Thus was developed the Romanistic religious basic motive of nature and supernature or nature-grace.

However, in this way Thomas divided life into two distinct spheres—the natural or "secular" sphere of reason and society (common to all men) on the one hand, and the supranatural or "sacred" sphere of faith and the Church (and limited only to the Christian) on the other. But once this dichotomy became established, it did, in fact, consequently make the sphere of faith inaccessible to reason and the "secular" sphere of reason unimportant to faith. It was only a question of time before this kind of Christianity became so heavenly minded that it was no earthly use, and before "secular" life, emancipated from the control of faith, apostasized into the neo-heathendom of the Renaissance and modern humanism with its new (yet scholastically caused) religious basic motives of (secularized) freedom and science!

But let us again return to Thomas, with his nature-grace synthesis between the Hellenistic religious motive of matter-form on the one hand and the Christian religious motive of creation-fall-recreation on the other, whereby he also hoped to save the shaky culture of the late middle ages (with its composite Platonic, Aristotelian, Islamic, Jewish, and Christian elements) from disintegration, and whereby he hoped to assert the clear superiority of "supernatural"(!) Christianity.

Theontologically, Thomas believed that God is the Highest Form, the Original Mover, the First Cause, the Necessary Being, and the Highest Perfection, Whose existence can be rationally proved to the satisfaction of all (unregenerate) men. Existontologically, being is omnipresent, and ranges from God the Supreme Being to matter, the lowest form of being (cf. Eriugena), whereas evil is mere privation of being (cf. Plotinus and, unfortunately, Augustine). Cosmogonically, God created the world, time, and space out of nothing, although the co-eternity of the universe is at least rationally(!) conceivable. And angelologically, the angels, as pure non-material "forms," are the highest created beings.

Anthropologically, Thomas maintained that man is com-posed of a "supranatural" soul and a "natural" body, the soul being the divine and rational immortal "form" which first gives shape to the non-divine and mortal (yet immortalizable) and material body (cf. Aristotle). Sociologically, individual man is subordinated to social man, and both the individual and the family are subordinated to the state as the highest "natural" or "secular" sphere (cf. Aristotle); but the state in its turn is, of course, itself subordinated to the "supranatural" or "sacred" Church. Epistemologically, reason is common to all men, and adequately enables man to understand the whole of the "natural" or "secular" sphere and also *that* there is a God; but faith (a special gift of God) is necessary to understand the "supranatural" or "sacred" sphere and *what* God is like. Consequently, philosophy and the special sciences are inferior to (sacred) theology. Soteriologically, all salvation is channeled to man exclusively through the (R.C.) Church as an institute, and then again largely through the sacraments. Ecclesiologically, the priests are superior to the laymen, the monks to the priests, the archbishops to the monks, and the Pope to the archbishops. And eschatologically, man will ultimately see God and partake of the divine essence, although not of the divine personality.

Thomas is correct in that God is supreme, but incorrect in that He should be described in such abstract Aristotelian terms as "Highest Form," "Original Mover," or "First Cause," etc., rather than in concrete and Scriptural terms such as the "Rock," the "Ancient of Days," or the "Father of Spirits," etc.; correct in that being (or rather, created existence!) is present throughout the universe, but incorrect in that there are diminishing degrees of created existence and that evil is the lack of existence (for evil, though ax-

135

iologically absurd, is nevertheless ontically very real); correct in that the world was created out of nothing, but incorrect in that its co-eternity is rationally conceivable—for this is only pseudo-rationally or rationalistically conceivable; correct in that angels are non-material, but incorrect in that they are "forms" or that they are the highest created beings—for *man* is (Gen. 1:26f; Heb. 1-2).

Thomas was correct in that man does consist of soul and body, but incorrect in that the soul is not divine but creaturely, and not merely rational but also voluntative and emotive, and not "form-al" but spirit-ual or non-material. He was correct in that the soul is immortal, but wrong in denying the co-immortality of the human body and wrong in asserting that the soul gives "form" to the body—for the body was originally already "form"-ed before it was in-anima-ted by the soul or anima—Gen. 2:7! Sociologically, Thomas was correct in distinguishing the various social spheres, but incorrect in subordinating the relatively sphere-sovereign individual to the family, the family to the state, and the state to the Church. Epistemologically, he was correct in distinguishing reason and faith, but incorrect in separating them; correct in assuming that all men have "reason," but incorrect in virtually denying its depravity; correct in that only the believers possess saving faith, but incorrect in virtually denying that all men have some kind of "faith"—either in God or in an idol; correct in subjecting reason to faith in the last analysis, but incorrect in not realizing that *all* (true or false) "reason" rests in (true or false) "faith"—as Augustine and Anselm had shown. Thomas was correct in distinguishing theology and philosophy, but incorrect in separating them—as if philosophy could be indifferent to theology, and as if all (and even apostate) theology was necessarily sacred and therefore necessarily superior to philosophy, or could dispense with at least the formal auxiliary aid of philosophy.

Thomas was correct in distinguishing between sin and grace, but incorrect in tending to limit sin to the "secular" realm and in tending to limit ("supranatural") grace to the "sacred" realm, rather than acknowledging the presence of sin and grace in both realms and regarding *everything* as sacred when done to God's glory and *everything* (including Church activities) as secular when not done to God's glory but done according to the "secular" spirit of wickedness and worldliness (cf. Rom. 12:1f). Soteriologically, Thomas was correct that the Church is the typical and generally instrumental channel of salvation, but incorrect in limiting salvation to this channel both in the production and in the expansion of saving grace. Ecclesiologically, he was correct in emphasizing the structural nature of the visible Church, but incorrect in identifying this with the apostate Church of Rome and its anti-Scriptural clerical hierarchy on the one hand and in subjecting the "secular" laymen to the "sacred" preacher-priests on the other. And eschatologically, he was correct in that the believers will one day see God, but incorrect in that they will (somewhat pantheistically) partake of the divine essence.

The importance of Thomas Aquinas in the history of philosophy can hardly be over-estimated. His schizocosmic division of reality into the "sacred" and the "secular" principially separated the Bible from science, and this tendency lives on today in both Roman Catholicism and semi-Reformed Protestantism and Pietism. Moreover, Thomas' "rigid" system was (and is) only apparently rigid. By virtue of its inherent dialectical tension between the religious basic motives of grace and nature, it necessarily had to give birth to a more consequential emphasis on each of these motives and lead to an other-worldly mysticism on the one hand and a this-worldly secularism on the other.

137

8. *Voluntaristic philosophy*

If Thomas' philosophy was too rationalistic, voluntaristic and emotionalistic reactions thereto would not be long in asserting themselves. The emotional reaction took the form of mysticism (see section 9, below), and voluntarism was spearheaded by Duns Scotus, after whom there also came an additional nominalistic reaction to the aforegoing universalism.

In the voluntarism of Duns Scotus (1270–1308), the anti-rationalistic and anti-Thomistic tradition of Augustine and Anselm to some extent re-asserted itself. Unfortunately, however, he completely separated (practical!) theology and (theoretical) philosophy, and argued that one thing could be true in theology and quite another in philosophy (cf. Averroës). A moderate realist (looking at particulars before universals), he did at least give an important place to empirical knowledge in his epistemology—as too had Bonaventure and Thomas—but in this manner paved the way for nominalism and its consequential methodological skepticism and empiricism.

In William of Ockham (1280–1349), these anti-rationalistic and voluntaristic tendencies were even further developed. Everything depends on God's absolutely free will, the Church's say in political affairs should be diminished, and theology and other sciences were so completely separated from one another that Ockham even denied that theology was a science! There were no "scientific" proofs of God's existence (*per contra*, Thomas); and one accepted God by faith alone (cf. Luther) irrespective of reason, the range of which he greatly diminished in favor of nominalistico-empirical observations.

There is definitely an irrationalistic and subjectivistic element in Ockham. On the one hand, his voluntarism and proto-sphere-sovereignty (in his limitation of the powers of the Church) prepared the way for the Reformation, but on the other hand his irrationalism prepared the way for existentialism, and his empiricism prepared the way for naturalism—as evidenced in Pierre d'Ailly of Paris (1350–1425).

9. *Mysticistic philosophy*

In the face of the increasing trend of nominalism and its resultant this-worldly empiricism, an anti-empirical other-worldly mysticism naturally developed as an unavoidable reaction.

Bernard of Clairvaux (1091–1153) had already characterized himself as a pious man but as a mystic who downplayed the value of all science. To him the highest philosophy was to know and enjoy the crucified Christ. As such, his mystique was at least purely Christian and devoid of pantheism, yet his attitude to life was under-analytical and over-contemplative, under-rational and over-emotional. Other early mediaeval mystics were Hugh of St. Victor (1096–1141), and Francis of Assisi (1182–1226).

The mysticism of the middle mediaeval age is dominated by the figure of "Meister" Johannes Eckhart of Cologne (1260–1327). Unlike the purely Christian mysticism of Bernard, he also drank from the syncretistic mysticism of Pseudo-Dionysius (q.v.) and pantheistically identified all things with God, Who manifests His existence in the heart of man. Eschatologically, man unites with God through the practice of silence. Eckhart was condemned for heresy by the Church in 1327; but even after that, he still had many followers, such as John Tauler of Strausbourg (1300–1361), who was particularly interested in the ethical and personal aspects of mysticism. Other mystics, such as Thomas à Kempis (1380–1471), more closely followed the purely Christian mystical tradition of Bernard.

An example of a late mediaeval mystic is Nicholas of Cusa (1406–1464). Interested in the reform of the Church, he repudiated scholasticism and taught that God cannot be found by reason but only by intuition. Nicholas is an interesting figure. On the one hand he heralded the advent of the Reformation, viz., in his love of the Bible and his denial of the Church's temporal sovereignty over the West. On the other hand, he was somewhat synthetistically influenced by the neo-Platonic scholasticism, Arabian mysticism, and the Jewish Cabbalah. Again, he sometimes mystically doubted the value of empirical knowledge and regarded God as the Ultimate Reality in Whom all things participate and from Whom all things emanate. And finally, he sometimes also promoted the development of the empirical sciences by advocating the integration of mathematics and metaphysics and by teaching the revolution of the earth around the sun and the existence of many worlds. One thing his philosophy did clearly establish, however, was the inability of the scholastic nature-grace motive to give a permanently satisfactory account of the universe.

10. *Summary*

In this chapter we have looked at mediaeval philosophy —the West's period of stagnation and synthesis. After the climax of Christian philosophy and its creation-fall-recreation motive attained by Augustine, there was no major Christian thinker for six centuries until Anselm. During that time, Islamic philosophy arose and the Jewish and neo-Hellenistic philosophy continued, but the overwhelming characteristic of each of these schools was its syncretism with the other schools.

Scholasticism arose in the middle mediaeval period as an attempt by some gifted Churchmen to establish the superiority of Christianity by adopting a common philosophical ground with the various non-Christian philosophies. This was done by producing a new scheme (the nature-grace

140

motive) by hybridizing Greek thought and Christian thought. However, the stability of the scheme was only apparent, for the dialectical tension between the two motives remained, as evidenced by the fact that the other-worldly "supra-natural" grace element ultimately resulted in mysticism and the nature element promoted nominalism and—via the Renaissance—naturalism and unbelief.

Philosophy had again arrived at the crossroads. It was exhausted in the fruitless irrationalism of late scholasticism, and needed to be born again. Two kinds of philosophical children would soon be born from their dying mediaeval mother—the anti-Christian philosophy of the unregenerate rebirth of unregenerate man: the Renaissance; and the Christian philosophy of the rebirth of the truth in the life of elect mankind: the Reformation.

It is to a consideration of the firstborn child, the philosophy of the Renaissance, to which we must now turn.

Chapter VII

WESTERN PHILOSOPHY IN DECLINE

The Apostasy of Humanism

1. Survey

The Renaissance or the unregenerative rebirth of apostate man and his humanistic philosophy was from one point of view a warm and vital reaction against the cold and moribund stagnation of scholastic thought at the end of the mediaeval period. Yet from another point of view it was a necessary product of the unavoidable disintegration of scholasticism—unavoidable on account of the unresolved dialectical tension between the nature-grace motive. When Aquinas elevated grace above nature, it was only a question of time before men consequently regarded nature as grace-less. And in the Renaissance, man would ultimately demonstrate his "creative" control over nature and "redemption" from nature *without* his acknowledgement of God's grace. And men did this in the tradition of the proto-rationalism and proto-empiricism already established in scholasticism itself.

Post-mediaeval man longed for freedom from scholasticism, and he began to regard knowledge and science as the means to achieve this. Thus arose the new religious basic motive of the Renaissance and its accompanying and resultant humanism—the new motive of nature-science and its humanistic outgrowth of freedom-science.

Although learned Greeks fled to Italy and the West after

the fall of Constantinople to the Turks in 1453, and although the Spanish Inquisition at about the same time drove thousands of learned Jews into Eastern Europe where they disseminated their views, and although the establishment of the sea route to India and the Americas opened up vast new perspectives, the Renaissance was not such a break with the past as is commonly supposed. Its attempt to turn nature into culture by subjecting nature to knowledge or science, is only a further extension of the empiricism of late scholasticism and of the rediscovery of the knowledge and culture of ancient Greece and Rome (and, more remotely and ultimately—although in an apostate direction— of Genesis 1:28). Rejecting the Christian elements of the mediaeval period, the Renaissance thinkers sought their roots in the heathen elements of the Mediaeval period, and especially in those elements derived from the paganism of ancient Greece. Token homage was still paid to the Christian religion for reasons of expediency, and the Renaissance's radical breach with Christianity was not immediately apparent to all on account of the time-lag required for its heathen consequences to be fully realized. When such realization did eventually occur, however, the Renaissance ultimately culminated in radical humanism.

Accordingly, we may perhaps distinguish the movement of apostasy into two successive periods: the Renaissance (ca. 1300–1600) and its more consequential successor modern humanism (ca. 1600–1970). The precise dating here is somewhat arbitrary, but we have taken Descartes (1595–1650), whom many consider to be the father of modern philosophy, as a convenient point of demarcation.

In the Renaissance prior to Descartes, we may perhaps again distinguish between the Pre-Renaissance and the Renaissance proper. And under modern humanism beginning with Descartes, we may (all too cryptically) perhaps distinguish: rationalism, empiricism, radical humanism,

143

neo-mysticism, phenomenalism, idealism, psychologism, socialism, evolutionism, positivism, pragmatism, neo-realism, logical positivism, existentialism, and pseudo-Christian philosophy.

This is of course, all too sketchy a classification, and many of the thinkers so classified below could be subsumed under different headings altogether. However, all systems of classification are defective, and in an introductory work of this nature such defective treatment is inevitable in what is essentially an attempt to avoid massive multiplication of the various headings. It is hoped, however, that the treatment of the subject matter here adopted will be of some value in yielding an insight into the widespread apostate progression of humanistic thought.

2. *The Pre-Renaissance*

One of the foremost figures of this period was the naturalistic necromancer Roger Bacon of Oxford (1214–1294). Sharply distinguishing between the theological and non-theological sciences, and continuing the proto-empirical tradition of the Greeks, Arabs, and middle ages, he repudiated Thomas and the schoolmen and concentrated on natural science where he championed observation and experimentation, made magnifying glasses and gunpowder and anticipated the later invention of suspension bridges, aeroplanes, and locomotives.

One of Bacon's contemporaries was Raymond Lully of Majorca (1235–1315). Drawing from Christian, Arabic, and Jewish (and especially Cabbalistic) tradition, he not only wrote a Utopian novel but also published his famous book *General Art*, which he proposed as a basis for all the sciences and in which he represented the ultimate principles of logic and metaphysics in symbolic letters and geometrical figures.

If the above two thinkers tended to emphasize the science

motive, others would stress that of freedom. The gifted priest Marsilio Ficino of Florence (1433–1499) translated Plato, Porphyry, Plotinus, and Pseudo-Dionysius and sought to promote humanism and harmonize Christianity and Plato by claiming that the latter was inspired (!). Ficino doubtless made this claim in order to make Christianity rationally acceptable. Significantly, Ficino based man's *summum bonum* or highest good not on the teaching of the Church, but on a universal human tendency.

John Pico della Mirandola of Padua (1463–1494) may perhaps be cited as one of the last representatives of the Pre-Renaissance. Thoroughly schooled in Hebrew and Arabic, and influenced by Ficino as well as by the Church Reformer Savanarola, Pico asserted man's freedom of choice in determining his own future. It was views like these (as well as his attempts to Platonize the prevalent Aristotelian philosophy) which led to friction with the Church.

3. *The Renaissance proper*

The Renaissance as such broke through with all its strength in the thought of men such as Da Vinci, Machiavelli, Pomponazzi, Erasmus, Montaigne, More, Paracelsus, Copernicus, Cardano, Telesio, Bruno, Galilei, and Campanella. In this section an attempt will be made to say something of each of them.

Leonardo da Vinci of Milan (1452–1519), artist, engineer, and scholar, was undoubtedly the dominant figure of the Italian Renaissance. Propounding basic principles of science such as the heliocentric theory of the universe and anticipating the mechanics of Galilei, he advocated experimentation as the basis of science instead of the old traditional scholastic views. Empirical observation is transformed into rational reflection and that in its turn into mathematical and mechanical formulation. With da Vinci, the age of natural science had begun in earnest.

The more humanistic implications of the Renaissance in its radical apostasy from revealed truth were developed by Niccolo Machiavelli of Florence (1449–1527). Disillusioned with the corruption of the Church, he sought his salvation in the state. In his amoral masterpiece of statecraft, *The Prince*, he indicated how a ruthless sovereign could gain and maintain power, eliminate opponents, and placate the masses.

In Pietro Pomponazzi of Mantua (1462–1525), a doctor of medicine and professor of philosophy, the Aristotelian, Averroëstic and Thomistic proofs of the immortality of the soul were denied. Belief in immortality was simply a matter of faith, and was in no wise necessary for moral conduct.

Perhaps the most famous figure of the Renaissance and certainly the best known in Northern Europe, was Desiderius Erasmus of Rotterdam (1466–1536). Although a translator of the Bible and a critic of the deplorable condition of the Church, he refused to join Luther in his separated stand against Rome, and fulminated against his doctrine of predestination. To Erasmus, the life of Christ was more important than His death; the Sermon on the Mount more important than the forensic event on Calvary; reason and ethics more important than faith and doctrine; and the happiness of man more important than the honor of God.

A contemporary and friend of Erasmus was Thomas More of London (1478–1535). Best known for his book *Utopia*, which described an imaginary island where war and oppression were taboo, More was a devoted Catholic humanist who was martyred for courageously defying King Henry VIII by questioning his right to divorce his wife and marry another.

Another Utopian thinker was Michel de Montaigne of Perigon (1533–1592). A skepticistic and naturalistic humanist, Montaigne, like Rousseau after him, proposed a return to primitive society and morality. Not culture but nature was to solve the problems of man.

A fascinating if confused individual was the alchemist and physician Theophrastus Bombast of Hohenheim or Paracelsus (1493–1541). Combining neo-Platonism, Cabbalism, and witchcraft, he asserted that a medical investigator should be competent in astrology, alchemy, and philosophy. Disease was the result of a struggle between nature and demons, and nature study and its supposedly mystical basis was essential to the diagnostician. Characteristically, he met his death by sampling alcohol, in his search for the elixir of life.

A major breakthrough in the field of natural science was achieved when Nicolaus Copernicus of Poland (1473–1543), the famous astronomer, discovered that the Ptolemaic theory of a geocentric universe was wrong and substituted in its place the heliocentric theory of the solar system. He also taught that the earth turned on its own axis, and attempted to prove these claims mathematically rather than teleologically. Not surprisingly, in an age of superstition he elected not to popularize his discoveries, even though a century later Johan Kepler justified his cosmology in accordance with Pythagorean mathematics.

Less circumspect thinkers, however, suffered for publicizing their views. Geronimo Cardano of Milan (1501–1576), for example, an Epicurean transmutationist, was arrested for heresy. Bernardino Telesio of Cosenza (1508–1588), although he did not leave the Church, renounced a papal nomination as Archbishop in order to devote himself to the empirical sciences and panpsychic cosmology. Giordano Bruno of Nola (1548–1600), a pantheistic and emanationistic Copernican, was burned at the stake by the Roman Inquisition. Galileo Galilei of Pisa (1564–1642), who publicized the Copernican system and his own astronomical discoveries, was continually plagued and even incarcerated by the Church authorities. And Tommaso Campanella of Calabria (1568–1639), who sought to combine mediaeval thought and empirical science in his Utopian *City of the Sun*, and who defended Galilei, was imprisoned by the Inquisition for twenty-seven years.

The Church had stupidly sought to suppress the advance of knowledge. The stage was now set for the development of a radical and anti-ecclesiastical modern humanism.

4. *Rationalism*

The tension between nature and grace inherent in scholasticism had now led to the Renaissance which progressively presented *man* instead of God as the center of the universe. Henceforth, science would develop to enable man to control the universe, albeit in an apostate manner. And to promote such science, man would alternatingly over-emphasize the role either of reason or of experimentation, thus resulting in either the heresy of rationalism (the absolutization of reason) or the heresy of empiricism (the absolutization of experience).

The grand architect of rationalism was undoubtedly René Descartes of La Haye (1596–1650). Always remaining a faithful Roman Catholic, his philosophy is but the Post-Renaissance humanistic explication of elements already germinally present in Roger Bacon and indeed even in the scholastic scheme. For in René Descartes, on the one hand the area of grace is separated from and placed in radical contradistinction to and over against the absolutized area of nature. And grace or authority is itself humanized and developed into the personality (or) freedom motive, whereas nature is progressively culturalized and developed into the science (or mechanical) motive.

Descartes deliberately adopted a skeptical methodology in order to arrive at certainty. Everything could be doubted except the fact that he could doubt; and in his opinion his very ability to doubt established his own existence, for one must exist in order to be able to doubt—*cogito* (or actually: *dubito*) *ergo sum*—"I think (or actually: I doubt), therefore I am." However, if the individual's mind or ego exists, much more must God, the Great Ego, of Whom the human ego is but a faint ontological reflection, exist—and exist as the Absolute and Uncreated and Unmoved and Perfect Substance and Creator.

But God created not merely mind or *res cogitans*, but also matter or *res extensa* or extension in space and time. This *res extensa* was to be apprehended by mathematical knowledge, the development of which was necessitated by the then ever-increasing navigational calculations — which mathematical knowledge Descartes held to be the root of all further scientific knowledge. In this way, however, Descartes divided the cosmos into two spheres, each relatively independent of one another—the realm of the mind or Spirit with its innate ideas on the one hand and the realm of science on the other. But thus was the Romish division between the "sacred" and the "secular" perpetuated, and even aggravated—for henceforth the "secular" would more and more develop totally independently from the "sacred," and itself be absolutized first under one denominator (as in Descartes' "mathematicism") and then under another (such as Engels' "physicism," or Bergson's "vitalism," etc.). The dilemma, however, remained—namely, the radical dualism between freedom and science. Even man, felt Descartes, was basically a machine (*res extensa*), apart from his spirit (which was *res cogitans*). In later thinkers this would soon lead first to the absolutization of (natural) science and then to the absolutization of (human) freedom in apostate philosophical idolatry.

The problem of interaction between the *res cogitans* and the *res extensa* so clearly dichotomized by Descartes, was acutely realized by Arnold Geulincx (1624–1669), who was originally a Catholic professor at Louvain and subsequently became a Calvinistic professor at Leyden. Whereas Geulincx did attempt to ground his axiology in ontology (*ita est, ergo ita sit*—"thus it is, so thus let it be"), and to establish the Sovereign God as the first cause of all things, instead of attacking Descartes' dichotomy, he attempted to justify it and to solve its difficulties by elaborating the doctrine of "occasionalism," whereby mind and matter do not interact upon one another but merely appear to as a result of the previous "occasion" of God having set each to run its own course without influencing one another, yet in a kind of "pre-established harmony" with one another. Unfortunately, this view to some extent derives from Aristotelian deism and anticipates Leibnizian rationalism.

This theory of occasionalism was particularly worked out by Geulincx's fellow-Cartesian, Nicolas Malebranche of Paris (1638–1715). Ascribing philosophical doubt to a free act of the human will, Malebranche denied all cosmic causality save God, with Whom all creatures are immediately united and without Whose will all creatures are powerless.

A more apostate degree of rationalism was reached in the thought of Baruch de Spinoza of The Hague (1632–1677), in whom we find a synthesis of rationalism, mysticism, and the Jewish philosophy (including the Talmud and the Cabbalah). Rejecting Descartes' dualism, he held that mind or thought and matter or extension are simply attributes of God the Ultimate Substance Who is neither mind nor matter but pantheistically omnipresent. God's will he held to be identical with the laws of nature, which will is not to be apprehended by revelation but rather by reason and more particularly "spatialistically" by geometry. God is therefore to be known and loved not by faith but by the intellect alone—*amor Dei intellectualis.*

Perhaps even more rationalistic, was Gottfried Leibniz

of Leipzig (1646–1716). Developing a synthesis between Plato and Democritus and Aristotle and Descartes, Leibniz sought to overcome the Cartesian dualism between matter and mind by reducing the world not to material atoms (as had Democritus), but to individual and psychical "monads," each an individual field of energy endowed with perception and regulated by a pre-established harmony (cf. Geulincx) by God as the Monad of monads. Reality is thus basically pluralistic, not monistic, and in this belief Leibniz anticipated the views of James and the American pragmatists. Space and extension are secondary and are only produced by the monads which are themselves governed by the laws of logiç and mathematics.

It was, however, Leibniz' student Christian Wolff of Breslau (1679–1754) in whom the false gospel of rationalism and the German Enlightenment reached its peak and in whom deism and rationalism coincided. To Wolff, man could be happy without divine revelation and grace—to be good was to live according to nature and reason, whereby man could perfect himself. And Wolff's disciple Alexander Baumgarten of Berlin (1714–1762), the pioneer and namer of the science of aesthetics, rationalistically misdirected the development of that scientific field from its very inception.

5. *Empiricism*

It should not be thought, however, that the false nature-grace motive of scholasticism resulted only in that subjective absolutization of man's reason called rationalism. At the other extreme, it also developed into that equally false absolutization of objective experience known as empiricism. If some Pre-Renaissance figures such as Ficino and Pico had heralded the emancipation of apostate reason, other figures of that period such as Roger Bacon and Lully had augured the emancipation of apostate scientific experience. And later, it was particularly in the thought of Francis Bacon and his successors that "secular" science was destined to be promoted.

Francis Bacon of Verulam (1561-1626) played the role in the development of empiricism which Descartes played in the development of rationalism. Writing the first philosophical treatises ever written in English, Bacon defended the secularization of science and philosophy and (post-scholastically!) promoted the distinction between natural and revealed religion in theology. In Bacon, man's ideal science controls nature in the interests of man rather than in the interests of God (cf. Gen. 1:26-28), and he anticipated man's dominion over the earth and the air and the sea (in his dreams of inventing perpetual motion machines and airplanes and submarines) as well as man's Utopian happiness (in his book *New Atlantis*).

When Galilei was condemned by the Catholic Church for his scientific claims, Pierre Gassendi of Provence (1592-1655), himself a Catholic priest, protested that the Church's condemnation had nothing to do with the pursuit of science(!). Gassendi himself, though a theist, sought to combine the heathen atomism of Democritus and Epicurus with the Christian doctrine, and empiricistically taught that knowledge is acquired from sensation rather than from reason.

The further consequence of Descartes', Galilei's, and Gassendi's secularization and emancipation of science from religion is clearly seen in the views of Thomas Hobbes of Malmesbury (1588-1679), who exalted empiricism as the only theory of true knowledge and who materialistically sought to finally abolish the Cartesian dualism by denying the separate and non-material substantiality of the soul. In actuality, all is corporeal movement, and processes of consciousness are, in the last analysis, nothing but individual particles of matter in motion. Coupled with this materialism, Hobbes also professed a post-scholastic nomi-

152

nalistic and equally atomistic individualism, and limited causality to such particular bodies. Sociologically, individual man is but a brute, but he may acquire a measure of personal security by entering into a "social contract" with other individuals and delegating some of his own sovereign rights to the state in the interests of the maintenance of law and order. But all this only illustrates the tragedy of humanism: unregenerate man's search for freedom by exploiting and applying scientific discoveries only enslaves him and renders him by nature "brutish and nasty," as Hobbes himself realized.

Hobbes's radical empiricism and social contract theory was further developed by John Locke of Wrington (1632–1704), whom many consider to have had a profound effect on the American Declaration of Independence. Locke strongly insisted on the separation of the Church and State, later developed by Charles de Montesquieu, and maintained that sovereignty ultimately rested with the people from whom it was originally derived. All men were potentially equal. They were not born with innate ideas, as Descartes had suggested, but their minds were originally blank or like a *tabula rasa*. All knowledge is originally acquired by sensational experiences or impressions, but these produce simple ideas and the latter in their turn produce complex ideas by reflection or reasoning. Christianity is acceptable because reasonable and practical, held Locke, although his views are really rather closer to deism.

In Isaac Newton of Woolsthorpe (1642–1727), one sees the traditions of both rationalism and empiricism. Deriving his mechanism from Descartes yet championing the experimental method, this pious author of many theological treatises was enabled to make such important discoveries as the theory of the spectrum, the reflecting telescope, and the theory of universal gravitation. Yet his anti-metaphysical method and belief in the neutrality of human reason, coupled with Locke's empiricistic epistemology, unwittingly helped promote the increasing secularization of natural science.

In Julien de Lamettrie of Paris (1709–1751), empiricism exhibited its radical consequences. Advocating atheistic metaphysics, he denied the immortality of the soul and insisted that man was essentially a machine genealogically related to other organisms by evolution.

The French Encyclopaedists Denis Diderot of Langres (1713–1784) and Jean Baptiste d'Alembert of Paris (1717–1783) were also firmly in the empiricistic tradition—Diderot pantheistically and antiteleologically traced even the formation of moral values to childhood experience, and the antitheistic d'Alembert pragmatistically held that truth is only useful as an hypothesis. Etienne de Condillac of Grenoble (1715–1780), a Catholic abbot, somewhat more conservatively maintained the Cartesian dualism of body and soul, even though limiting the origin of psychological experiences to sensation alone; but Paul d'Holbach of Paris (1723–1789) radically condemned both Christianity and deism and materialistically and evolutionistically regarded nature as a workshop full of tools whereby man may improve his life. Europe was now ripe for the godless French Revolution of 1789.

As a last example of empiricism, we may perhaps refer to Joseph Priestley of Yorkshire (1733–1804), a Unitarian clergyman and the discoverer of oxygen. Priestley was a philosophical materialist, and denied the difference between the body and the soul. Moving from England to America, he had a profound effect on leading thinkers of both countries such as Erasmus Darwin, James Watt, Thomas Jefferson, and Benjamin Franklin.

6. *Radical humanism*

Regardless of whether philosophy degenerated in the direction of rationalism or in the direction of empiricism, the net result was the same: namely, the general absolutization of the science motive at the expense of the consequently threatened freedom motive. Not surprisingly, therefore, the pendulum was now to react rather sharply in favor of the promotion of a radical humanism or the glorification of man.

Henry St. John or Viscount Bolingbroke of Battersea (1678–1751) continued the tradition of British deism. Violently hostile to Christianity, he reduced all morality to self-love, and had a profound effect even on French unbelief.

Claude Helvetius of Paris (1715–1771) maintained that all men were potentially equal, and that all differences were the result of solely environmental factors. There are no absolutes in ethics, and personal interest is the basic rule of all human behavior. Helvetius had a marked influence on later British utilitarianism via Jeremy Bentham, who studied his writings.

Francois Marie Voltaire of Paris (1694–1778) is perhaps the best known of all the radical humanists. A forerunner of the French Revolution, he adopted Bolingbroke's deism, tolerated every form of unbelief, and believed in man's ability to shape the future by employing the results of secular science. He was greatly admired by Benjamin Franklin, who brought his grandson to be blessed by him.

Another famous naturalist infected by deism was Jean Jacques Rousseau of Paris (1712–1778). Deeply influenced by the naturalism of Montaigne, the social contract theory of Hobbes, and by Locke's theory of the sovereignty of the people, Rousseau nominalistically exalted the individual in his natural state and fulminated against the degenerative effects of culture. A law unto himself, Rousseau's life was oddly characterized by 'both a passionate sense of social justice and an appalling condition of personal immorality.

Less radical but more dualistic was Friedrich Jacobi of

155

Düsseldorf (1743–1819), who proto-existentialistically championed feeling against reason, holding that not knowledge but feeling guarantees the individual's contact with the outside world. To Jacobi is attributed the saying that one can be a heathen with one's head as long as one is a Christian in one's heart. Such a dichotomy is, however, ultimately untenable.

Johann Pestalozzi (1746–1827) is often regarded as the father of modern education. A profound humanist, he believed that man was a social animal, capable of evil yet certainly perfectable by progressive training of the mind, the heart, and the head.

The seeds of the principles of Helvetius and of the American and the French Revolutions all found fertile ground in the thought of Jeremy Bentham of London (1748–1832). He held that the aim of all government should be to promote the greatest pleasurable happiness for the greatest number of people and to harmonize public and private interests. It is clear that this, the so-called utilitarian principle, is absolutely humanistic and radically opposed to all absolute values.

An example of the many nineteenth century American preachers who apostasized into humanism was Ralph Waldo Emerson of Boston (1803–1882). He absolutistically exalted individual man—whose worth, however, he derived from the universe as the great Oversoul; for Emerson's philosophy was a synthesis of romanticism, Hinduism, humanism, and neo-mysticism.

7. *Neo-mysticism*

Whereas the scholastic nature motive devolved into empiricism, the grace motive not only secularized into rationalism and radical humanism, but also irrationalized into mysticism as yet another avenue whereby man sought his freedom. Mysticistic tendencies were already manifested in the middle ages in Bernard of Clairvaux, Meister Johann Eckhart, and Nicholas of Cusa. And this tradition was now to be continued in the thought of men like Boehme, Fox, Swedenborg, Shem-Tov, and Schopenhauer.

Jacob Boehme of Altseidenberg (1575–1624), a self-taught cobbler influenced by reading the writings of Eckhart, saw in all creation reflections of the fierce conflict between (good) spirit and (evil) matter. To him, evil is a necessary pre-condition for the existence of all things, and heaven and hell are here on earth. Salvation is by renunciation of evil and progressive illumination.

George Fox of Drayton (1624–1691), also a cobbler, claimed to have been "opened up" by an inner light which he regarded as the Holy Spirit. Rejecting the Bible and the institutional Church, Fox, who was much influenced by Boehme, founded the Society of Friends or Quakers and advocated peace with men and silent meditation as means of illumination.

By far the most learned of the neo-mystics was Emmanuel Swedenborg of Stockholm (1688–1772). An erudite engineer, scholar, scientist, mathematician, mechanist, physiologist, and astronomer, he suddenly started having dramatic dreams and visions in his early fifties, claiming to be sent by God to announce the end of the Christian and the beginning of the New Jerusalem age. To Swedenborg, God is Love yet not trinitarian, and reveals Himself in visions; Christ is Savior, but the Pauline epistles are uncanonical.

An example of Jewish neo-mysticism is Baal Shem-Tov of Miedziboz, alias Israel ben Eliezer (1700–1760). The pioneer of modern Chassidism (cf. Buber), Shem-Tov pantheistically and anti-intellectualistically sought God through prayer and everyday life. Contrary to Boehme, he held that pleasures are not sinful, and that God must be served with the body as well as with the soul and even in the simplest activities.

As an example of a thoroughly humanistic mysticism, attention may be drawn to Arthur Schopenhauer (1788–1860). The world is governed by an evil will, held Schopenhauer, who also pessimistically exalted Indian mysticism above optimistic Western thought. Salvation is impossible, except through cultivation of art, sympathy, and (ultimately) the extinction of the self and complete indifference to living.

8. *Phenomenalism*

After a period of natural scientific empiricism devolving from Francis Bacon on the one hand and of rationalism inaugurated by Descartes on the other, it looked as if the further development of epistemology had polarized. In David Hume of Edinburgh (1711–1776), empiricism took on a skeptical and principially amoral aspect and prepared the way for the later development of phenomenalism on the one hand and positivism on the other. Rejecting the principles of induction and the "fictions" of God, causality and the self, Hume reduced knowledge to a bundle of sensations bound together in simple phenomenalistic association irrespective of the sensing subject or the sensed object—which latter—if it exists at all—is unknowable. Hereby Hume sounded the ultimate death-knell of both the personality ideal and the science ideal of humanism, and heralded the ultimate breakthrough of both Husserlian phenomenology and radical existentialism as the end of the road of autonomous man.

First, however, the world was about to be offered a genial attempt to resolve the polarization of humanism's twin motives of freedom and science, and such a solution was presented in the epoch-making philosophy of Immanuel Kant of Köningsberg (1724–1804).

The son of pietistic parents, this brilliant man clearly saw how the absolutization of the empiricistic science motive was threatening the other basic motive of humanism, the freedom or personality motive, and indeed threatening all transcendental values such as ethics and even faith in God Himself.

In order to reserve a (sacred!) area for religion and morality, Kant delineated the limits of (secular!) science and reason. Pure reason is linked to empirical experience, and cannot know the invisible and supra-sensational, such as God and truth, nor even the objective and noumenal "thing-in-itself," but can only know the phenomenal "thing-for-me," the thing as it *appears* to be and as it presents itself to the senses and as it is then apprehended by reason in terms of the intellectual categories of space and time into which the mind then orders it.

But all this only has reference to the realm of "pure reason." In addition, man also has a "practical reason" or conscience or heart, in which he is apriorically and necessarily aware of being bound by transcendental ideas of God, virtue, and immortality and which it is categorically imperative that he obey, even though man himself is radically evil.

The ultimate result of Kant's well-intentioned demarcation of life into two spheres—one of science and the other of freedom and religion—was, however, far different than he intended. Science and freedom became dualistically opposed to one another—religion no longer had to be scientifically (or even historically) accurate, as long as it promoted human freedom; and it is human freedom that posits God and morality, not vice-versa! The way was now open for the development of all kinds of religious liberalism and even existentialism, for there was no longer an appeal from religion to science—or vice-versa! In future it would be easy to write off religion and indeed the entire noumenal or metaphysical world as "unscientific," even when neo-Kantianism was mixed with idealism, as was frequently the case.

A good example of this is even Hermann Lotze of Bautzen (1817–1881), a professor of medicine, who attempted to combine a mechanistic physiology with an anthropocentric idealism. The natural world can be adequately explained in terms of physics. But at a higher level, God, the Supreme Personality, controls the panpsychic monads of which the universe consists (cf. Leibniz), and amongst which the soul of man occupies a leading place in its cosmic goal of teleologically realizing moral values.

Lotze influenced many thinkers, including James Ward of Hull (1843–1925), a Congregational clergyman who became a psychologist and also a professor of philosophy. A panpsychist, he established the limitations of the natural sciences and demonstrated their inability to yield an adequate account of the entire cosmos.

A leading neo-Kantian and founder of the Marburg school was Hermann Cohen (1848–1918). Going beyond Kant, Cohen denied the very existence of the thing-in-itself. There are no data, and it is thought which creates both the "subject" and the "object." Even the idea of God is neither vital nor personal, and can only be rationally understood.

A more unorthodox brand of Kantianism is found in the thought of Georg Simmel of Berlin (1858–1918). Although somewhat relativistic and pragmatistic, Simmel nevertheless believed in the self-transcendence of life, and took a deep and balanced interest in the philosophical implications of psychology, sociology, economics, science, art, and religion.

An independent neo-Kantian who stressed the value of Kant's aesthetical, ethical, and legal views was Wilhelm Windelband of Potsdam (1848–1915). A noted authority on the history of philosophy, Windelband sharply distinguished between the "factual" natural sciences, "normative" philosophy, and "unique" history, which latter deals scientifically with every activity of the human spirit.

An independent student of Windelband was the modern Dutch psychologist and philosopher Gerard Heymans of Ferwerd (1857–1930). Proceeding towards an ontological formulation of the results of psychology and physics, Heymans arrived at the theory of psychical monism, in terms of which the visible world is but the outside of the psychic processes of the cosmic spirit. Epistemologically, Heymans followed Kant, but sought to ground aprioric thought in psychology.

A most important philosophical figure is Edmund Husserl of Prossnitz (1859–1938). The father of the so-called "phenomenological" school, he sharply separated logic from psychology and advocated a type of realism in terms of which objects are considered to exist independently of their human recognition and which analyzes only immediate data, after they have been phenomenologically isolated from everything else (such as the empirical conditions necessary for their detection and even their ontic existence). In this way, the data are believed to be allowed to speak for themselves without any metaphysical or epistemological presuppositions whatsoever. Husserl's work was continued by others such as Max Scheler of Munich (1874–1928), who applied the phenomenological method to anthropology and religion, and it also influenced the thought of the radical existentialist Martin Heidegger.

In the twentieth century, neo-Kantianism was applied in many fields. Paul Natorp of Düsseldorf (1854–1924), a disciple of Hermann Cohen, applied it to epistemology, psychology, ethics, education, and social philosophy. Ernst Cassirer of Breslau (1874–1945) applied Kantianism to the task of systematization of science in linguistic and symbolic forms and to the task of co-ordinating knowledge with ideas of religion and art. And José Ortega y Gasset of Madrid (1883–1955), trained in the neo-Kantianism of Hermann Cohen, the phenomenology of Husserl, and the positivism of Dilthey, applied the principle of relativity particularly to the field of history.

9. *Idealism*

The word "idealism" is indeed very elastic, and can be used to designate any philosophy which puts the primary stress on or absolutizes the non-material factor in an attempt to explain the cosmos; and it is in this broad sense that the word is here used. The empiricism of Hobbes and Locke had stressed that nothing exists in the mind which is not first apprehended by the senses—*nihil in intellectu nisi prius in sensu*—and this certainly tended to promote a materialistic outlook. The rationalism of Descartes and Malebranche would now have its reactionary effect in promoting the opposite tendency, as manifested in a long line of thinkers of whom George Berkeley of Cloyne (1685–1753) was one of the first.

Bishop Berkeley's solution was at least partially Christian. Proceeding from Locke's empiristicistic epistemology and writing before Hume, Berkeley maintained that sensations never exist by themselves but always in the mind of some or other knower. In fact, only mind really exists—matter only "exists" dependently, as a perception—dependent on the fiat of the mind which creates and sustains the perception. To be is therefore to be perceived—*esse est percipi*. And as the human mind can only perceive things temporarily and as long as it "looks" at them, in order to guarantee cosmic continuity, the eternal Mind of God is introduced as an ontic necessity. The price that Berkeley had to pay to establish this Christian truth, however, was the annihilation of matter—a manifestly absurd solution.

Later, the phenomenalist Immanuel Kant did at least reserve an important epistemological function for the thinking mind, but the essentially irrational in his noumenal realm was clearly brought out in the absolute idealism of

162

Johann Fichte of Rammenau (1726–1814). To Fichte, morality is more important than science, and man's will is the microcosmic reflection of the moral order of the universe, alias God, the Transcendental "I" or Absolute Spirit Which controls the dynamic development of history. Firstly, the I posits Itself by its own free thought—thesis. Secondly, the I posits the non-I over against Itself—antithesis. And thirdly, the I and the non-I limit and to some extent absorb one another—synthesis. From this point of view, Fichte is the bridge between Kantian dualism on the one hand and Hegelian (and Marxian!) dialectics on the other.

An interesting if changeable follower of Fichte was Friedrich von Schelling of Leonberg (1775–1854). Basically a pantheistic idealist, his thought developed through at least three stages. In the first period, Schelling accepted Fichte's dualism between the I and the non-I, regarding the non-I as the historical unfolding of the I's progressive self-consciousness in which the I recognizes Itself in Its unconscious state. In his second period, Schelling maintained that the I or Spirit and the non-I or nature were parallel explications of one and the same more basic Absolute. And in his third period, Schelling, under the influence of Boehme's neo-mysticism, regarded God as pure Spirit, Who objectifies Himself in the world of ideas, but Whose creation is the source of apostasy from Himself via human freedom. Salvation lies in man's return to God through world history in art, science, and morality.

The dialectical idealism of Fichte and Schelling reached its zenith in the well-known advocate of objective idealism, Georg Hegel of Stuttgart (1770–1831). To Hegel, the real is the rational, and reality is the Self-unfolding of the Idea of Reason through a system of triads. The non-material idea or the Idea-in-Itself is the thesis Whose fundamental science is logic, which Idea objectifies and partially materializes Itself in Nature or the Idea-outside-of-Itself—as the antithesis Whose fundamental science is geometry. This Nature now develops into Spirit, the Idea-in-and-for-Itself, into man as the synthesis between Idea and Nature and into Jesus Christ as the acme of mankind in whose consciousness the Idea becomes Self-conscious through history as the fundamental science of the Spirit, through history as the "autobiography of God." In this way, the Idea achieves Freedom (through man)—achieves it also through religion, but particularly through philosophy.

The acme of subjectivism, however, was perhaps reached in the thought of Kaspar Schmidt of Bayreuth, alias Max Stirner (1806–1856). The founder of theoretical anarchism, he solipsistically asserted the absolute independence of his own ego, and called for the abolition of God, the Pope, the German Kaiser, nationality, and even the Fichtean transcendental "Ego." As far as Schmidt alias Stirner was concerned, he himself was Independent and Unique—there was but one God, Kaspar Schmidt; and Max Stirner was His prophet.

Eduard von Hartmann of Berlin (1842–1906) idealistically sought to combine Hegel's rationalism and Schopenhauer's voluntarism into what he called "transcendental realism." In this system, the Unconscious Will originates and promotes the development of the entire cosmos; but the end is always pessimistic, so that the best thing man can do is to renounce the will to live.

Francis Bradley of Glasbury (1846–1924) was initially a disciple of Hegel, although he also supported the categorical imperative of Kant against Bentham's ethical utilitarianism. Basically monistic, Bradley held that only the suprapersonal Absolute Whole is strictly real, in Which the lack of truth, beauty, and righteousness is resolved without being abolished.

A more theistic viewpoint was adopted by the American

George Howison of Maryland (1834–1916), who advocated a "Personal Idealism" in which God, the Perfect Person and Final Cause, unites all other persons who have their own responsible freedom. So far this sounds rather Biblical, until one learns that Howison's God is not Creator and Ruler, but only ideal and end.

A famous American neo-Hegelian philosopher was Josiah Royce of California (1855–1916). Regarding religious faith as the ground of social cohesion, Royce combined the absolute idealism of Hegel and Fichte with Schopenhauer's voluntarism into what he called "synthetic idealism." While yet guaranteeing the freedom of the individual, Royce rejected all relativism and regarded every aspect of the cosmos as a particular manifestation of the Absolute.

The early twentieth-century swing away from materialism and positivism towards idealism in the important field of modern physics followed on epoch-making discoveries by men such as Planck, Einstein, and Driesch. Max Planck of Kiel (1858–1947), who formulated the quantam theory and thereby shifted the age-old emphasis in physics from matter to energy, believed in the possibility of reconciling science and religion. Albert Einstein of Ulm (1879–1955), the discoverer of the special and general theories of relativity of such great cosmological importance, also ventured into the field of political idealism and humanistically advocated total disarmament, international Zionism, a socialistic society, and world government. And the famous biologist Hans Driesch of Kreuznach (1867–1941), originally a firm disciple of the materialist Ernst Haeckel, abandoned mechanism in favor of a theistic and teleological vitalism, as a result of his experiments with the blastomeres of eggs.

The famous Italian aesthetician and politician Benedetto Croce of Percasseroli (1866–1922) opposed both materialism and Kantian dualism. Stressing the importance of intuition in acquiring knowledge and of the intellect in ordering it, Croce developed an idealistic liberalism in which history plays an important role.

A female American philosopher who combined the idealism of Hegel and Royce and the neo-realism of S. Alexander, was Mary Calkins of Wellesley (1863–1930). The cosmos, though itself an Absolute Person, nevertheless consists of different emergent minds distinct therefrom. Her view is thus similar to Howison's, but more pantheistic.

The influence of Hegel is also found in the thought of the famous liberal theologian W. E. Hocking of Cleveland (1873–1966). Combining absolute idealism with pragmatism, Hocking advocated a political synthesis between *laissez-faire* individualism and centralized collectivism.

The idealistic historian and cultural philosopher Johan Huizenga of Leyden (1872–1945) sought to balance spiritual and material interests in society. He advocated an emphasis on vocation and a return to morality (rather than the development of psychology) as the best way to improve our modern society so plagued with its intellectual superficiality and lack of love.

A modern American thinker in the personalist tradition of Howison and Calkins, is Edgar Brightman of Middletown. To Brightman, the rationality of the universe and the existence of human personality evidences the existence of God. Brightman's God, however, is limited by a factor which he terms "The Given" (which explains the phenomena of evil and suffering), and is therefore not the sovereign and unlimited God of Scripture.

Archbishop William Temple of Canterbury (1881–1944) sought to combine the idealism of Plato and Hegel with the social philosophy of Karl Marx, while yet holding to the uniqueness of and necessity for Christianity as an instrument of social and cultural progress. Rather obviously, such a syncretism did justice to none of its ingredients.

As a last example of modern idealism, we mention Albert

Schweitzer of Alsace-Lorraine (1875–1965). A world-famous theologian, philosopher, musicologist, and historian, he turned down every professorship offered him and spent his life on his medical mission station at Lambarene in West Central Africa. Almost deifying reverence for life and human solidarity and the principle of altruism, his theology was certainly not that of orthodox Protestantism.

10. *Psychologism*

Before the middle of the nineteenth century, psychology was technically a branch of philosophical epistemology. As a result of the work of Wundt, Brentano, Freud, Adler, Wertheimer, Watson, Jung, McDougall, and others, however, it has now obtained recognition as a full-fledged science distinct from philosophy.

The first psychological laboratory was established at Leipzig in 1879 by Wilhelm Wundt of Neckarau (1832–1920), a philosopher who sought to synthesize Hegel and positivism. In Wundt's opinion, the *will* and its attendant emotions was the basic factor in psychological experience.

This position was opposed by Franz Brentano of Marienburg (1838–1917) who, while exaggerating the value of natural science, almost scholastically characterized psychological data as those which intentionally embrace their objects in themselves. Though the content of psychology is physical, the act is *mental*.

Perhaps the most famous of all psychologists or rather psychologicists is Sigmund Freud of Vienna (1856–1939). The founder of the psycho-analytical school, Freud employed hypnotism and the interpretation of dreams as attempted cures for neuroses. In his opinion, the past repression of expression of the *libido* or the sexual factor is one of the most important factors in psychology.

Freud's disciple, Alfred Adler of Vienna (1870–1937), ultimately withdrew from him and formed the school of individual psychology which emphasized the *ego* or "I" instead of the libido. To Adler, the desire to acquire authority is the most fundamental formative factor in psychology.

Closer to the Christian position is the Gestalt school of psychology founded by Max Wertheimer of Frankfort (1880–1943) and his co-worker Wolfgang Köhler. Wertheimer refused to limit his investigations to only one element, but insisted on looking at psychological phenomena as coherent *wholes* which transcend and impart their character to all their component elements.

A totally different and essentially materialistic theory was advocated by Ivan Pavlov of Russia (1849–1936), who reduced psychology to the study of the conditioned *reflex reaction* in man and animals—the basic principle of communistic "brain-washing." And the environmental and mechanistic principles of animal psychology were also summarily applied to human beings by John Watson of Chicago (1878–1958), the founder of the behaviorist school.

Of much greater value is the work of Carl Gustav Jung of Zürich (1875–1961). Originally an advocate of psychoanalysis, he later drew away from Freud and founded his own school of analytical (or "complex") psychology. Refusing to limit the cause of neuroses to past experiences and substituting the principle of *energy* in the place of Freud's sexual factor, Jung believed that individual, social, national, and racial factors should all be considered in psychological analysis and in the cultivation of personal harmony.

As a last example of an influential figure in the development of psychological philosophy, William McDougall of Oxford and later of Harvard (1871–1938) may be cited. To McDougall, there are at least fourteen motives or instincts which regulate social strivings, ranging from self-preservation through amusement. This is a sane viewpoint, and Mc-

Dougall's defense of the psychological interaction between body and mind merits close attention.

11. *Socialism*

During the last two centuries, there has been an ever-increasing trend to relate philosophy to social problems particularly, yet by no means exclusively, in the various socialistic movements. To some extent, this has been an exaggerated and apostate absolutization of the freedom motive as a protest against the miseries of that stepchild of the science motive—the industrial revolution.

A pioneer in this field was undoubtedly Claude Henri de Saint-Simon of Paris (1760–1825), an advocate of utopian socialism. To St. Simon, philosophical changes cause social changes. In the industrial age, the factory worker has become more important than all other classes of society, and should accordingly be entrusted with the control of the government. Of Christianity, only its social and ethical doctrines are worth preserving, and for the rest it should be supplanted by a sensualistic pantheism.

One of the early Russian revolutionary socialists was the philosopher Alexander Herzen (1812–1870). To him, chance governed the development of history, but the free individual too could to some extent also determine the course of events. Like Mao-tse-tung and unlike Marx, Herzen held that an agrarian country such as the then Russia could indeed unfold into socialism without the intervening stage of urbanization and the development of a capitalist economy.

An early advocate of revolutionary socialism in Western Europe was Moses Hess (1815–1875), whose writings converted Friedrich Engels to the communist cause. A staunch advocate of violence, Hess was, however, motivated by humanitarian rather than by economic considerations, and later became an ardent Zionist.

Perhaps the leading revolutionary in Western Europe

was the exiled Russian, Michael Bakunin (1814–1876). A violent anarchist who seemed to delight in revolution for its own sake, he was finally written off by Karl Marx as "a man devoid of theoretical understanding."

The atheistic communist Karl Marx (1818–1883) believed that economic factors were the cause of philosophical, religious, and social benefits—not vice-versa; and that the course of history was inevitably determined by such factors. Industrialized society was bound to produce a class of propertyless proletarians, who would ultimately overthrow the capitalists and establish socialism.

Much subtler but perhaps even more dangerous were the views of the American social philosopher Henry George (1839–1897), who advocated the nationalization of all land and its redistribution as the common property of all people and the establishment of the single tax. His views had much influence on British Socialists like William Morris and Fabians like George Bernard Shaw.

Altogether different were the social views of Henry Sidgwick of Skipton (1838–1900). A disciple of John Stuart Mill (who combined utilitarianism with positivism), Sidgwick rejected individualistic hedonism and sought to further a social utilitarianism founded on common sense morality.

The attitude of the Hegelian Bernard Bosanquet of Rock Hall (1848–1923), is even more balanced. The cosmos is a totality of individual parts, each of which is unique and each of which has a role to play in the welfare of the whole. In the field of social ethics, this means that both the individual and society have their rights and duties towards one another.

One of the founders of what is now the science of sociology is Émile Durkheim of Les Vosges (1858–1917). Denying metaphysical values, he insisted that each community had a coercive and changeable collective consciousness distinct from its members, which consciousness was also relative because it was different from that of other communities. Certainly this dominant viewpoint in sociological thought is no bar to the steady advance of Marxism.

The founder of Russian Marxism was Georgi Plekhanov of Tambov (1856–1918). Rejecting Herzen's (and Mao's) thesis of progressing directly from feudalism to socialism, Plekhanov promoted Marx's thesis of the necessity of intermediate capitalism. As leader of the Russian Social-Democratic Labor Party, he had a profound effect on Lenin, even though he sided with the Mensheviks against Lenin's Bolsheviks in the 1904 Party split.

It was, however, Lenin or Vladimir Ulyanov of Simbirsk (1870–1924) who brought communism to power in Russia in 1917. Combining the Russian anarchistic tradition with Marxist doctrine, Lenin worked out and successfully applied the tactics of revolutionary take-over. As a philosopher, he condemned the epistemology of Mach and Avenarius and also elaborated the political philosophical distinction between revolutionary socialism and pure communism.

The influence of economics on sociology was also elaborated (and from a quite different viewpoint) by the great German scholar Max Weber of Berlin (1864–1921). According to Weber, it was Protestantism—and Calvinism in particular—which promoted the spirit of capitalism; an opinion also broached previously by the communist Friedrich Engels himself.

12. *Evolutionism*

In one sense the theory of evolutionism or transmutationism as a life and world view is very old, and may be traced back to Empedocles as regards organic beings, and as a cosmic principle even as far back as Heraclitos. The theory has, however, received particular prominence since the formulation of freedom-threatening apostate natural scientific hypotheses from the time of Lamarck onwards, and it is here that we shall now begin.

Jean Lamarck (1744–1829) was one of the first modern scientists to adopt an evolutionistic view of the cosmos instead of the traditionally Christian and more static one. Lamarck clearly distinguished the Creator from the creation and lifeless beings from living beings, but he did hold that environmental changes can modify living beings and cause them to produce new characteristics.

The most famous of the evolutionists is, of course, Charles Darwin of Shrewsbury (1809–1882). Abandoning Christian theism though maintaining Christian ethics, Darwin was an acute observer and world traveler. Noting many variations in animals and plants, Darwin concluded that, as more living beings are born than are able to survive, only the fittest specimens survive in the struggle for life. This ensures that only the fittest specimens can reproduce over a long period of time and, coupled with the averred hereditary transmission of acquired characteristics, this gradually brought about profound changes in the species themselves.

Friedrich Engels of Barmen (1820–1895) applied Darwin's views to the universe as a whole but particularly to the supposed evolution of man, combining it with labor and with the dialectic principle as the causative factors of such development. The result has been that evolutionism is now an integral part of communist philosophy throughout the world.

Non-communistic evolutionists have helped to spread the evolutionistic philosophy—and sometimes even in its dialectical form—throughout the Western world. The famous agnostic Thomas Huxley of Ealing (1825–1895) championed "evolution-by-leaps" in biology, and the British engineer Herbert Spencer of Derby, who encyclopaedically if unprofoundly applied the principle of evolution to the entire range of human thought, and particularly to the fields of ethics, sociology, psychology, and biology, interpreted the more complex in terms of the less. Optimistically equating evolution with progress, Spencer did more to popularize this philosophy amongst the masses than probably anybody else.

Another engineer turned evolutionist but a man of deeper learning was C. Lloyd Morgan of South Africa (1852–1936), an eminent biologist, geologist, and psychologist. Developing Huxley's "evolution-by-leaps," Morgan arrived at the theory of emergent evolution, thus heralding the advent of the holism of Bergson and S. Alexander.

The popularizer of evolutionistic philosophy in continental Europe was Ernst Haeckel of Potsdam (1834–1919), who elaborated a hylozoistic metaphysics reminiscent of the Ionian materialists. God and immortality were exchanged for a monistic naturalism—although it is ironic that Haeckel did later feel obliged to assume the existence of a property similar to sensation "in the foundation-stones of the structure of matter itself!"

13. *Positivism*

The development of positivism or radical empiricism did to some extent parallel the development of both socialism and evolutionism. The three are, however, quite distinguishable, and it will be well to begin the treatment of positivism with the thought of Auguste Comte of Montpellier (1798–1857).

In his youth, Comte was influenced by the utopian socialism of St. Simon. Later, however, he outgrew utopianism in favor of positivism. According to Comte, humanity goes through three stages of growth: firstly, the theological or mythical stage, when the supernatural is employed to explain nature; secondly, the philosophical or metaphysical stage, when aprioric speculations and abstractions are used to attempt to understand the universe; and thirdly, the positive stage, when the methods of the so-called "exact sciences" such as mathematics and physics are summarily applied in respect of all the other sciences too. These latter methods alone, he felt, were truly scientific, and absolute presuppositionlessness was a *sine qua non* of all scientific research. Of course, this is impossible—for absolute presuppositionlessness is in itself an absolute presupposition!

The Left-Hegelian Ludwig Feuerbach of Landshut (1804–1872) paved the way for the adoption of views similar to positivism in Marxist circles. Reducing the idea of God to the mere skyward projection of human impotence, Feuerbach rejected all idealistic philosophy in favor of the radical empiricism of a materialistic natural science.

The famous British logician and social reformer John Stuart Mill of London (1806–1873) sought to combine positivism with utilitarianism. Empiricistically exaggerating the logical importance of induction and downgrading the deductive syllogism as circular reasoning, he defended the liberty of the individual—because of its social utility.

Positivistic materialism was promoted in Germany by Jacob Moleschott. Originally of Utrecht (1822–1893), he was a psychologist, and taught that the whole of human life was physically determined—"no thought without phosphorus!" And similar views were espoused by Ludwig Büchner of Darmstadt (1824–1899), an atheistic lecturer in medicine at Tübingen who identified the mind and the brain. These are both representatives of "vulgar materialism," and they were both rejected by Lenin the dialectical materialist because they believed that the brain secretes thought just like the liver secretes bile.

Although he did distinguish between the natural sciences and the disciplines of the spirit, Wilhelm Dilthey of Biebrich (1833–1911) empiricistically and positivistically opposed any metaphysical investigation of the supernatural whatsoever. Especially history analyzed man—but history is merely a physical discipline and not a science—for only the natural sciences, he held, are scientific.

174

Ernst Mach of Turas (1838–1916) may perhaps be cited as a last example of an empiricistic philosopher who tried to interpret science positivistically, entirely free from metaphysics. Yet Mach attached as much importance to the psychical as he did to the physical. Reminiscent of Hume's epistemology, Mach regarded both matter and personality as but a complex of sensations, and was severely attacked by Lenin on account of his influence on the thinking of many communists, which Machian influence the Russian leader considered to be dangerously antimaterialistic.

14. *Pragmatism*

The system of philosophy known as pragmatism is an All-American discovery, even though continental thinkers like Simmel, Vaihinger, and Poincaré did adopt positions somewhat similar thereto.

The term "pragmatism" was first coined by the American thinker Charles Peirce of Cambridge (1839–1914), whose views also reflect the influence of Kant and Darwin. To Peirce, the significance of ideas should be tested by examining their empirical results. Being is a unityless, polylateral, and pluralistic phenomenological unfolding of different actualities, whereas knowledge, which is social or "pragmaticistic" in its nature rather than individual, is alway provisional and fallible. This theory Peirce called "fallibilism," and it logically involves the denial of absolute truth.

Peirce's better-known contemporary William James of Cambridge (1842–1910) differed from the former in at least two important respects: ontologically, he made room for God in his "pluriverse"; and epistemologically, the verification of knowledge was a more personal and less social matter. The knower vitally interacts with the known world and does not merely reflect objective reality. As a psy-

175

chologist as well as a philosopher, James made a major contribution to pragmatistic epistemology.

The great mathematician and physicist Henri Poincaré of Nancy (1854–1912) asserted that what determined the selection of one scientific hypothesis instead of a score of other equally possible hypotheses, is simply what he calls the "convention" of choosing the simplest hypothesis which yields a consistent and verifiable explanation. This notion therefore combines pragmatism with the principle of economy of thought known as "Ockham's Razor."

A different kind of pragmatism is encountered in the thought of the German idealistic positivist, Hans Vaihinger of Nehren (1852–1933). To Vaihinger, religious and metaphysical ideas are beautiful myths—yet useful fictions if they are successful means of promoting man's will to live. This is done by believing the fiction "as if" it were true; if the fiction proves to be pragmatically workable, Vaihinger's "Philosophy of As-If" has proved its worth.

A last example of pragmatic philosophy is that of the famous American educationalist John Dewey of Burlington (1859–1952). To Dewey, knowledge is participating in the funded experience of society, instrumentally interacting with one's experiential surroundings. Dewey was an activist. Total social involvement as opposed to individual contemplation was to him the requirement for true education and true philosophy.

15. *Neo-realism*

After the Kantian and Hegelian period of phenomenalistic and idealistic dominance of philosophy, there has been a saner reaction towards a greater degree of acceptance of the existence of objective reality, particularly in England and America. This reaction, known as neo-realism, has stressed the existence as well as the material and mental nature (albeit the neutrality) of the objective world.

One of the best known of the neo-realists is undoubtedly the independent British mathematician Bertrand Russell of Trelleck (1872–   ). To Russell, objective being is a multiplicity of events in space and time distinct from the perceiver thereof, even though sense data (as distinct from objects) are themselves subjective and do not exist apart from the perceiver.

Another neo-realist and the founder of the modern common sense school, is G. E. Moore of Cambridge (1873–1958). To Moore, philosophy should analyze and elucidate common sense, not destroy it. Reality exists independently of man's cognizance thereof, and the latter does not alter the sense data, even though, contrary to Locke, it is the sense data which exist independently of their perception and it is the "objects" which are subjective.

Neo-realism underwent a degree of change in the philosophy of George Santayana of Madrid (1863–1952), who called his system "critical realism." To Santayana (cf. Plato), being consists of a variety of existences which subsist in what he calls "essences." The existences themselves are not apprehendable by epistemological processes—as are the essences—but only by "animal faith." The essences, however, give an adequate albeit a critical representation of the real existences.

A follower of William James, who in addition advocated neo-realism, is Ralph Barton Perry of Harvard (1876–1957). Correctly placing ontology before epistemology, Perry concluded that reality is independent of human cognizance thereof, which latter can only "reveal" the former's existence.

More complicated is the position of the emergent evolutionist Samuel Alexander of Sydney (1859–1938). Matter is primary, for complex mind has evolved—albeit differentiatedly—from less complex matter, even though it interacts therewith. Knowledge is cognizance of objective reality, and hence (neo-)realism is the true theory of epistemology.

Originally a neo-Kantian, Nicolai Hartmann of Riga (1882–1950) steadily moved towards (neo-)realism. To him ontology came to be at least as vital as epistemology, and one should seek to understand the actual thing-in-itself, even though complete rationality is not achievable.

A more complex position was adopted by the Englishman Alfred North Whitehead of Cambridge (1861–1947), who later taught at Harvard. Although he later to some extent moved away from realism towards idealism, he insisted that reality should be interpreted as interwoven events rather than as isolated objects, although they are in fact individuated by eternal "objects" (cf. Plato). God establishes which forms shall be actualized, and reason, the function of which is to apprehend such forms, is an aid to promote better human living.

16. *Logical Positivism*

Together with radical existentialism, modern logical positivism alias logical empiricism alias scientific empiricism is indeed the end of the road and the tacit declaration of the bankruptcy of humanistic philosophy.

The founder of the Vienna Circle of logical positivism was Moritz Schlick of Rostock (1882–1936). To Schlick, the establishment of logical meaning was the most important task of philosophy. Positivistically limiting knowledge to the empirical and the logical, Schlick and his school regarded all values as factually meaningless and as mere emotivism.

Perhaps the best-know promoter of this theory and the successor to G. E. Moore at the Cambridge School was Ludwig Wittgenstein of Austria (1889–1951). Originally an architect, Wittgenstein later devoted himself to investigating the logical structure of linguistics, regarding the whole of philosophy merely as a critique of language. To him, logical and mathematical truths are tautological, and the most important characteristic of symbolism or ideal language is sameness. That this theory, in spite of its praiseworthy emphasis on the necessity of philosophical clarity, tends to promote intellectual sterility, need hardly be demonstrated.

To Rudolf Carnap of Vienna (1891–), logical syntax or the study of the structure and interrelationship of statements is of great importance. All the sciences should have a common language—the language of mathematicized logic whereby their unity can be advanced. Metaphysics are irrelevant, and only the verifiable is scientific.

Hans Reichenbach of Berlin (1891–1953) attempted to clarify particularly the geometrical ideas of space and time. He insisted that all knowledge is merely probable and is founded on the statistical frequency of occurrences as presented to human experience. Consequently, he rejected traditional logic with its absolute values in favor of a new "probability logic" of higher and lower degrees of truth.

A last example of logical positivism is the Englishman Alfred Ayer of Cambridge (1910–). To him, only the verifiable is real. Sharply distinguishing between factual and value judgments, he holds that the former are publicly provable, whereas the latter—such as religion and ethics—are meaningless and pure emotivism.

17. *Existentialism*

The philosophy of existentialism is perhaps the most influential stream of thought in Western Europe today, particularly among the masses. It is characterized by a search for freedom, a rejection of authority, and an irrational absolutization of the present moment of the individual human being's existence to the exclusion of the past and the future and to the exclusion of all other beings.

The first advocate of radically anti-Christian existentialism was perhaps Friedrich Wilhelm Nietzsche of Röcken (1844–1900), who glorified in life for its own sake and who attacked reason, science, morality, and especially Christianity. God is dead, and kindness towards one's fellow man is a manifestation of the lack of living a self-assertive life as a superhuman antichrist. Many of these evil ideas later re-asserted themselves in Nazism.

A different type of existentialism altogether is found in the thought of the creative evolutionist Henri Bergson of Paris (1859–1941). To Bergson, reality is an incessant stream of time or duration moved by a vital impulse which unfolds in freedom in all possible directions, but which is resisted by the mechanism of matter. Man knows all this by intuition, which sympathetically identifies the knower with the ever-moving known object and which dynamically and existentially transcends static reason.

Karl Jaspers of Oldenberg (1883–), a psychiatrist turned philosopher, believes in God yet rejects both Christianity and atheism. To him, the historical individual's existential awareness is the same as certainty that God is the root of all cosmic plurality. God exists for an individual to the extent to which that individual himself really exists. This arises from and is accompanied by freedom, and it results in life as the primordial power out of the ground of the individual's being himself.

Existentialism reaches barren and pessimistic depths in the thought of Martin Heidegger of Masskirch (1889–), who follows the phenomenology of Husserl and the secularized individualism of Kierkegaard. Apprehending guilt and dread in the very heart of human personality, man is isolated and lost in his loneliness. Yet he is doomed to exist, to be sick even unto death. His freedom consists merely of his acceptance of this endless fate of nihilistic individualism.

Heidegger's disciple Jean Paul Sartre of Paris (1905–) is, if anything, even more radical. An atheistic existentialist,

Sartre combines this view with a radical and almost solipsistic individualism. Man cannot escape from his isolation, and is doomed to be free. Mere "being-*in*-itself" is impersonal and neutral, and leads to nausea and disgust. But "being-*for*-itself" or self-conscious personality confronting nothingness, is to be strived for; it does not exist, but it must act and *become*—in order to avoid non-being. To genuinely "exist" is therefore to act by "carving out a hole" in being, by one's world "being-*for*-itself" instead of being-*in*-itself" from which it must be separated.

Existentialism has sometimes been combined with theology with truly ruinous consequences, as in the thought of Rudolph Bultmann of Marburg (1884–   ). In his attempt to get the gospel accepted as existentially relevant by "scientific" modern man, Bultmann not merely "demythologizes" but also "degospelizes" the gospel. Nearly all the fundamentals of the Christian faith are regarded as myths formulated by the early Christian Church—including Christ's resurrection from the dead! (Cf. I Cor. 15:17-18).

Paul Tillich of Prussia and later of Harvard (1886–1965) also tried to adopt the gospel existentially to modern man. As God Himself is the "Ground" of all being—and only symbolically conceived of as a Person—the question as to His "existence" is absurd. It is man's very imprisonment in the anxiety of non-being which makes God a living God. Jesus Christ is the new existential being, here and now; and His pre-existence before His mythical virgin birth and His post-existence after His mythical resurrection are neither existential nor historical.

However, it is not only the Christian world which has experienced the impact of existentialism. The Chassidic Jew Martin Buber (1878–1966) no less struggled with the problem. A profound student of Judaism, Christianity, and the various oriental religions, Buber propagated the universal importance of the existential realization of God's immanence as taught in the Talmud and as mystically experienced in prayer.

18. *Pseudo-Christian philosophy*

This is a somewhat comprehensive category, and will include miscellaneous philosophers who all claim(ed) to be Christian thinkers. We, however, have classified them all as "pseudo-Christian philosophers." This does not, of course, imply that all of them are lost as far as their salvation is concerned, but it certainly implies that their philosophical views are not in accordance with Biblical Christianity.

The Protestant Reformation in the first half of the sixteenth century was almost immediately opposed by the Papistic Counter-Reformation which was called into being by way of antithesis. The Jesuits were particularly active in the Romish reaction, and Francisco Suarez of Granada (1548–1617) is a good example of that school. Suarez perpetuated the scholastic elevation of "revealed" theology above "natural" philosophy, although he did rise above Aristotle in teaching the utter ontic transcendence and independence of God and in ascribing the principle of individualism to substantial essence rather than to matter. On the other hand, however, he anti-empirically taught the auto-intuitive nature of human knowledge, and jesuitically maintained that moral norms and natural law are not absolutely unalterable.

It should not be thought, however, that Protestantism was free from the old Romish dualism between nature and grace; and such dualism here led either to emotionalistic pietism on the one hand or to rationalistic supranaturalism on the other.

A dangerous kind of individualistic and irrational religious idealism was advocated by Friedrich Schleiermacher of Breslau (1768–1834). Nominally a preacher of the German Reformed Church, he was steeped in pietism from childhood and he very uncalvinisticly accepted Kant's dualism between religion and science. The result was that Schleiermacher sought the essence of religion in the individual's personal emotional experience of absolute dependence on what he believed was Christ (rather than in the cosmic Christ Himself as presented in Holy Scripture, for which presentation Schleiermacher, like his modern liberal disciples, had very little respect indeed).

William Paley of Peterborough (1743–1805) is an example (like Bishop Butler before him) of the other extreme. Although doing much valuable work in the field of Christian apologetics in which he sought to refute deism (e.g., by his famous "watch argument"), Paley synthesized Biblical revelation with hedonism, and utilitarianly maintained that it is the beneficial tendency of a moral action that makes it right—even though he did concede that it is the Will of God which is the ultimate ground of morality.

The gaping chasm between faith and science in pseudo-Reformed Protestantism became particularly apparent in the thought of Albrecht Ritschl of Germany (1822–1889). To Ritschl—under pressure from an apostate and hostile natural science created by the very dualism he himself sought to perpetuate—religion is independent of science. It embraces value judgments of the heart distinct from those of reason.

This familiar distinction and false antithesis between the heart and the head is reminiscent of Jacobi (*supra*), the forerunner of existentialism. And in the Lutheran Sören Kierkegaard of Copenhagen (1813–1855), the first recognized "Christian existentialist," it is instructive to note that he too (like his admirers) ignored the importance of a Christian philosophical view of the universe. To Kierkegaard, the existentiality of the individual—albeit with Jesus Christ— is the sole concern of philosophy. The body belongs to the temporal (the "secular"?!), but the spirit is the real self and belongs to the eternal—and to the moment! In the eternal moment, the individual passionately lays hold of the eternal, and thus freely chooses his own eternal salvation. By faith in Christ, the individual absurdly renounces his own existence in favor of that of Christ, cf. Luther (q.v.). Quite apart from his enormous influence on Christians through dialectical theologians like Barth, it is evident that Kierkegaard's hyperindividualism is radically opposed to the Biblical concept of covenantal solidarity.

The Romish tradition was forcibly continued in the thought of men like Pope Leo XIII of Rome (1810–1903), who elevated the thought of Thomas Aquinas to the status of the official philosophical system of the Roman Catholic Church. Thomas should be studied in the original sources, and scholasticism should be up-dated to agree with the post-Aquinian Romish doctrines.

This pronouncement gave great impetus to the work of Romish intellectuals like Maritain and Gilson and resulted in the movement known as neo-scholasticism or neo-Thomism. Jacques Maritain of Paris (1882–) systematically presented Thomism as a theocentric humanism, and sought to ground his humanism in God's cosmonomic and teleological world order. And Étienne Gilson of Paris sought to defend Thomism historically. On the one hand Gilson contrasted Thomism with non-Thomistic scholasticism, but on the other hand he to some extent tried to reconcile it with existentialism.

Not all Roman Catholic thinkers endorsed the return to Thomas. Maurice Blondel of Dijon (1861-1939) rejected Thomism, sought to reconcile pragmatism with idealism, and showed affinity with Augustine and Pascal, in his views of grace and faith—even though he did not overcome the nature-grace dialectic of scholasticism. The modern palaeontologist Pierre Teilhard de Chardin sought to reconcile the transformistic life and world view with Romanism in terms of a Christogenic, Christocentric, and Christotelic evolutionism. And Gabriel Marcel of Paris (1889–) has synthesized Romanism and existentialism—only in God can man perform existential deeds and thus participate in the acts of God.

The Russian Orthodox Church has also had its great syncretistic thinkers. Vladimir Soloviev (1853–1900), like Kierkegaard, distinguished between true Christianity and an apostate Church hopelessly enslaved to the Russian state and ruling classes. A passionate humanitarian, he protested against the very distinction between those inside the Church and those outside, and his profound realization of the humanitarian importance of the incarnation made him extremely sympathetic to the claims of Rome.

The great Leo Tolstoy (1828–1910), a Russian nobleman appalled by the Tsarist oppression of the poor, upheld the Sermon on the Mount and preached and practiced social repentence—opposing a worldly Church and working with the serfs in the fields. Yet Tolstoy all but denied the personality of God and the meaning of Calvary.

A dynamic kind of Christian syncretism was advocated by Nicholas Berdyaev of Kiev (1874–1948). On becoming a Marxist, he was exiled and threatened with excommunication from the Russian Church. Later, he returned to Christianity yet not to Churchianity, and he was accused of insulting the Synod and put on trial. Saved by the Red Revolution of 1917, the communists themselves expelled him from Russia five years later for supporting true Christians. According to Berdyaev, man was created by a finite God, but must himself be creative in order to establish his own creativity.

An American thinker also originally quite influenced by Marxism is Reinhold Niebuhr of Missouri (1892–). Under the influence of neo-orthodoxy, he also promoted a syncretism between Scripture, existentialism, and secularism. Conscious of man's evil nature, he does, however, falsely regard original sin as man's present free choice against God and his own humanity, which sin precedes(!) that of "Adam."

The most famous "Christian existentialist" is, of course, Karl Barth of Basel (1886–1969). To him, God is the Wholly Other, Who in creation disdainfully rejected non-being and created a suprahistorical "Adam" who is essentially Jesus Christ of Nazareth, the Word-in-the-flesh, God's "yes" to righteousness and "no" to sin. In Christ alone does God reveal Himself, and fallible Scripture merely points to Christ —and even then only when the Holy Spirit is pleased to use it for this purpose. Here, in spite of other contributory factors, we see the result of the scholastic and Kantian dualism between nature and grace and reason and faith— for according to Barth, philosophy is opposed to faith, and a Christian philosophy is impossible.

Some who claim to be Reformed have, however, tried to reconcile immanentistic (or non-Christian) philosophy and Scripture, and to construct what they consider to be a philosophy acceptable to Christians. Such are contemporary thinkers like the existentialistically relevant A. E. Loen and the anti-antithetic C. A. van Peursen of the Netherlands. However, in spite of many valuable elements in their thought, they are nonetheless both promoters of syncretism, and can therefore in our opinion not be regarded as advocates of a Biblically-true and Christian philosophy.

19. *Summary*

In this chapter, an attempt has been made to demonstrate that the false nature-grace motive of scholasticism ultimately and necessarily had to result either in the complete secularization of philosophy on the one hand, or in the complete abandonment thereof on the other—both tragic alternatives, from the point of view of a Biblical life and world view.

In the Pre-Renaissance and the Renaissance proper, man progressively emancipated himself from the dictatorship of the false Church and subjected himself to the new dictatorship of natural science, which manifested itself either in an absolutization of created reason (as in rationalism), or in an absolutization of created experience (as in empiricism). Each tendency in its own way led to the development of a radical humanism in which not God but man was glorified, resulting in deism, the French Revolution, and the no less humanistic British liberal utilitarianism; while otherworldly religionists reactionarily yet falsely sought their salvation not in consistent Christianity but in escapist neomysticism.

An immanentistic attempt to bridge the dichotomy between the traditions of rationalism and empiricism was made in the phenomenalism of men like Hume and Kant and their successors; but this soul-deadening theory did not ultimately satisfy, and only helped promote the more vital philosophy of idealism as a reaction of the freedom-living human spirit thereagainst.

In the nineteenth century the human spirit was remarkably stimulated by the unfolding of psychology, social philosophy, and evolutionism. But when the logicistic spirit of positivism, pragmatism, and neo-realism had exhausted its genius, it terminated in the poverty of logical positivism— while idealism petered out into the despair of modern existentialism. Some syncretistic attempts were made to promote theoretical thought by combining some of these systems with the Biblical world view, but this only resulted in pseudo-Christian philosophy—which by its very nature could convincingly satisfy neither the Christian nor the infidel.

Tired and syncretistic mediaeval philosophy had needed a new lease of life centuries earlier. The apostate Renaissance had sought to give philosophy this new lease of life

Chapter VIII

THE REBIRTH OF TRUE PHILOSOPHY

The Continuing Reformation

1. Survey

Unfortunately this final chapter will not be as long as the previous one. Unfortunately—for the quantity of Christian philosophy is unimpressive compared to the arsenal of apostate thought. Yet at least a start has been made to philosophize to God's glory. A start had been made earlier in Eden and in the Hebrew and Patristic philosophy. And a new start was now to be made again in the late middle ages even amidst the asphyxiating atmosphere of scholasticism—made in power in the Reformation period of the sixteenth and seventeenth centuries, and made again during the last hundred years in Holland and South Africa and—to a lesser yet fortunately ever-increasing extent—in North America and elsewhere too.

2. The Pre-Reformation

True Christian thought did indeed burn very low during the dark ages, though it never completely petered out. For God kept alive the flame of truth, and handed it down from Paul and John through men like Irenaeus, Athanasius, Augustine, Gottschalk, and Anselm to mediaeval minds like Bradwardine.

Thomas Bradwardine of Canterbury (1290–1349) reacted against the increasing Pelagianism and scholasticism by ap-

189

pealing back to that greatest of all early Christian philosophers and theologians, Augustine of Hippo. Re-establishing the truths of unregenerate man's total inability and the sovereignty of God, Bradwardine thought largely in Biblical terms, despite his adoption of the voluntarism of Duns Scotus and Ockham, and he had great influence on later thinkers such as Wycliffe and Huss.

John Wycliffe of Yorkshire (1320–1384), besides being a lecturer at Oxford, was also King's chaplain, and he championed the right of a government to deprive unrighteous clergy of their ill-gotten property. In his work *Trilogy*, he rejected transubstantiation and criticized the ecclesiastical indifference towards the social conditions of his age. He rejected papal imperialism in favor of the sphere sovereignty of the British government, and grounded his beliefs on the authority of Scripture, reason, and conscience, rather than on tradition.

One of Wycliffe's followers in Bohemia was Johan Huss of Husinetz, rector of the University of Prague. Criticizing particularly ecclesiastical corruption and the selling of indulgences in his work *On the Church*, he was treacherously invited to the Council of Constance, arrested there, and condemned for heresy and burned at the stake.

3. *The Reformation proper*

The thought of late scholasticism and particularly of the Pre-Reformation, coupled with the greater accessibility of the Holy Scriptures as a result of the invention of printing at the end of the fifteenth century, was destined to result in the mighty Reformation at the beginning of the sixteenth, under the initial leadership of Zwingli in Switzerland and Luther in Germany.

Huldreich Zwingli of Wildhaus (1484–1531) was a classicist and Greek scholar who put great stress on theocentricity and the divine omnipresence, even ascribing the "good" among the heathen to the omnipresent Logos (cf. John 1:5, 9). Augustinian in his view on election and sin and Anselmic on the doctrine of the atonement, Zwingli elaborated his ideas in his *Commentary on the True and False Religion.* Zwingli was killed in battle against the Catholic armies, but his views prepared the way for and were much improved and later stabilized by John Calvin.

Martin Luther of Eisleben (1483–1546), however—lawyer, Bible translator, and theologian—was the real spearhead of the Reformation. Rejecting scholasticism and Aristotelianism outright in favor of the Bible, he was expelled from the Romish Church for rediscovering and especially for advocating the great Pauline doctrine of justification by grace through the individual's personal faith alone. Faith in God's Word and not natural reason (as in Thomism) is what is required. And this strong emphasis broke the Church's stranglehold over the individual and the state.

It was, however, particularly Jean Calvin of Noyon (1509–1564) who systematized and elaborated the implications of the Reformation. Calvin repudiated the apostate Church of Rome, and set about developing a radical life and world view based on the absolute sovereignty of God Who was above all law (cf. Dooyeweerd), yet Whose laws in every sphere expressed the rationality of His will (*per contra,* Duns Scotus and Ockham). Primarily a theologian, Calvin opposed the Scriptural concept of the prophethood, priesthood, kingship, and equality of all believers and their mutual covenantal solidarity to the Romish concept of ecclesiastical hierarchy; and, like Zwingli, he appreciated the elements of truth even in the works of the unregenerate (cf. his elaboration of the doctrine of common grace).

But Calvin's Biblical views had profound implications in the sphere-sovereign non-theological fields too—particularly in the areas of politics, public morality, economics, and education, where Calvin moved for better municipal health

191

laws, employment opportunities, private industrial development, and God-centered academies. For to Calvin, the development of the heart and body and mind, of the arts and the sciences and everything else to the glory of God, was a *vocatio Dei* or divine calling. "Philosophy," Calvin wrote to Bucer, "is therefore an excellent gift of God, and learned men in every century who zealously devoted themselves thereto were influenced by God Himself, so that they would give to the world the information of the knowledge of the truth."

The Thomistic distinction between *opus servile* or "secular" manual labor and *opus spirituale* or "sacred" spiritual work, was foreign to Calvin's understanding of the teaching of Holy Scripture. "*All* human labor is of *equal* value; after all, all [Christians] are in the Lord's service, and contribute towards the maintenance of human society." [1] "*All* craftsmen of whatever kind, who serve the needs of men, are *ministers* of God." [2] Even "agriculture is *commanded* by God." [3] (See further my article: "Calvin on the Sciences" [4]) After Calvin, who unshakeably asserted that "the fear of the Lord is the beginning of wisdom," [4a] the world would never be the same again—creaturely ecclesiastical imperialism over the whole of life was beaten back, and the Creator's total authority in every field of human endeavor was once again proclaimed.

The first Christian *Encyclopaedia of Theology* was written by Andreas Gerhard of Yperen, thus alias "Hyperius" (1511–1564), who regarded both theology and philosophy as "gifts of God." Even if God calls a man to be a preacher, the latter should, in Hyperius' opinion, first study grammar, logic,

[1] Calvin: *Opera Omnia*, XXVII, 14.
[2] Calvin: *Opera Omnia*, XXXVI, 83.
[3] Calvin: *Opera Omnia*, XXIII, 83.
[4] Lee: *Calvin on the Sciences*, Sovereign Grace Union, London, 1969.
[4a] Prov. 1:7.

rhetoric, arithmetic, geometry, music, astronomy, physics, history, architecture, and agriculture, before starting on theology!

It was particularly Pierre Ramus of Picardy (1515–1572) who questioned the authority of Aristotle. Leaving the Romish Church for Calvinism in 1561, Ramus broke radically with all scholasticism and Aristotelianism and propounded the idea of the coherence of all the sciences under the sovereignty of God. Ramus even published a new logic and the first textbook on natural science ever printed in French. For Ramus, in spite of a certain amount of superficiality in his approach, the Word of God was the only norm in matters of faith and practice; for the human brain and will was totally depraved as a result of the fall.

Jerome Zanchius of Italy (1516–1590), who was later a professor at Heidelberg, although incorrectly reducing philosophy to a sub-division of theology, clearly emphasized the scientific character of theology and the central role of Scripture in the construction of every branch of science. To Zanchius, mathematics and physics occupy a place of honor alongside of theology, and wherever the great Aristotle disagrees with the creational teaching of Moses, Aristotle is to be corrected by Moses, and never Moses by Aristotle.

Zacharias Ursinus of Germany (1534–1583), a co-author of the blessed Heidelberg Catechism which sought to draw Lutherans and Calvinists together, although primarily a theologian and Hebrew scholar, had the following[5] to say about the value of philosophy:

". . . *true* philosophy, although much different from Christian doctrine, does not conflict therewith, . . . and was impressed into the mind of man at creation as *a beam of the wisdom of God*. For philosophy is a doctrine of God, of the *creatures*, and *other good things* profitable to the human

[5] Ursinus: *Schatboek*, chapter II of the foreword.

race, formulated by wise men in the *light of nature* and on grounds naturally well-known. Whence it is not only permissible but also *useful* for the Christian to *study philosophy. . . .* Philosophy also teaches other arts and sciences useful to man, particularly the art of reasoning and the arts of calculating, land-surveying and the knowledge of the course of the heavens and such like which are not taught in the congregation, although they are nevertheless useful in understanding the doctrine of the Church and in making it understandable to others."

Johann Heinrich Alsted (1588–1648), a Calvinistic professor of theology, supplemented and elaborated the views of Zanchius and Ursinus. Regarding theology, jurisprudence, and medicine as the three principal disciplines, he sought to derive them all from Holy Scripture and discussed them after "theoretical and practical philosophy" in his highly esteemed 1630 *Encyclopaedia of the Sciences.* Philosophy he described as a divine gift which teaches one a knowledge of God, increases one's love for Him, and which is indispensable even for the formal systematic treatment of theology. All theologians, he felt, should study philosophy in general and logic, physics, mathematics, mataphysics, ethics, economics, politics, the scholastics, and history in particular.

Even within the Church of Rome there were some who advocated a considerable degree of Scriptural reformation. Cornelius Jansen of Holland (1585–1638), for instance, opposed scholasticism and stressed predestination, rejected Aquinas and championed Augustine, and wanted Belgium to be an independent Catholic republic like Protestant Holland was. Even though Jansen opposed the great Calvinist Voetius, his views were nevertheless papally anathematized in 1713. And Jansen's admirer Blaise Pascal of Paris (1623–1662), the great natural philosopher and discoverer of the mathematical theory of probability, although remaining a Roman Catholic, opposed Descartes and was sympathetic to Protestantism. As a devoted Bible student and advocate of Augustinian theology, he firmly believed in predestination and in the sovereign saving grace of God.

In the Reformed Churches, the chief issue at the beginning of the seventeenth century was the fight between the Arminians and the Calvinists over the meaning of predestination. The leader of the Calvinist party was Franz Gomarus (1563–1641), a student of the great Ursinus. Seeking to stress the absolute sovereignty of God in salvation, it is under Gomarus' leadership that the Synod of Dordt (1618–1619) formulated the famous five points of Calvinism or "TULIP"—T, total depravity; U, unconditional election; L, limited atonement; I, irresistible grace; and P, the perseverance of the saints (that is: once saved, always saved).

One of the delegates at the Synod of Dordt who later became a world-famous Christian philosopher of law and theologian, was the great Gijsbertus Voetius (1588–1676), the thoroughly Calvinistic professor of Oriental Science who stoutly resisted the advance of Cartesian rationalism. A godly man of encyclopaedic knowledge, he set a very high standard of academic achievement as a useful prerequisite for theological study, namely: knowledge of languages (Latin, Greek, Hebrew, Aramaic, Samaritan, Arabic, Ethiopian, Persian, Turkish, Armenian, Coptic, Italian, Spanish, French, English, High German, and Low German or Dutch); of rhetoric; of poetry; of history; of archaeology; of theoretical philosophy (logic, mnemonics, metaphysics, physics, [including medicine], and mathematics [including arithmetic, geometry, statics, architecture, cosmography, astronomy, geography, optics, acoustics, music, painting, sculpture, etc.]), and of practical philosophy (ethics, economics, politics, and jurisprudence).

We may perhaps close this discussion of the Christian philosophy of the Reformation period by referring to the work of the great Christian natural scientist of Puritan England, Robert Boyle of London (1627–1691). Dedicating his life to natural scientific research to the glory of the Triune God, Boyle is particularly famous for his investigation of the properties of air, the mechanical properties of matter, and the transmutability of metals, although he was opposed to anatomical dissection for what he considered to be Biblical reasons. Even though Boyle was also an amateur theologian and a keen student of the Scriptures, Hebrew, Aramaic, and Greek, as well as a promoter of the Gaelic translation of the Bible and of missions to India, he flatly refused the offer of a clerical provostship on the ground that he could do more for the Lord as an ecclesiastical layman than as a clergyman. And in his will, this mighty man of God made provision for the establishment of the *Boyle Lectures* for the scientific defense of trinicentric Christianity against "notorious infidels, viz., atheists, theists[!], pagans, Jews and Mahommedans."

4. *Modern Dutch Christian philosophy*

After the demise of Puritanism in England and the growth of a cold Protestant scholasticism in Europe, Christian thought shrunk and stagnated as pietism, supranaturalism, and finally liberalism plagued the people of the Lord. But under the blessed providence of Almighty God, a revival of true theology and philosophy started in Holland during the nineteenth and continues to endure even through this twentieth century, and has now taken root elsewhere too, particularly in South Africa and also in North America.

The first to raise his voice like a trumpet against the humanistic apostasy of the French Revolution of 1789 and its ruinous consequences, was the famous Dutch Calvinistic poet, jurist, librarian, and anti-revolutionary historian, Willem Bilderdijk (1756–1831), who was followed by the equally famous poet, jurist, orientalist, and theologian, the great converted Jew Isaac de Costa (1798–1860). But a man of even greater influence was the famous mentor of Abraham Kuyper himself, Guillaume Groen van Prinsterer (1801–1876).

Groen was an influential Christian nobleman, lawyer, writer, and politician. Seeking to apply and develop the views of the great German Lutheran philosopher and politician Dr. F. J. Stahl, who had sought to guarantee the freedom of the various spheres of life by appealing to the law of creation as their charter, Groen, the leader of the Anti-Revolutionary (Calvinistic) political party and the doughty opponent of Thorbecke's liberalism, first distinguished the sphere-sovereignty of church and state and later of the other social spheres—even though he sought to ground such sphere-sovereignty in national historical development rather than in the law of creation.

The greatest impetus to Christian philosophy in the nineteenth century, however, was undoubtedly given by that many-sided Christian genius, preacher, theologian, journalist, encyclopaedist, educationalist, trade unionist, and statesman, Abraham Kuyper Snr. of Amsterdam (1837–1920), who further worked out Groen's system of sphere-sovereignty and elaborated his philosophical views particularly in his works *Encyclopaedia of Holy Theology* (three volumes),[6] *Common Grace* (three volumes),[7] and *For the King* (three volumes).[8]

Kuyper sought to ground theology, philosophy, and every other science solely in a Christian life and world view based on the Holy Scriptures, and his fundamental presupposition in all fields of knowledge was that the Almighty God and Creator of the universe has subjected all His creatures (including all social relationships) to divine ordinances

[6] Kuyper: *Encyclopaedie der Heilige Godgeleerdheid.*
[7] Kuyper: *Gemeene Gratie.*
[8] Kuyper: *Pro Rege.*

based on His Own Sovereign Will.[9] Consequently, everything in nature and society has a relative sphere-sovereignty (over against every other creature, but not, of course, over against the wholly Sovereign God). Hence: individual, family, school, university, factory, business, church, state, and nation all have their own sphere of influence free from the intrusion of the other spheres—and this "sphere sovereignty" is grounded not in national historical development (thus Groen), but in the order of creation itself (cf. Stahl). For, as Kuyper remarked, there is not even so much as a thumbbreadth of the universe in respect of which the Sovereign God cannot say: "That is mine." [10]

However, although the Triune God created the universe, the whole world has been cursed as a result of the fall of man. Yet the Second Person of the Trinity has become the Mediator of salvation, and as the risen Messiah and glorified Son of man is right now exercising full authority over *all* spheres of life—not only in the Church where His authority is recognized, but even in the extra-ecclesiastical spheres where His authority is not recognized. But still, held Kuyper—perhaps somewhat inconsequentially in the light of the aforegoing—the work of Christ as Mediator of salvation and as Recreator is restricted to the field of particular or special grace—to the Church and its members alone; in the other spheres where common grace is operative, Christ only rules as Mediator in creation.[11]

To Kuyper, all men are religious, and possess the divinely implanted *semen religionis* or seed of religion as well as the *sensus divinitatis* or sense of deity—not merely in their intellect, will, and emotions, but in their entire being, which is still the image of God in the broader sense even after the fall.[12] But man's religion is now twisted by sin, and can

[9] Cf. Ps. 119:90-91.
[10] Cf. Kuyper: *Souverein in eigen Kring*.
[11] Cf. Gen. 1:3,26f; Ps. 33:6; John 1:1-4,9; etc.
[12] Cf. Gen. 9:5-6; Jas. 3:9.

only be corrected by a divine act of regeneration. Regeneration, however, affects not merely man's intellect or will or emotions, but his entire being—with his heart as its religious root. So that when once a man is truly regenerated, his views of everything and therefore even of all the sciences (which previously rooted in the apostate faith of his apostate heart), must now root in the Christian faith of his regenerated heart. And therefore, "to say that a Christian has less need of philosophy [than does an unbeliever] is thus nothing else than an expression of spiritual sluggishness and misunderstanding." [13]

If Kuyper was the greatest advocate of Christian philosophy in Holland around the beginning of the twentieth century, he was not the only one. Adriaan Steketee (1846–1913), a professor of classical languages at Kampen, who lived not only in the Scriptures but also in the writings of Plato and Augustine and Dante and Pascal and Goethe,[14] wrote articles on the value of science and on Platonic studies and the significance of art to theological candidates. Jan Woltjer (1849–1917), a professor of philology and philosophy, elaborated the cosmological and epistemological importance of the Logos,[15] the essence of matter,[16] and the relationship between realities and ideas.[17] And Willem Geesink (1854–1929), a professor of philosophy and Christian ethics, not only wrote an authoritative work on moral philosophy,[18] but also pioneered Christian cosmology in his masterpiece *Concerning the Lord's Ordinances*,[19] in which he gave a scriptural analysis even of such phenomena as bacteria and thunderstorms! [20]

[13] Kuyper: *Encycl.*, II, 1909, p. 569.
[14] Steketee: *Beschouwingen van een Christen-denker*.
[15] Woltjer: *De Wetenschap van den Logos*.
[16] Woltjer: *Het Wezen der Materie*.
[17] Woltjer: *Ideëel en Reëel*.
[18] Geesink: *Gereformeerde Ethiek*.
[19] Geesink: *Van 's Heeren Ordinantiën*.
[20] Cf. Ps. 146:1-6.

Another very great thinker almost of the calibre of Kuyper himself was the famous dogmatician, philosopher, psychologist, politician, and educationalist Herman Bavinck (1854–1921), whose philosophy is found chiefly in his books: *Philosophy of Revelation*,[21] *Christian View of Life*,[22] *Christian Scholarship*,[23] *Knowledge and Life*,[24] and here and there in his masterpiece *Reformed Dogmatics* (four volumes).[25]

Bavinck was a moderate realist whose philosophy proceeded from everyday experience, and who grounded all epistemology in ontology, which latter is itself grounded in "revelation"—the key word in Christian thought. The Three Persons of the Trinity eternally reveal Themselves to One Another (theontologically), and epistemologicoarchetypically know whatever comes to pass ontically. The entire cosmos, both in its origin and in its present structure, is a revelation of God, Who thus reveals Himself to man externally in nature, internally in human consciousness, and also in the Logos—the creative Word, the Word made flesh and the inscripturated Word—as the source of all the principles of theology, philosophy, and all the special sciences.

Bavinck's successor Valentine Hepp turned his attention to the solution of the epistemological problem created by the doctrine of common grace.[26] To Hepp, the Holy Spirit is the source of *all* truth, and He not only gives a special assurance of salvation to God's elect, but He also gives a general assurance of the truth of every fact to every investigator whether he is saved or not, and is thus Himself the Final Ground of the certainty of all human knowledge.[27]

There were also other Christian philosophers during this

[21] Bavinck: *Wijsbegeerte der Openbaring.*
[22] Bavinck: *Christelijke Levensbeschouwing.*
[23] Bavinck: *Christelijke Wetenschap.*
[24] Bavinck: *Kennis en Leven.*
[25] Bavinck: *Gereformeerde Dogmatiek.*
[26] Hepp: *Het Testimonium Spiritus Sancti*, I.
[27] Cf. Job 32:8; Prov. 20:27; John 1:5,9,33; I Cor. 2:11; I John 5:6.

period between the two world wars—T. Hoekstra (1880–1936), who concentrated on developing a Christian history of philosophy; B. Wielenga ((1873–1949), who elaborated a Christian philosophy of aesthetics; Jan Waterink, who did a great work in developing the theory of Christian education and Christian psychology; and Ph. Kohnstamm (1875–1951), whose philosophical research into personality and cosmology led him to become an adherent first of the cosmonomic philosophy of Amsterdam in Holland and later of the creationistic philosophy of Potchefstroom in South Africa. But no one did more to develop Christian philosophy during this period and since than the two founders of the cosmonomic school or the *Wijsbegeerte der Wetsidee* ("Philosophy of the Idea of Law")—D. H. Th. Vollenhoven (1892–) and his brother-in-law Herman Dooyeweerd (1894–).

In 1926, Vollenhoven, an ordained pastor, succeeded Geesink as professor of philosophy at the Free University of Amsterdam, where he immediately set about applying the Scriptures and their idea of the covenant[28] to every field of human endeavor, even subjecting the time-honored Aristotelian logic to a thoroughly Biblical critique and to a reconstruction which pointed to Jesus Christ the Logos or Word of God as The Basis of all syllogistic reasoning. His books *Logos and Ratio (Word and Reason)*,[29] *Headlines of Logic*,[30] and *The Necessity of a Christian Logic*[31] develop this position.

Not only has Vollenhoven pioneered Christian logic, but he has also pioneered the development of a Christian approach to mathematics. His doctoral dissertation dealt with *The Philosophy of Mathematics from the Theistic*

28 Cf. Gen. 1:26f and Hos. 6:7 marg.
29 Vollenhoven: *Logos en Ratio.*
30 Vollenhoven: *Hoofdlijnen der Logica.*
       De Noodzakelijkheid eener Christelijke Logica.
31 Vollenhoven: *De Wijsbegeerte der wiskunde van theïstisch standpunt.*

Viewpoint,[31] and his later writings include *The Activity of the Soul in Arithmetical Education*,[32] *The Place and Value of Mathematics and Natural Science according to the Calvinistic Doctrine of Science*,[33] *The Principles of the Faculty of Mathematics and Natural Science*,[34] *Problems and Schools in the Philosophy of Mathematics*,[35] and *Is Space Euclidian or Non-Euclidian?* [36]

Vollenhoven has also written on the introduction to philosophy, on the principles of Christian philosophy, on psychology, and on evangelism, in which latter he remains vitally interested. But it is particularly in the field of the history of philosophy that he has been active. Specializing (though not exclusively) in ancient Greek philosophy, Vollenhoven has written works on Zeno of Elea, Zeno the Stoic, Platonism and neo-Platonism, Aristotle, Tertullian, Origen, Nestorius, Augustine, Boëthius, Thomas, Erasmus, occasionalism, Kuyper, Barth, etc.

Finally, to understand something of the Christian dedication of Vollenhoven, we cannot do better than quote from his Opening Address as Chairman of the international Association for Calvinistic Philosophy at its first meeting, in 1935:

". . . it is something glorious that brings us together here. It is not philosophy, for that is not the first thing in our lives. It is much rather the tie to God's Word, because by grace we have learned to desire to live on Christ alone, and religion as a matter of the heart has become the nucleus of our entire existence; because we have learned that peace and life are to be found only in heeding the commandments of the Lord. . . .

[32] Vollenhoven: *De activiteit der ziel in het rekenonderwijs.*
[33] Vollenhoven: *Plaats en waarde van de wis- en natuurkunde naar Calvinistische wetenschapsleer.*
[34] Vollenhoven: *De wis- en natuurkundige Faculteit en de principia.*
[35] Vollenhoven: *Problemen en richtingen in de wijsbegeerte der wiskunde.*
[36] Vollenhoven: *Is de ruimte euclidisch of niet-euclidisch?*

"... current philosophy knows nothing of all this which is so close to our hearts: knows nothing of a God, if by that you mean the God of Scripture; nothing of a heart, which can only find rest in Him; nothing of a world history, which is rooted in the first and the last Adam. ...

"If we concentrate all our strength against the enemy, on the antithesis, God will not withhold His blessing from us."

If Vollenhoven is the great historian of the cosmonomic philosophy, Dooyeweerd is its great systematician. Dooyeweerd became a doctor of law at the age of twenty-three (with a dissertation on *The Cabinet in Dutch Constitutional Law*)[37] and a professor of Legal Philosophy, Encyclopaedia of Legal Science and Ancient National Law at the age of thirty-two—with an inaugural address on "The Significance of the Cosmonomic Idea [*"Wetsidee"*] to Legal Science and Legal Philosophy."[38] And since then, he has written other legal works such as *The Crisis of Humanistic Statecraft in the Light of a Calvinistic Cosmology and Epistemology*[39] and *The Struggle Around the Concept of Sovereignty in Modern Jurisprudence and Statecraft.*[40]

Although he has also pioneered Christian sociology, Dooyeweerd's chief emphasis has been in the field of systematic philosophy, where he has sought to develop a Christian cosmology and anthropology, but especially a Christian epistemology. And these ideas he has formulated in Dutch works like his *Philosophy of the Cosmonomic Idea* (three volumes),[41] his *Reformation and Scholasticism,*[42] and his *Renewal and Reflections,*[43] but particularly in his monu-

[37] Dooyeweerd: *De Ministerraad in het Nederlandsche staatsrecht.*
[38] *De beteekenis voor die Wetsidee voor Rechtswetenschap en Rechtsphilosophie.*
[39] Dooyeweerd: *De Crisis der Humanistische staatsleer in het licht eener Calvinistische kosmologie en kennistheorie.*
[40] Dooyeweerd: *De strijd om het souvereiniteitsbegrip in de moderne rechts- en staatsleer.*
[41] Dooyeweerd: *De Wijsbegeerte der Wetsidee.*
[42] Dooyeweerd: *Reformatie en Scholastiek.*
[43] Dooyeweerd: *Vernieuwing en Bezinning.*

mental English work *A New Critique of Theoretical Thought* (four volumes) and its lesser English popularization *In the Twilight of Western Thought.*

Dooyeweerd's philosophy is characterized by a constant appeal to Scripture as its principal basis. God has given laws and ordinances for the government of each of His creatures "after his kind" [44] in its own createdly-sovereign sphere, and these laws form the boundary between the Creator and His creation.[45] Every philosophy, even that of an infidel, proceeds from such a cosmonomic idea (or idea of law), which either correctly or incorrectly determines the nature of law and its place in creation. This determination is a religious choice—either for Christ or against Him, and it is made in the heart of man as the epistemological Archimedes' point or center of human existence from out of which are "the issues of life." [46] Where the choice is made against Christ, we have "immanence philosophy," whereby one or more aspects of creation are worshiped instead of the Creator.[47]

There are indeed such aspects or "modal law spheres" of creation—just as those of number, space, movement, matter, life, feeling, thought, history, language, society, economics, aesthetics, law, ethics, and faith—each createdly-sovereign in its own sphere yet analogically reflecting something of all the other spheres, and each imbedded into created time as the first and most basic of all creatures, and each reflecting something of the wisdom of that one true God on Whom they and all other creatures are utterly dependent.

To understand something of Dooyeweerd's burning love for the Lord Jesus Christ, one should listen closely to the words of his inaugural address to his new students on his being appointed a university professor.

[44] Gen. 1:21.
[45] Ps. 119:90-91; 148:1-6.
[46] Prov. 4:23.
[47] Cf. Rom. 1:25.

"Which of you can hesitate and tarry, when the King of our science summons you to the battlefield of the spirit? . . . Never forget—the demand of science comes to you not as a demand of human culture, but as a divine demand of Christ your King, Who has directed you to labor in the field of science."

And then Dooyeweerd closed his address with the following prayer to the Triune God: "Unto Thee, O Lord my God, do I direct my prayer in this hour. To thank Thee for every trial, for every chastisement; to thank Thee that Thou hast finally called me to serve Thee at this School.

"Inspire Thou my labor at this University, may my weakness be made perfect in Thy strength, and grant, O Father of all mercy, that love for Thee and for the existence of Thy Kingdom will always continue to burn in my heart, so that my steps will never depart from the way of truth which Thou hast revealed to us in Thy holy Son.

"And when our weak strength fails us, in that our heart is always inclined towards sin, worldliness, and lack of courage, O Father, confirm Thyself Thy kingdom in our science and disturb even there the kingdom of lies, so that the labor of men may be sanctified by Thy Spirit."

Vollenhoven and Dooyeweerd have inspired many other Christian scholars to philosophize to God's glory. Amongst those in Holland, most of whom are still alive, we merely mention the names of professors: Zuidema (1906–), who has given brilliant Christian-philosophical refutations of existentialism, communism, and the ecumenical theology; Mekkes (1898–), who has elaborated the importance of the structure of creation and of the development of Christian statecraft; Van Riessen (1911–), who has struggled with the problems of modern technology and their socio-political implications; and Popma, who has especially sought a Biblical answer to the relationship between philosophy, theology, history, culture, and faith.

205

Mention must also be made of the genial spirit of Klaas Schilder. A theological professor at Kampen, and much disturbed by developments within the Reformed Churches especially in the area of relationship between the covenant, faith, and baptism, Schilder not only authored a beautiful *Trilogy*[48] on the philosophical, psychological, and theological implications of the life and death of Christ; but his books on *Heaven*[49] and *Hell*[50] are standard works in those fields and contain much philosophical material, and his famous book on *Christ and Culture*[51] articulates his philosophical views in detail.

To Schilder, God is the Owner of the earth, and from Adam onwards to the end of the world man is covenantally obligated to develop it. This development centers especially in the work of Christ and the Spirit, Whose conquest of the world is God's reconquest. Christ, the Alpha and Omega, binds the beginning of history to the end of history. Man must serve God, and with his talents he must investigate and extract everything from the world that God put into it, and he must use all things in promoting the further extension of the universe.

Adam started to do this when he cultivated the earth as his covenantal work for God. Christ the Second Adam and God Incarnate fulfilled this covenant and its cultural requirements. And Christ continues to expand culture through His children as they fulfill their obligations of investing all their talents in their cosmic service to God as He guides the entire universe through all its labors into its eschatological cosmic sabbath rest, culminating in the cultural city of the New Jerusalem. The weekly sabbath, the everlasting sabbath rest, and the cultural mandate are all inter-related.

[48] Schilder: *Christus in zijn Lyding; Christus in zijn Doorgang; Christus in zijn Opstanding.*
[49] Schilder: *Wat is de Hemel?*
[50] Schilder: *Wat is de Hel?*
[51] Schilder: *Christus en Cultuur.*

All men (Adam, the wicked, Christ, and the Christians) *must* unfold all history, science, and culture. In man's unfolding of the fullness of creation, God Himself perfects His creation and elect mankind enters into God's cosmic sabbath rest.

Other modern Dutch thinkers—to mention only a few—are: Wurth and Troost, the Christian ethicists; Dengerink and Van Dijk, the Christian sociologists; Groenman, the Christian physical educationist; Rookmaaker, the Christian aesthetician; Spier, who has given much thought to the philosophy of Jaspers and particularly to the relationship between time and eternity; Smit, the Christian historian; Schoep, the medical philosopher; F. Kuyper, the Christian cultural philosopher; Goudzwaard and Van der Kooy, the Christian economists; and Diemer and Groen, the Christian natural scientists, etc., etc. The influence of Christian philosophy and scholarship in Holland is still increasing, and looks forward to a bright future.

5. *Modern South African Christian philosophy*

Modern South African Christian philosophy not only roots in the European thought of Calvin, Voetius, Kuyper, Bavinck, Vollenhoven, and Dooyeweerd, but also roots in its own soil in that it grounds itself in the Bible and in the Reformed faith in a very distinct manner. For even when the first settlers arrived in South Africa in 1652, their governor, Jan van Riebeeck, immediately prayed to the Triune God that "Thy true Reformed Christian doctrine . . . be propagated and disseminated" throughout the land.

On the whole, it may perhaps be said that Christian Afrikaner thought in South Africa, now some three centuries old but only really coming into its own during the past hundred-and-fifty years and particularly in this twentieth century, has developed through three originally more or less successive and progressive (yet overlapping and now parallel) stages, namely: theological philosophy, pure philosophy in general, and the philosophies of the various special sciences.

The first stage was what we may perhaps call "theological philosophy," and consists of men like: the great Calvinistic statesmen Krüger and Steyn; the great patriot, theologian, and poet Totius (on the significance of whose life the Dutch philosopher Vollenhoven has written an article); the theologian and Calvinistic patriot Kestell; the dogmatician, Church historian, and Christian thinker E. E. van Rooyen; and the dogmatologian, ecclesiologist, psychologist, anti-evolutionist, philosopher, and Christian educationalist Potgieter.[52] Significantly, all of these three latter men rank as experts in the thought of John Calvin. Younger contemporary theologians who are also philosophers, are men like Heyns the apologeticist and philosophical anthropologist, and Durand the missiologist and cultural philosopher.

The second stage in South African Christian thought is that of pure philosophy in general, and the thinkers in this group generally follow either the cosmonomic philosophy of Vollenhoven and Dooyeweerd or the indigenous creationistic philosophy of Stoker—or something in between the two systems.

Hendrik Stoker of Potchefstroom is certainly a Christian philosopher every bit the equal of Vollenhoven and Dooyeweerd, and is regarded by them as such. Promoting under Max Scheler with a doctoral dissertation on *Conscience*,[53] although Stoker writes against a wealthy background of psychological experience, he tends to stress the cosmological and phenomenological aspects of philosophy rather than the epistemological as does the Amsterdam School.

Stoker's thought is nowhere presented systematically in

[52] Potgieter: *Die Verhouding tussen die Teologie en die Filosofie by Calvyn.*
[53] Stoker: *Das Gewissen.*

a set of volumes as is Dooyeweerd's, but rather consists of scores of monologues (nearly all of them in Afrikaans) on a variety of subjects, the most important of which are perhaps his largely ontological works: *The Philosophy of the Idea of Creation*,[54] *Calvinism and the Doctrine of the Law Spheres*,[55] *The Newer Philosophy at the Free University*,[56] and *Something About a Calvinistic Philosophy*;[57] his largely epistemological works: *Problems of a General Gnoseology*,[58] *Something About Reasonableness and Rationalism*,[59] *The Snail's Shell Theories of Consciousness*,[60] and *The Crisis in Modern Psychology*;[61] his methodological works: *Principles of a Christian Doctrine of Science*,[62] *Christianity and Science*,[63] *Scriptural Faith and the Pursuit of Science*,[64] and *Something About Causality*;[65] his works on moral philosophy: *The Basis of Morality*[66] and *Theological, Philosophical and Special Scientific Ethics*; [67] and his political writings, such as: *The Battle of the Orders*,[68] etc., etc. Only now (1968) have some of his major writings been collected into the anthology *Origin and Direction*,[69] volume two of which has yet to appear.

To Stoker, the idea of creation is more encompassing than is the Amsterdam School's idea of law—hence his "creationistic philosophy" (or *The Philosophy of the Idea of Creation*).[70] Within the unity of this creation, there are a variety

[54] Stoker: *Die Wysbegeerte van die Skeppingsidee.*
[55] Stoker: *Die Calvinisme en die Leer van die Wetskringe.*
[56] Stoker: *Die Nuwere Wysbegeerte aan die Vrije Universiteit.*
[57] Stoker: *Iets oor 'n Calvinistiese Wysbegeerte.*
[58] Stoker: *Probleme van 'n Algemene Gnoseologie.*
[59] Stoker: *Iets oor die Redelikheid en Rasionalisme.*
[60] Stoker: *Die Slakkehuisteorieë van die Bewussyn.*
[61] Stoker: *Die Krisis in die Teenswoordige Sielkunde.*
[62] Stoker: *Beginsels oor 'n Christelike Wetenskapsleer.*
[63] Stoker: *Christendom en Wetenskap.*
[64] Stoker: *Skrifgeloof en Wetenskapsbeoefening.*
[65] Stoker: *Iets oor Kousaliteit.*
[66] Stoker: *Die Grond van die Sedelike.*
[67] Stoker: *Teologiese, Wysgerige en Vakwetenskaplike Etiek.*
[68] Stoker: *Die Stryd om die Ordes.*
[69] Stoker: *Oorsprong en Rigting.*

of ontic differences of modalities, degrees, qualities, values, and being—not just different "law spheres," and each of these different ontic realities not only possesses "sovereignty-in-its-own-sphere" [71] but also "universality-in-its-own-sphere.[72] Furthermore, each ontic reality or "substance" also possesses "freedom-in-its-own-ability"[73] (or a peculiar nature whereby it develops and expresses itself) and "universality-in-its-own-ability" [74] (whereby each substance affects and is affected by every other substance in the universe). Consequently, the cosmos consists not merely of fifteen Dooyeweerdian ("numerical" though "pistic") spheres or modalities strung together in cosmic time like beads on a necklace, but it rather consists of various "cones" wedged together like cut but unseparated slices of a Christmas cake, each cone supporting the others, only one of which cones contains the "law spheres," while the other cones contain substances such as values, causation, qualities, etc. All the cones are necessary to explain the cosmos, and individual created beings or "existents" cut right across the conical schemes. It is only in the divine "createdness" of the cosmos as a whole that the ontical unity can be established.

Stoker has also insisted that what Dooyeweerd regards as the modal sphere of history is really a distinct cone of events quite different from all the law spheres; and he has advocated a new motive for the understanding of existentialism distinct from that of humanism—the "contingency-meaning" motive. To Stoker, theology is not the special science of the pistic sphere dependent upon the principles of the one and only general science of philosophy, but the general science which studies the Creator's Self-revelation (in Scripture) alongside of both the other general science

[70] Stoker: *Die Wysbegeerte van die Skeppingsidee.*
[71] "soewereiniteit in eie kring"
[72] "universaliteit in eie kring"
[73] "vryheid in eie bevoegdheid"
[74] "universaliteit in eie bevoegdheid"

210

of philosophy which studies the creation revelation as a whole (in nature) as well as alongside all the special sciences (each of which studies a part of the creation revelation)—all these sciences borrowing from and lending to one another in subjection to the teaching of the Word of God.

Stoker was not the only South African thinker to question the propriety of one of Dooyeweerd's modal spheres—in his case, the historical. The Dooyeweerdian order of the spheres was also questioned by G. H. T. Malan, emeritus professor of philosophy at the University of the Orange Free State, who believed that the numerical sphere presupposes prenumerical and numberable objects.

The present[75] professor of philosophy at the University of the Orange Free State, the preacher-philosopher E. A. Venter, is not only a firm advocate of Christian philosophy in general, but particularly of the Christian history of philosophy in particular.[76] His specialized studies of Aquinas (whom he radically opposes) and Calvin (whom he enthusiastically champions) also deserves a wide audience.

Venter's colleague, the preacher-philosopher P. de B. Kock, is more the systematician. Currently engaged in a monumental eight-volume introduction to Christian philosophy,[77] he sharply delineates the philosophy of Dooyeweerd (which he largely but not entirely follows) from that of Hepp, Stoker, F. Kuyper, Brümmer, and A. L. Conradie; and especially from that of Van Peursen and Loen, whom he regards as syncretistic.

Brümmer, another young South African preacher-philosopher currently a professor at the University of Utrecht in Holland, has written an impressive critique of Dooyeweerd in English entitled *Transcendental Criticism and Christian*

[75] Died: October 1968.
[76] Cf. especially Venter: *Die Ontwikkeling van die Westerse Denke.*
[77] Kock: *Inleiding in die Christelike Wysbegeerte.*

Philosophy, in which he claims to detect the latent influence of Kantianism in Dooyeweerd's thought, and in which he especially questions the Dooyeweerdian view of time and of the relationship between theology and philosophy and between common sense and scientific knowledge. To Brümmer, the divine Logos is the ultimate ground of all—the creative ground of all existence, the revelatory ground of all knowledge, the incarnative ground of all redemption, and the teleological ground of all consummation.

A remarkable philosopher is the female thinker Professor A. L. Conradie, of the University of Natal. Dr. Conradie has sought to give a historical outline of the development of the neo-Calvinistic concept of philosophy with special reference to the problem of communication (in which she discusses Calvin, Kuyper, Bavinck, Woltjer, Hepp, and especially Dooyeweerd, and in which she analyzes Dooyeweerd's thought and contrasts it with the various Immanentistic and Romish systems of modern philosophy), concluding that if a Christian philosophy is impossible, all philosophy is impossible.

Other contemporary Christian philosophers in South Africa we only mention in passing: D. F. M. Strauss, who has written on the philosophy of mathematics, aesthetics, and linguistics; P. J. Meyer, the philosopher of natural culture and existentiality; N. T. van der Merwe, the promising Christian logician and epistemologist; and a host of relatively young philosophers such as Taljaard and Van der Walt of Potchefstroom, H. Rossouw of Stellenbosch, and P. G. W. du Plessis of Port Elizabeth.

Coming finally to the last stage in the development of South African Christian Afrikaner thought, the elaboration of the philosophies of the various special sciences, we can be briefer. More or less following the order of the Dooyeweerdian modal spheres, we enumerate the following: Christian mathematicians like D. J. van Rooy, A. J. van Rooy, and Heidema;

Christian physical scientists like Van den Berg, Schutte, Vrey, and Gerritsma; Christian biologists like Eloff, P. J. Botha, and the internationally known late Duyvene de Wit (who refuted the Russian Oparin's evolutionism); Christian psychologists like W. A. Smit and A. B. van der Merwe; Christian historians like Swart and Hanekom; Christian sociologists like Keyter, G. Cronjé, and P. O. le Roux; Christian educationalists like J. Chr. Coetzee, Greyling, and J. J. Pienaar and Christian physical educationalists like I. R. van der Merwe and Fleischmann; Christian economists like Diederichs and F. J. du Plessis; Christian aestheticians like D. F. Malherbe, Dekker, and D. P. van der Walt; Christian legal and political philosophers like L. J. du Plessis, H. J. Strauss, G. F. de Vos Hugo, Wessels, Treurnicht, etc., and Christian criminologists like P. J. van der Walt and Swanepoel; and Christian theologians too numerous to mention.

Against the background of international politics, many are asking today: "Can there any good thing come out of South Africa?" And at least in respect of the above thinkers, we think the answer is justified: "Come and see!" [78] Of course, the author of this present work is a very prejudiced person. For he himself is a Christian South African.

6. *Modern North American Christian philosophy*

The New World was colonized in Massachusetts and Connecticut by the godly Pilgrim Fathers from 1620 onwards, and even their early civil laws reflected their high view of the absolute sovereignty of the Triune God. Thus, in 1656 Governor Eaton enacted that "whosoever shall profane the Lord's day, or any part of it, by work or sport, shall be punished by fine or corporally. But if the court, by clear evidence, find that the sin was proudly, presumptuously, and even with a high hand, committed against the command and authority of the blessed God, such person therein de-

[78] Cf. John 1:46.

spising and reproaching the Lord shall be put to death. Num. 15:30-36." The initial life and world view of those early settlers was thus the well-known motto of John Calvin himself, namely that "the fear of the Lord is the beginning of knowledge." [79] As John Winthrop had maintained before the General Court of Massachusetts even earlier in 1645: ". . . the kind of liberty I call civil . . . is the same kind of liberty wherewith Christ has made us free"; and he then enjoined his brethren citizens: ". . . if you will be satisfied to enjoy the civil and lawful liberties such as Christ allows you, then will you quietly and cheerfully submit unto that authority which is set over you, in all administrations of it, for your good."

Yet the early colonial life was intensely active and practical. There was not much time for meditative thinking. Consequently, a Christian philosophy of any real depth—as opposed to a widespread and blessed non-philosophical Christian life and world view—only found a few advocates in those dynamic early days; advocates such as Cotton Mather and Jonathan Edwards Snr.

Cotton Mather of New England (1663–1728) was the first great thinker. A philosopher of nature, historian, and theologian, Mather also wrote against witchcraft, but later mitigated his views somewhat. A keen student of medicine too, he was persecuted by his less-enlightened brethren for advocating vaccination against smallpox.

An even greater figure and one whose philosophical stature was unparalleled right down to the twentieth century, was the great Jonathan Edwards Snr. of Northampton (1703–1758). Firmly rooted in the absolute sovereignty of God and the truth of divine election, and convinced of the total depravity of man and the enslavement of the human will, he fulminated against deism and Arminianism in his many theological works, whereas his philosophical works

[79] Cf. Prov. 1:7.

dealt particularly with the problems of virtue and the will. However, although Edwards was a mighty man of God and a Christian educationalist (he was later elected President of Princeton University), it is only fair to mention that his unorthodox view of original sin as well as the Platonistic, Newtonian and Lockean elements in his otherwise Christian writings did not have a salutary effect on the further course of American thought.

After deism and unitarianism had crippled American thought for many decades, God raised up the Old Princeton theology in the nineteenth century to defend the faith. Especially in the writings of the Hodge's (Charles and A. A.), of Shedd and Warfield, and particularly of the Baptist A. H. Strong, there is much of philosophical importance. However, it must be remembered that all these men were primarily theologians and not philosophers, and so it is not surprising that they did not attempt to offer a Christian philosophy as such.

The twentieth century saw the almost universal collapse of American orthodoxy—long undermined since the days of deism and unitarianism. Christian thinkers are indeed few, but the names of two theologians should be mentioned who, unlike the Old Princetonians, have (in addition to their theological and apologetical pre-occupations) even attempted to work out a genuine Christian philosophy too: J. Oliver Buswell, Jr., who has sought to clarify the relationship between ontology and epistemology in his book *Thinking and Being*, and who has undertaken valuable studies on Aquinas and Tennant from a Christian perspective; and C. Van Til.

Cornelius Van Til, whose *Defense of the Faith* in particular has sought to re-establish belief in the absolute sovereignty of the Triune God in the classic Pauline-Augustinian-Calvinistic tradition, has incisively proposed the oneness and the threeness in the divine Tri-unity as the root and solution

215

of the problem as to the relationship between universals and particulars.

Van Til is a consequential Calvinist. By correctly exalting the ontological Trinity as the *only* starting point for *all* brands of human knowledge, he has not only exposed the remnants of scholastic evidentialism in the Old Princetonians, but he has also drawn attention even to the inconsistencies of the Amsterdam Dooyeweerdians.

God made everything in the universe solely for His own glory, asserts Van Til. Everything is covenantally interrelated and subjected to man as the head of creation—and man is subjected to God. In subduing the earth, man—both individually and as a community—also subdues himself unto God as his reasonable religion. And this he does in obedience to his covenantal obligations to the Triune God.

Although primarily an apologetician, Van Til (b. 1895) cannot be ignored in his own right as a Christian philosopher too. His influence especially in North America and Asia is still expanding.

A small group of full-time Christian philosophers, however, has finally emerged in the United States and in Canada. This group includes men like Gordon H. Clark, who has written Christian philosophical works on the history of philosophy, education, cosmology, anthropology, and religion; D. H. Freeman, who has developed a philosophy of religion, and who, with the logician W. Young, the author of *Towards a Reformed Philosophy*, has translated Dooyeweerd's major work into English; Runner, the Christian epistemologist and political philosopher; Knudsen, the Christian philosopher of existentialism; Rushdoony, the Christian educationalist and political philosopher; Reid and Farris, the Christian historians; Kooistra, the Christian sociologist; Seerveld, the Christian aesthetician; and North, the Christian political economist.

America got off to a great and glorious start with the

godly Pilgrim Fathers and Jonathan Edwards. May the God of history take her back to "the old paths," [80] revive His work in the midst of the years[81] and lead her forward till Jesus comes.[82]

7. Modern Christian philosophy in other countries

This section will be pitiably short, because the only well-known Christian philosophers of this group have been the great Austrian Calvin scholar Bohatec, the German Calvinist thinker Kolfhaus, the Hungarian-German Varga von Kibéd, the French thinkers Auguste Lecerfe and Pierre Marcel, and, more recently, the English political and legal philosopher Hebden Taylor.

The harvest truly is plenteous, but the laborers are few. "Pray ye therefore the Lord of the harvest, that He will send forth labourers into His harvest!"[83]

8. Summary

In this chapter we have attempted to trace the rebirth of true Christian philosophy from the point reached in the Pauline-Athanasian-Augustinian-Anselmic line up to the present day.

Starting with the Pre-Reformational opposition of Biblical Augustinianism to syncretistic scholasticism, which, after the invention of printing, resulted in the Reformation itself, it was seen that of all the early Reformers it was especially Calvin who presented the germ of a Christian life and world view. In this respect, his Trinitarian Theocentrism and emphasis on the doctrines of cosmic creation and regeneration, common grace, and the priesthood and kingship of all believers, laid down a solid basis for the later development of Christian philosophy.

[80] Cf. Jer. 6:16.
[81] Cf. Hab. 3:2.
[82] Cf. Rev. 22:20.
[83] Cf. Matt. 9:38.

217

Although the Christian development of philosophy and the other non-theological sciences was encouraged particularly by Ursinus, Alsted, Voetius, and especially the natural scientist Boyle, it was really not until the middle of the nineteenth century that there was any really significant further development of an uncompromisingly Biblical Christian philosophy. But then, inspired by Calvin and Groen van Prinsterer, Abraham Kuyper developed his philosophy of sphere-sovereignty and principially applied it to the entire universe; while particularly Woltjer, Bavinck, and Hepp respectively worked out the implications of the philosophical importance of the Logos, revelation, and the Holy Spirit.

It was, however, particularly the philosophical work of Vollenhoven, Dooyeweerd, and Stoker in the twentieth century which—after that of Augustine, Calvin, and Kuyper—has given developing Christian philosophy perhaps its greatest impetus; Vollenhoven surveying it historically, Dooyeweerd being its principal systematician, and Stoker grounding it solidly in creation. Since the time of this first contemporary Christian philosophical activity, whole hosts of Christian philosophers have mushroomed up, chiefly in Holland, South Africa, and North America. Some of the prominent thinkers have been men like Zuidema, Popma, Mekkes, and Van Riessen in Holland; Venter, Potgieter, Kock, and Brümmer in South Africa; and Gordon Clark, Van Til, and Runner in North America. Kindred thinkers in other countries than these are few and far between, but fortunately their numbers are increasing slowly but surely, even amidst the ever-increasing apostasy of this present wicked world.

This then summarizes this chapter on the rebirth of True Philosophy. However, to put our whole introduction to the history of philosophy in a correct perspective, we will close off this undertaking with a conclusion on the following page.

218

CONCLUSION

"In the beginning God created the heaven and the earth. And the earth was without form, and void; and darkness was upon the face of the deep. And the Spirit of God moved upon the face of the waters. And God said: 'Let there be light!'" [1]

"And God said, 'Let Us make man in Our image, after Our likeness: and let them have dominion over the fish of the sea, and over the fowl of the air, and over the cattle, and over all the earth, and over every creeping thing that creepeth upon the earth.'" [2]

But men fell into sin. The majority, the children of the devil, loved their sin, and remained "vain in their imaginations, and their foolish heart was darkened." Their multitudes of apostate philosophers, "professing themselves to be wise, . . . became fools, and changed the glory of the uncorruptible God into an image made like to corruptible man, . . . [and]changed the truth of God into a lie, and worshipped and served the creature more than the Creator." [3] Thus arose the "isms" of immanentistic philosophy; the "profane and vain babblings, and oppositions of science falsely so called" [4]—the babblings of the false philosophers of Ancient Egypt, Mesopotamia, India, China, and Greece; of the Gnostics, Jews, Moslems, and Romanists; of the Renaissance, rationalism, empiricism, and existentialism—and so on, almost *ad infinitum—philosophia perennis!*

[1] Gen. 1:1-3.
[2] Gen. 1:26.
[3] Rom. 1:21-25.
[4] I Tim. 6:20.

219

But God did redeem at least His elect from sin! He redeemed a minority of mankind, the children of God, including even some philosophers: *redeemed* philosophers, who would think *not* "after the rudiments of the world," but "after *Christ*." [5] And the holy line of such philosophers runs down through history like a golden thread: the holy line of thinkers like GOD, His image the redeemed Adam, Noah, Moses, David, and Solomon, centering in JESUS CHRIST AND HIS HOLY SPIRIT, and thenceforth unfolding still further in the thought of Paul, John, Augustine, Anselm, Calvin, Voetius, Kuyper, and the modern cosmonomic and creationistic trinicentric philosophers in this year of our Lord 1968 and, we trust, tomorrow too, and even until Jesus comes to fully reveal His redeemed universe and to reward even His faithful philosophers and to continue to use them in His glorious service on the new earth unto all eternity (see ch. I, sec. 10, above).

But while our Lord tarries, let us think on! As a small but elect band, let us oppose His many enemies, including all their apostate philosophers, with all our might. And let us also think positively to the glory of God with all our *mind*,[6] and "in *understanding* be men." [7] Let us meditate about the universe that astonished the first Adam and was astonished by the Second. Let us ground our cosmic meditations in our God and in His Christ, and let us try to understand as much as possible of "the manifold wisdom of God." [8] Let us learn to love His knowable Triunity and search for its reflection even in the as yet still unknown triunities in every modal sphere and in every corner of this His universe.

Let us do all this as unto the Lord Himself, for "of Him, and through Him, and to Him are all things, to Whom be glory for ever." [9] And let us glorify Him even in our philosophizing about His cosmos, as in worshipful adoration we all

[5] Cf. Col. 2:8.
[6] Cf. Matt. 22:37.
[7] I Cor. 14:20.
[8] Eph. 3:10.
[9] Rom. 11:36.

acclaim in the words of the philosopher John,[10] "Thou are worthy, O Lord, to receive glory and honour and power: for Thou hast created *all* things, and for Thy pleasure they are and were created!"

[10] Rev. 4:11.

APPENDIX

CHRISTIAN PHILOSOPHY IN TWENTIETH CENTURY NORTH AMERICA

(Address given at the 12th National Congress of South African Philosophers, 1970)

Mr. Chairman and my fellow philosophers! At this Twelfth Congress of Philosophy in South Africa. I have been requested to address you in English and on the subject of "Christian Philosophy in Twentieth Century North America." I myself would have preferred to have addressed you in Afrikaans, particularly had my subject been on South African or European philosophy. But as I have been requested to speak in English instead, I shall accordingly comply. And perhaps this is just as well after all for the purposes of my present address, seeing that the majority of North American philosophical works are recorded in the English language, so that speaking in English on this subject does at least obviate the task of translating citations.

* * *

First of all, I feel I should give a short critical account of my own epistemological limitations in respect of the subject under discussion. I am only aware of the existence of about eight thousand professional philosophers in North America,[1] of whom perhaps several hundred are Catholic thinkers (chiefly Thomists), and of whom perhaps fifty or less are that kind of Protestant philosophers who seriously attempt to think Biblically. This is, at least, the impression I received while teaching philosophy for more than two and a half years in the United States. I readily admit that an observation of such short duration is indeed not the most sufficient basis on which to draw firm conclusions, but honesty demands that I should reveal this necessary limitation of my approach.

Honesty also demands that I should also at the very outset confess my own adherence to the Calvinistic life and world view and admit the fact of its decisive orientation of my whole life and therefore also of my whole philosophical thinking.

There is also a time limitation. With less than an hour at my disposal, I shall obviously only be able to do little more than refer to the more important twentieth century Christian philosophers in North America and their works, and perhaps also elaborate just a little on the views of a few of the more prominent ones.

Next, I must clearly demarcate the subject under discussion. I shall not attempt to deal with the philosophers of Mexico and French-speaking Canada, but I shall limit myself to the philosophers of the United States and English-speaking Canada. I shall further limit myself to an examination only of Christian philosophy (which is not at all widespread in North America), and I shall therefore not deal with the influential schools of pragmatism, logical positivism, and linguistic analysis which dominate the current North American scene.[2] Again, I shall not deal with Catholic-Christian thought, as I do not really consider it to be a purely Christian philosophy but rather a conscious syncretism which has traditionally combined Greek philosophy (and particularly Aristotle) with Christian thought[3] and which has more recently sometimes added an existentialistic dimension hereto.[4] Nor shall I deal with Lutheran[5] and other non-Calvinistic Protestant Christian philosophies,[6] but confine my remarks to Calvinistic philosophers whom I consider to be making a conscious attempt to be consistent Christian thinkers about everything. And lastly, I shall only say a few words about Christian philosophers in America prior to the twentieth century; and this I shall do only in order to lead up to our subject proper, namely: "Christian Philosophy in Twentieth Century North America."

* * *

The American mind, even more so than the English, has long been overwhelmingly practical and rather anti-theoretically orientated. Even the early Puritans were practical activists, and building the new colonies in the teeth of extreme climatic conditions and constant Redskin attacks did not leave much time for meditative thinking. Consequently, a Christian philosophy of any real depth—as opposed to a then widespread and blessed non-philosophical Christian life and world view—only found a few advocates in those dynamic early days: advocates such as Mather and Edwards. *Cotton Mather* concentrated on the philosophy of nature, and *Jonathan Edwards, Sr.,* on the problems of virtue and the will[7]—yet even they were primarily theologians rather than philosophers,[7] although even current humanistic philosophy in America still takes considerable note of them.[8]

Even in Edwards there are Platonistic, Newtonian, and Lockean elements in his otherwise Christian writings, which foreign elements did not have a very salutary effect on the further course of American thought.[9] And after the headway made by the social ideas of Hobbes and Locke and the French Encyclopaedists and humanists via the American Revolution of 1776,[10] radicalized by the rise of American transcendentalism,[11] New England unitarianism, and social Darwinism in the nineteenth century[12]—in spite of Christian philosophical elements in the writings of thinkers like the Old Princetonians such as *A. A. Hodge, Charles Hodge,* and *Warfield*[13]—the twentieth century saw the almost universal collapse of American orthodoxy.

Yet "Orthodox Calvinistic Thought"—for want of a better name—continues to live on in the hearts and minds of a small minority of American philosophers. And within this minority we may perhaps distinguish at least three main trends, which trends I somewhat cryptically propose to call: (i) Calvinistic scholasticism, (ii) the cosmonomic philosophy, and (iii) the Westminster school. This is not a watertight classification, however, and many thinkers display features of more than one of these trends. In what follows, however, I shall attempt to say something about some of the leading Christian philosophers in America against the background of each of these three trends.

* * *

One of the leading twentieth century exponents of the Old Princetonian evidentialistic school of Calvinistic scholasticism—which school semi-scholastically sought to establish the credibility of the

Christian faith by rational enquiry supposed to lead to the establishment of clear "evidences"—is *J. Oliver Buswell, Jr.,* the Dean of the Graduate Faculty of Covenant Theological Seminary. Buswell's main philosophical ideas are found in his *A Christian View of Being and Knowing* and in his *Systematic Theology,*[14] as well as in his smaller philosophical studies on Tennant and Dewey and Aquinas.[15]

Buswell considers himself to be a thoroughgoing Calvinist—yet traces of Romish scolasticism are still very visible in his writings. For instance, Buswell holds with the Arminian scholasticist Bishop Butler that "the inductive arguments [for the proof of God's existence —the cosmological, teleological, anthropological, moral and ontological arguments,[16] do] . . . establish a presumption in favour of faith in the God of the Bible," so that "the Christian Gospel *might* be true";[17] and he also states that God's "being is a brute fact."[18]

In some respects, Buswell is even more removed from Scripture than is Rome. Not drawing the full consequences of the ontic distinction between the uncreated God and the qualitatively different created universe, Buswell dislikes the term "Aseity"[18] when applied to God, and insists that God's eternity is not timelessness,[19] for time to Buswell is an abstraction analogous to number.[20] Buswell even crypto-pantheistically erases the sharp distinction between God and man with statements like: "If the past is not past for God as well as man, then we are yet in our sins";[21] and: "We must insist that whatever in the Bible is univocal for man is univocal for God."[22] Then again, there is Buswell's almost Hegelian statement that, "The incarnation proves the immutability of God to be dynamic rather than static."[23] And elsewhere Buswell most uncalvinistically refers to human choices as the "free, undetermined acts of moral agents,"[24] and he further declares that, "Our moral choices are choices in which we are ourselves the ultimate cause."[25]

However, in spite of these serious inconsistencies in his Christian thinking Buswell has also made many acute and accurate observations. "I am well aware that the Thomists hold that God is 'Pure Being,' " he writes. "My contention is that such statements are mere combinations of syllables without intelligible connotation. . . . I still insist that the words 'pure being' are absurd. . . . [For] in the

225

horizon of the Judeo-Christian tradition, the words 'God is' clearly mean [that] the God described in the Bible exists as a substantive entity, a non-material spiritual Person, 'infinite, eternal and unchangeable in His being, wisdom, power, holiness, justice, goodness and truth.' This is much more than a category of 'pure being.' "[26] And Buswell comes very near to Dooyeweerd's adherence to Calvin's own position of *Deus legibus solutus est, sed non exlex,* where he criticizes Jonathan Edwards for arguing "that God has no freedom of will whatsoever, but is completely bound by the laws of logic and ethics . . . , adhering rigidly to the 'law of sufficient reason' not only for the creature, but also for the Creator Himself."[27] And Buswell also realizes the error of Aquinas in dividing the cosmos into natural and supernatural realms, and he very aptly describes this error as "schizocosmia." [15]

Unlike many modern American thinkers, Buswell believes as does Dooyeweerd that, "Man was intended and is destined to have dominion over all the earth and all the creatures upon it. . . . The command to rule the earth, given before man became a sinner (Gen. 1:26ff.), was repeated to Noah and his posterity, after the devastation of the flood (Gen. 8:15 - 9:17), after mankind had become a sinful race"; and Buswell further believes that, "God's image in man, which is related to man's intended rule over the earth," should be regarded "as a key for interpretation of the entire biblical doctrine of human culture,"[28] which human culture embraces history, physical and cultural anthropology, morality, the family, the state, economics, and the church.[29]

Part of Buswell's encyclopaedic arrangement of the sciences and branches of learning is also rather reminiscent of Dooyeweerd, Buswell commencing with mathematics and proceeding through physics, chemistry, biology, psychology, and metaphysics to philosophy.[30] Yet, writes Buswell, "Dooyeweerd's is an *a priori* Christian philosophy," and although "I have sincere respect for the scholars who adhere to this view in Holland and America, . . . I am not convinced that they have, as yet, produced a great Biblical system of philosophical thought."[31]

With an appeal to common grace[32] and even to Calvin's Institutes,[33] Buswell also feels that even unregenerate and "fallen man may hear and understand something of the Word of God. . . . This is the assumption of Christ in dealing with the most perverse of men. 'Ye hypocrites, *ye can discern* the face of the sky and of the earth. . . .' "[31] And therefore, believes Buswell, "The unbeliever, since he denies that God is the Creator of red cows, cannot even [truly] know a red cow."[31] Personally, I believe that Buswell has here misunderstood the relationship between a true knowledge of something on the one hand and an awareness of a state of affairs on the other. Only the regenerate may truly know; the unregenerate know not, but are merely vaguely aware. As St. Paul remarks to St. Timothy (I Tim. 6:3-5): "If any man teach otherwise, and consent not to wholesome words, even the words of our Lord Jesus Christ, and to the doctrine which is according to godliness; he is proud, *knowing nothing,* but doting about question and strifes of words, whereof cometh envy, strife, railings, evil surmisings, perverse disputings of men of *corrupt minds,* and *destitute of the truth. . . ."*

Yet Buswell surely does have a point where he declares: "As Christians, we begin not with the evidences for the existence of God but with the assumption of God's existence. . . . On the other hand, we are dealing with a considerable number of people in the world who are intellectually committed to positions antagonistic to Christian theism. When we speak to people of this kind in terms of our Christian faith in God . . . , it is frequently necessary to outline our reasons for faith in the God of the Bible. . . . It is one thing to say, 'Arguing from theistic evidences is often not the best approach,' and quite another thing to say, 'The inductive arguments for the existence of God are to be totally abandoned.' "[34] Paul's words that the heathen "should seek the Lord, if haply they might feel after him, and find him, though he be not far from every one of us," writes Buswell, were actually "addressed to the Areopagus, that is, the Athenian Philosophical Association. The members were Epicureans, and Stoics. Paul had to explain to them that the 'God that made the world and all things therein, seeing that he is Lord of heaven and earth, dwelleth not in temples made with hands; neither is he worshipped with men's hands, as though he needed anything, seeing

227

he giveth to all life, and breath, and all things.' "[35]

Buswell's integrity and earnestness is evidenced in his contention, which I happen to share, "that the philosophical jungles of our day are just as dense and just as dark as any to be found in tropical Africa or South America. The [philosophical] worshippers of 'an unknown God' are just as entitled to a presentation of the Gospel in terms of their language as are those we commonly call 'heathen.' The student of philosophy must understand that the jungles through which he must penetrate, if he is to be faithful to his commission in our so-called civilized areas, are just as difficult as any jungles ever penetrated by Livingstone."[35]

The next philosopher I wish to deal with is *Gordon H. Clark,* Professor of Philosophy at Butler University. Like Buswell, Clark too is a strong adherent of the Old Princetonian school of rationalistic Christian apologetics, holding that reason is common to all men by virtue of all men being created in the image of God, so that reason may lead to faith—a basically scholastic position. For Clark believes that, "A Christian must commit himself to rationalism or rationality on pain of being irrational, and he must be logical, on pain of being illogical, and also on pain of denying that God is wisdom and truth, and on pain of asserting that God is the author of paradox and confusion."[36]

However, unlike Buswell, Clark is thoroughly Calvinistic in his theology in general and his soteriology in particular, and he is also much more systematic and uncompromising in his attempt to develop a specifically Calvinistic philosophy. Indeed, Clark actually calls himself an "evangelical . . . Calvinist,"[37] and while insisting that the very basis of his thought "is the inerrancy of Scripture,"[38] he even admits to being supralapsarian as regards election and reprobation.[39] Moreover, Clark has expressed himself very Calvinistically indeed on the problems of knowledge, ethics, methodology, revelation, language, education, politics, natural science, history, and theology.[40]

In many respects Clark occupies a position nearer to Van Til's presuppositionism than to Buswell's apologeticism. "Basic world-views are never demonstrated, they are always chosen," asserts Clark, adding that "no demonstration of God is possible; our belief is a voluntary choice."[41] To Clark, the non-Christian is not neutral, but filled with "a bitter hatred of the doctrines of Jesus Christ."[42] In this matter of the irreconcilable antithesis between Christianity and all other systems of thought, as well as his insistence that God is even above the moral law,[43] Clark is even stronger than Dooyeweerd and hardly weaker than Van Til.

Yet although Clark regards God as being above the moral law, he does not regard God as being above the laws of logic.[43] As Rushdoony states, "The point of difference [between Clark and Van Til] is the role he [Clark] permits to rationality, the extent of God's comprehensibility, and the place of Greek logic in Christian philosophy."[44] To Clark, somewhat scholastically, it is not just God that is impossible, for "the immutable," declares Clark, "is what is meant by reality."[45] And for Clark, "This immutable reality is God, logic, the forms of thought and the rational structure of the universe."[46]

To Clark, Christ *is* Logic. Hear Clark's rendition of the beginning of John's Gospel: "In the beginning was Logic, and Logic was with God, and Logic was God. . . . In Logic was life, and the life was the light of men." "The law of contradiction," continues Clark, "is not to be taken as an axiom prior to or independent of God. The law is God thinking. . . . Not only was Logic the beginning, but Logic was God."[47] ". . . the Bible," declares Clark, "is the mind [the Logos, the Word] of God, or, more accurately, a part of God's mind. . . . Romans 4:2 is an enthymematic hypothetical destructive syllogism. Romans 5:13 is a hypothetical constructive syllogism. I Corinthians 15:15-18 is a sorites. Obviously, examples of standard logical forms such as these could be listed at great length."[48] And now Clark draws his disturbing conclusion from all this. He asserts that because "man is the image of God, man is basically logical,"[49] and "the fact that the Son of God is God's Reason, . . . plus the fact that the image [of God] in man is so-called 'human reason,' suffices to show that this so-called 'human reason' is not so much human as divine."[50]

This startling view of Clark's does, I think, somewhat tend to equate

229

creaturely logic with the Creator God, and it also erases the radical distinction between the knowledge possessed by God the Creator and the knowledge possessed by man the creature. Long before Clark did, *Dr. S. O. Los* of Potchefstroom had described I Corinthians 15 as a sorites;[48] but Los did not draw a semi-pantheistic conclusion herefrom, namely that God is logic, as did Clark! Hence it is more than understandable that Clark's ordination into the Orthodox Presbyterian Church in the mid-forties was challenged by Van Til and others on the grounds that Clark's epistemology was incompatible with the doctrine of the incomprehensibility of God,[51] Van Til holding that the knowledge possessed by God is qualitatively different from that possessed by man.[52] To Van Til, Clark's position on this point is basically "Romantist-Arminian" or scholastic, in that Clark "seems to hold that man may obtain a certain amount of information about God apart from revelation," which knowledge is presumably "to be obtained by 'reason' operating independently of revelation."[53] And this "reason," declares Clark, enables man to choose the "plausible solutions" offered by one system which "tends less to skepticism" than another [system].[54] The result is that Clark believes that "Christians and non-Christians have certain 'common ground.' That is to say, a regenerate and an unregenerate person may believe the same proposition."[55] Significantly, Clark, while not objecting to being called an idealist, prefers to be called a realist, holding as he does that the human "mind can actually possess the truth, the real truth."[56]

Clark concedes as regards the anti-realistic cosmonomic philosophy that "Herman Dooyeweerd is to be congratulated for his attempt to cover all the fields of knowledge,"[57] but Clark questions the correctness of what he calls the "linear filiation" in the Dooyeweerdian modal spheres. Particularly does he question the precedence of history before language, the dependence of aesthetics on economics, and the significance of aesthetics as the foundation of jurisprudence.[58] Still less can Clark appreciate how Dooyeweerd's logical sphere can be *central* in the modal scale, instead of *fundamental* in order to be able to guarantee the rationality even of mathematics.[58]

To Clark, of course, logic is supratemporal because it roots in *the* Logos, Jesus Christ, and is in fact *identical* to Him.[58] From the cosmonomic viewpoint, however, not only the logical modality roots in Christ but so do all the *non*-logical modalities too—and *none* of the modalities are identical to Christ! Clark's absolutization of the logical modality actually means that he is (at least theoretically) a Christian logicist, or, as he himself admits, a rationalistic Calvinist.[59] And it is submitted that it is this self-confessed rationalism or logicism which also causes Clark difficulty in accepting the cosmonomic order of the law spheres in the cosmonomic modal scale.

Finally, Clark also questions the wisdom of Dooyeweerd's description of the creation days of Genesis as non-historical. The Dooyeweerdian description is unwise, declares Clark, "in view of the neo-orthodox antithesis between time and eternity, in view of paradox and supra-temporal contemporaneity."[60] But Clark apparently fails to realize that Dooyeweerd hereby merely means that the creative days were *non*-historical because *pre*-historical and pre-*human,* because history as such necessarily presupposes the existence of man.

* * *

Concerning the American *cosmonomic* school itself, I am going to be shorter. This is not at all because I consider its contributions to the development of Christian philosophy to be less significant than that of the Calvinistic scholasticism dealt with above—to the contrary! I am personally acquainted with some of the American cosmonomists and I share many of their views. But I am going to be shorter here, because the cosmonomic philosophy of Dooyeweerd and Vollenhoven is comparatively better known in South Africa than is the North American Calvinistic scholasticism I have just been describing, and also because the American cosmonomists do not much deviate from the relatively well-known Dooyeweerdian position, apart from being too antagonistic towards other Calvinistic philosophical positions, too anti-conservative in their social and political views,[125] as well as somewhat too philosophistical and anti-theological—no doubt as an understandable over-reaction against centuries of Puritanically Protestant scholastical theological imperialism over the legitimate aspirations of a Christian philosophy striving to be free from conservative theological strictures as opposed to the always relevant Biblical guidelines.

It was *David Hugh Freeman,* Professor of Philosophy at the University of Rhode Island, who, with his colleague William Young, translated into English both Dooyeweerd's three-volume *De Wijsbegeerte der Wetsidee* and, singlehandedly, Spier's *Inleiding in die Christelijke Wijsbegeerte,* under the respective titles: *A New Critique of Theoretical Thought*[61] and *An Introduction to Christian Philosophy.*[62] As such, American philosophers owe Freeman a huge debt of thanks. Freeman's own article, "The Neo-Augustinianism of Herman Dooyeweerd,"[63] gives us a useful if objectivistic outline of the views of the great Dutch thinker, and Freeman's book, *A Philosophical Study of Religion,*[64] is still quite an acceptable approach to that subject. But Freeman's *Logic: The Art of Reasoning*[65] neutralistically avoids all antithetic clashes with humanistic logic and thus compares very unfavorably with the radical Christian approach of Freeman's fellow Christian logician, *D. H. Th. Vollenhoven,* in the latters works, *Logos en ratio, Hoofdlijnen der logica,* and *De noodzakelijkheid eener Christelijke logica.*[66] Freeman's colleague, *William Young,* is at least more refreshing and challenging. Frankly acknowledging his debt towards his mentor Gordon H. Clark, Young, although differing from Dooyeweerd on several points, does not hesitate to say so in his book, *Towards a Reformed Philosophy.*[67] And in his other book, *Foundations of Theory,* Young boldly declares: "My indebtedness to Professor Herman Dooyeweerd will speak for itself. If some of the views expressed in this book appear to differ sharply from those of the pioneer in the field of Critique of Theoretical Thought, this is in part only because I owe so much to his masterly achievement.[68]

Doyen of the Dooyeweerdians in America is perhaps *H. Evan Runner,* Professor of Philosophy at Calvin College in Michigan and the power behind the American Groen van Prinsterer Society. Runner wrote his doctoral dissertation under Vollenhoven in Amsterdam on *The Development of Aristotle illustrated from the earliest Books of the Physics*[69] and after returning to America he produced his four printed lectures on "The Relation of the Bible to Learning,"[70] which trace the Christian theory of knowledge, the place of the Law, the necessary antithesis between Christian theory and all immanentistic theories. Insisting on the permanence of the Law even after the fall, and denying the scholastic concept of substance as contrary to the sovereignty of God,[71] Runner masterfully discloses the all-embracing religious pre-conditioning of all human knowledge, points out the errors of Greek and humanistic thought, graphically traces the downward trend of American philosophy even amongst Christian thinkers, and demands the rejection of all synthetic thought in favor of the undiluted Christian philosophical approach grounded in the triune basic religious motive of the creation, fall, and redemption of the entire cosmos.[70]

In his later writings, *Scientific and Pre-Scientific* and *Sphere-Sovereignty,* Runner discusses these subjects with a penetrating brilliance and an absorbing freshness;[72] and in his still later three printed lectures on "Scriptural and Political Task,"[73] Runner arrestingly presents the Christian political thesis in all its virility, the humanistic political antithesis in all its actuality, and the pseudo-Christian political synthesis [of both Catholic and Protestant scholasticism] in all its futility. Violently anti-Heppian and anti-substantialistic, it was Runner who warmly endorsed and first drew my attention to the very existence of the recently published doctoral dissertation of Dr. D. J. Malan entitled: *'n Kritiese Studie van die Wysbegeerte van H. G. Stoker vanuit die standpunt van H. Dooyeweerd.*[74]

But perhaps the most versatile of all the American cosmonomists, and certainly the most brilliant of the younger members of the school, is *Calvin Seerveld,* Professor of Philosophy at Trinity Christian College. After his doctoral dissertation under Vollenhoven in Amsterdam on *Benedetto Croce's earlier aesthetic theories and literary criticism,*[75] the aesthetically gifted Seerveld wrote his *Christian Critique of Art,*[76] in which he discusses the necessity and nature of art. Next he produces his *Christian Critique of Literature,*[77] in which he discusses literature among the arts and the office of literary criticism. Then followed other works, such as his socio-political *Christian Workers, Unite!*[78] and his beautiful dramatization of the Song of Solomon, as well as his educational writings, *A Reformed Christian College,*[79] *What the Lord Requires of Trinity [Christian] College,*[80] *Cultural Objectives for the Christian Teacher,*[81] and *The Song of Moses and the Lamb: The Joke of [the] Association for Reformed Scientific Studies' Education.*[82]

It should not be thought, however, that Seerveld the dedicated Dooyeweerdian is an uncritical Dooyeweerdian*ist*. As Seerveld himself remarks:[83] "An unbelieving student from the Chicago community who did a long list of readings in a course of mine at Trinity [Christian College], said at the end: 'I see now—Calvin was reforming Augustine; Kuyper reformed some of Calvin; Dooyeweerd reforms Kuyper, and now you are out to reform Dooyeweerd.' Right [replied Seerveld]."

Other North American cosmonomists worthy of note are *Robert D. Knudsen* (who wrote his doctoral dissertation under Zuidema in Amsterdam on *The Idea of Transcendence in the Philosophy of Karl Jaspers*[84]), *Paul C. Schrotenboer,*[85] *Maarten Vrieze, Remkes Kooistra,*[86] *Hendrik Hart* (writer of *The Democratic Way of Death*[87]), *B. Zijlstra, J. Olthuis, P. Schouls, P. Vanderstelt, H. Van der Laan,*[88] *C. T. McIntire,* and *A. De Graaff*[89]—which list is not exhaustive—but I think enough has already been said to show their growing significance on the American philosophical scene.

* * *

The last main trend in American Christian philosophy which I wish to outline is what I shall call the *Westminster school,* under the dynamic leadership of Van Til and Rushdoony.

Cornelius Van Til, Professor of Apologetics at Westminster Theological Seminary in Philadelphia, if not the most influential Christian thinker, is indeed the prince of presuppositionalism and of trinitarian transcendent theocentrism in North America today. Born in Holland and raised in the United States, Van Til combines the very best Reformed thought of two continents. With rare skill he extracts and combines the best of Hodge and Warfield with the best of Kuyper, Bavinck, and Schilder. An independent thinker, Van Til is also a warm advocate of the presuppositionalistic philosophy of Vollenhoven, Dooyeweerd, and Stoker.[90] Van Til would be faithful to Calvin and to St. Paul, but above all would he unquestionably follow that glorious Being, the Triune God, the Maker of heaven and earth.

I shall not even attempt to give a detailed outline of the works and philosophy of Cornelius Van Til in a paper of this length. This has already been attractively and adequately done by Rushdoony in his book, *By What Standard?*[91] I would commend it to anyone interested in acquiring an introductory knowledge of Van Til's thought. In what follows here, however, I shall merely try to outline the general thrust of his thought, and can only hope that my description does him sufficient justice.

Van Til is a consequential Calvinist. By correctly exalting the ontological Trinity as the Self-contained and Self-sufficient God and *only* starting point for *all* brands of human knowledge, he has exposed the remnants of scholastic evidentialism in the Old Princetonians, Lutherans, Arminians, Romanists, and others.

God made everything in the universe solely for His own glory, asserts Van Til. The divine Trinity or Tri-unity is the root and solution of the problem as to the relationship between all universals and particulars in the universe which He created and which reflects His glory, albeit in a creaturely manner. Everything is accordingly inter-related with everything else under God, and all creation is covenantally subjected to man as its head and crown. Man in his turn is subjected to God, and in subduing the earth, man—both individually and as a community—also subjects himself unto God as his reasonable religion by virtue of his covenantal obligations towards the Triune God, the Creator, Sustainer, Redeemer, and Consummator of heaven and earth.[7]

Van Til is the very apostle of antithesis.[92] He hates Arminianism with a holy hatred.[93] He hammers at Heidegger[94] and tilts at Teilhard[95] and Toynbee.[96] He regards the heresy of Karl Barth as a greater heresy than those refuted at Nicaea or Chalcedon[97]—to the bewilderment of Berkouwer.[98] But Berkouwer's bewilderment does not deter Van Til, for by reprobating reprobation (like Barth) Berkouwer himself has betrayed the Decrees of Dordt.[99] And just as Dordt merely reflected the views of *all* the Reformers of the sixteenth century—both Lutheran and Calvinist—"including even the gentle Melanchthon and the compromising Bucer,"[100] so too in these present syncretistic and ecumenical days of the liberal United Presbyterian Church's Confession of 1967[101] and the Romish Church's Vatican II

235

must Dordt still be upheld without apology and without compromise.[102]

In the light of his extremely critical faculty of judgment, I was indeed very humbled and not a little encouraged when Van Til, whom I am privileged to have met personally, wrote me that he had read my own defense of the Westminster Confession "with delight," and expressed the hope that I would "keep on working in this direction."[103] For Van Til, like me, holds to a doctrine of particular redemption,[104] cosmic in its scope and eschatological in its tendency.[105] The supralapsarian covenant with the historical Adam is worked out in depth and in great detail.[106] "Common grace must support special or saving grace," declares Van Til. "Saving or special grace cannot be adequately presented except in relationship to and in connection with common grace. Together they form the covenant framework in which the sovereign God deals with man."[107]

In his two books, *The Doctrine of Scripture* and *A Survey of Christian Epistemology,* Van Til is set *In Defense of the Faith*[108] against all comers. Because Van Til loves the Lord God Omnipotent and His Most Holy Word alone with all his heart, he does not hesitate to differ sharply even from his fellow Calvinists. Hence Van Til exposes Buswell's semi-Arminianism and scholasticism in the latter's apologetical system derived from "the Aquinas-Butler method" of apologetics.[109] Van Til also assails Hepp's "central truths" supposedly recognized by all men, on the grounds that the Heppian doctrine here undermines the truth of man's total depravity.[110] And Van Til even opposes Potgieter's allegation that Dooyeweerd is subjectivistic for making the *ego regeneratus* the immediate starting point and concentration point in philosophy—a very relevant matter in Christian philosophical circles in South Africa right at the present moment![111]

To Van Til, "We must know all things if we are to know anything about anything."[112] This does not mean that Van Til is irrational. To the contrary, Van Til believes in the absolute rationality of God, while stressing the creaturely and therefore incomprehensive rationality even of regenerate man.[113] Those who, like Clark[58] and Buswell,[109] believe in the logical reasoning powers of fallen man on account of man's creation in the image of the Logos-God have not

236

taken man's intellectual sinfulness seriously enough. "The more consistent his logical reasoning is, the more certainly will he end up with a finite God which is no God."[114]

Ronald H. Nash, Professor of Philosophy at Western Kentucky University, agrees with Clark's attack on Van Til on account of the latter's "pietistic depreciation of a so-called human logic as opposed to some unknowable divine logic."[115] But even Nash has to concede: "Perhaps, after all, Van Til is the more consistent Calvinist. At least Van Til does not draw back from the assumption that both God's morality and God's logic are a result of His own free choice and thus qualitatively different from man's."[116]

To Van Til, the logic of Clark and Buswell is Arminian logic.[117] Reformed logic, however, insists that it is only because God as Creator knows *all* things that men as creatures can know anything. And man only knows at all because as the image of God he reflects something of God's perfect knowledge like a mirror reflects its object.[118]

Van Til's work is being carried on and given a more concrete application by *Rousas John Rushdoony,* the editor of the Philosophical and Historical Studies in the International Library of Philosophy and Theology. Not only has Rushdoony endorsed Dooyeweerd to the American public[119] and summarized Van Til's own views,[120] but he also has independently developed them still further, especially in the fields of theology,[121] education,[122] and politics,[123] in which latter field Rushdoony, like many of our own South African philosophers, is a very conservative Calvinist. I am sure most of us here today will be delighted to know that our country has a firm friend in Rousas John Rushdoony. In 1967 he wrote to me: "I believe South Africa, although unfortunately now showing signs of drifting, is still more Christian than any other country of today and has a major contribution to make. South African Reformed believers are more aware of the basic issues of our time. Too many American Reformed thinkers are prone to sentimental humanism as they view social issues."[124]

As South African philosophers we should indeed be grateful for but also humbled by these words. May we not disappoint Rushdoony.

237

May we check the "signs of drifting" he sees in some of us, and make the "major contribution" he expects us to perform!

Other members of the Westminster school are *Gary K. North* of the University of California, the Christian economist who has refuted Marx[125] and also engaged in a running debate against Troost on property rights in terms of the eighth commandment;[126] the late *Henry Van Til,* author of the well-known book, *The Calvinist Concept of Culture;*[127] *C. Gregg Singer,* Professor of History at Catawba College in North Carolina;[128] and others such as *Nic. Van Til* of Dordt College in Iowa, *Robert B. DeMoss* of Covenant College in Tennessee, and *George Christian* of King's College in New York, the latter two of whom I have had the privilege of meeting at Conferences of the Association for Reformed Scientific Studies.

* * *

I shall say a final word about a few more American Christian thinkers that I have decided to classify as *Miscellaneous Calvinist Philosophers* because I have difficulty in fitting them with ease into any of the above three main trends. And here I must content myself with a mere enumeration of these men.

Clearly Calvinistic are *W. Stanford Reid,* Professor of History at McGill University in Montreal, Canada,[129] and *Robert L. Reymond,* a professor at the Covenant Theological Seminary.[130] The Old Dutch pre-Dooyeweerdian Calvinistic philosophy still lives on in Calvin College professors like *W. Masselink,*[131] *William K. Frankena,*[132] *D. Jellema,*[133] and *Alvin Plantinga.*[134] And rather unclassifiable are *William W. Paul,*[135] Professor of Philosophy at Central College in Iowa, and *Francis A. Schaeffer,*[136] who now resides in Switzerland.

But Southern Africa has also given America two great Christian philosophers in the persons of Hughes and Hebden Taylor. *Philip Edgecumbe Hughes,*[137] who grew up in South Africa, has not merely been a professor at several colleges first in England and now in the United States, but he is also a leading light in the International Association for Reformed Faith and Action. And *E. L. Hebden Taylor,* born of missionary parents in Katanga in the Congo, and currently a professor at Dordt College in Iowa, the author of quite the most comprehensive work on Christian political science available in the

English language,[138] has dedicated one of his other books[139] to "my revered spiritual father HERMAN DOOYEWEERD in appreciation of his great contribution towards the reformation of science." The book of Taylor's in question has as its full title: *Evolution and the Reformation of Biology—A Study of the Biological Thought of Herman Dooyeweerd of Amsterdam and J. J. Duyvene de Wit, late Professor of Zoology at the University of Bloemfontein, South Africa.*

* * *

Mr. Chairman and fellow philosophers. I was asked to address you on the subject of "Christian Philosophy in Twentieth Centurry North America." In this paper, I outlined my own limitations and presuppositions at the very outset, and then, after a short historical introduction, I attempted to give you an outline of the views of some of the more prominent North American Calvinistic scholastics, cosmonomists, and Westminster philosophers; and I ended up by enumerating miscellaneous other Calvinistic philosophers. I trust I have now discharged my commission to your satisfaction, and I am very grateful indeed to you all for your kind attentiveness. I thank you.

NOTES AND REFERENCES

1. Archie M. Bahan, *Directory of American Philosophers* (Albuquerque, N. M., 1968).
2. Cf. Schneider, *A History of American Philosophy* (New York: Forum Books, Inc., 1957), p. 197ff.; cf. also Whittemore, *Makers of the American Mind* (New York: Morrow and Co., 1964), p. 287ff.
3. Cf. Thomas Aquinas and Maritain.
4. Cf. Blondel and Gabriel Marcel.
5. Cf. Leander S. Keyser, *A System of Christian Evidence* (Burlington, Iowa: The Lutheran Literary Board, 1926); *A Manual of Christian Psychology,* and *A Manual of Christian Philosophy;* John Warwick Montgomery, *The Shape of the Past: An Introduction to Philosophical Historiography.*
6. Carnell, *An Introduction to Christian Apologetics* (Grand Rapids, Mich.: Eerdmans, 1966); *A Philosophy of the Christian Religion* (Eerdmans, 1964); Ferm, *A History of Philosophical Systems* (ed.), (New York: The Philosophical Library, 1950); *An Encyclopaedia of Religion* (ed.), (The Philosophical Library, 1945); Gates, *Adventures in the History of Philosophy* (Grand Rapids, Mich: Zondervan, 1961); Holmes, *Chris-*

239

tianity and Philosophy (London: Tyndale Press, 1964); "Philosophy," in *Christianity and the World of Thought,* ed. Armerding (Chicago: Moody Press, 1968); Mollenkott, *Adamant and Stone Chips;* Ramm, *The Christian College in the Twentieth Century* (Eerdmans, 1963); *The Christian View of Science and Scripture* (Eerdmans, 1966); Wilbur M. Smith, *Therefore, Stand* (Boston: W. A. Wilde Co., 1945); and Warren C. Young, *A Christian Approach to Philosophy* (Grand Rapids, Mich.: Baker Book House, 1966).

7. Cf. N. Lee, *A Christian Introduction to the History of Philosophy* (Nutley, N. J.: The Craig Press, 1969), *in loco.*

8. Cf. Schneider, *op. cit.,* pp. 8-17; Whittemore, *op. cit.,* pp. 15-16, 32-45; Peter Gay, *A Loss of Mastery: Puritan Historians in Colonial America* (New York: Vintage Books, 1968), pp. 53-117, 146-157.

9. Cf. C. Gregg Singer, *A Theological Interpretation of American History* (Philadelphia: Presbyterian and Reformed Pub. Co., 1964), pp. 28-29.

10. *Ibid.,* pp. 24-50; cf. Schneider, *op. cit.,* pp. 18-61; cf. Whittemore, *op. cit.,* pp. 47-153.

11. Cf. Singer, *op. cit.,* pp. 51-91; cf. Scheneider, *op. cit.,* pp. 168-196.

12. Cf. Singer, *op. cit.,* pp. 92-178; cf. Schneider, *op. cit.,* pp. 197-237; cf. Whittemore, *op. cit.,* pp. 287-418.

13. Cf. A. A. Hodge, *Outlines of Theology* (London: Nelson, 1879); *The Confession of Faith* (London: Banner of Truth Trust, 1958); Charles Hodge, *Systematic Theology,* I-III (London: Nelson, 1873); Warfield, *Calvin and Augustine* (Philadelphia: Presbyterian and Reformed Pub. Co., 1956); *The Inspiration and Authority of the Bible* (London: Oxford University Press, 1927); etc. More of a rationalistic Calvinist is the great Union Theological Seminary systematic theologian, W. G. T. Shedd, cf. his *History of Christian Doctrine,* I-II (Edinburgh: T. and T. Clark, 1867); *Dogmatic Theology,* I-II; and his *Orthodoxy and Heterodoxy* (New York: Scribner, 1893).

14. Cf. J. Oliver Buswell, *A Christian View of Being and Knowing,* 1960, and *A Systematic Theology of the Christian Religion,* I-II (Grand Rapids, Mich.: Zondervan, 1962).

15. Cf. Buswell, *The Philosophies of F. R. Tennant and John Dewey* (New York: The Philosophical Library, 1950); *Thomas and Bible* (New Jersey: Shelton College Press).

16. Buswell, *Systematic Theology,* I, p. 9.

17. *Ibid.,* p. 100.

18. *Ibid.,* p. 41.

19. *Ibid.,* p. 42.

20. Buswell, *Being and Knowing,* pp. 44-45.

21. Buswell, *Systematic Theology,* I, p. 47.

22. *Ibid.,* p. 39.

23. *Ibid.,* p. 55.
24. Buswell, *What Is God?,* p. 40.
25. *Ibid.,* p. 50.
26. Buswell, *Being and Knowing,* pp. 64-65.
27. *Ibid.,* p. 155; cf. Dooyeweerd, *A New Critique of Theoretical Thought,* I (Philadelphia: Presbyterian and Reformed Pub. Co., 1953), p. 93.
28. Buswell, *Systematic Theology,* I, pp. 344-345.
29. *Ibid.,* pp. 345-429.
30. Buswell, *Being and Knowing,* pp. 19-20.
31. *Ibid.,* pp. 175-177.
32. Buswell, Letter to Van Til, Jan. 30, 1937; cf. Cornelius Van Til, *A Survey of Christian Epistemology* (Den Dulk Christian Foundation, 1969), p. 224.
33. Calvin: *Institutes of the Christian Religion,* II:2:12-13 and II:6.
34. Buswell, *Being and Knowing,* pp. 171-173.
35. *Ibid.,* pp. 114-145.
36. Gordon H. Clark, "Reply to Roger Nicole," in Ronald H. Nash (ed.), *The Philosophy of Gordon H. Clark—A Festschrift* (Philadelphia: Presbyterian and Reformed Pub. Co., 1968), p. 479.
37. *Ibid.,* p. 484.
38. *Ibid.,* p. 478.
39. *Ibid.,* p. 479; cf. Roger Nicole, "The Theology of Gordon Clark in *ibid.,* p. 396.
40. Cf. *ibid.,* pp. 125-398.
41. Clark, *A Christian Philosophy of Education* (Grand Rapids, Mich.: Eerdmans, 1946), pp. 20, 48.
42. *Ibid.,* p. 78; cf. Clark, *A Christian View of Men and Things* (Grand Rapids, Mich.: Eerdmans, 1952), pp. 25, 33.
43. Cf. Clark: "Reply to Ronald H. Nash," in Nash (ed.), *op. cit.,* pp. 417-419.
44. Rousas J. Rushdoony, "Clark's Philosophy of Education," in Nash (ed.), *op. cit.,* p. 282.
45. Clark, *Thales to Dewey* (Boston: Houghton Mifflin Co., 1957), p. 19; cf. too his *A History of Philosophy* (with Martin, *et al.*), (New York: Crofts and Co., 1941).
46. Nash, "Gordon Clark's Theory of Knowledge," in Nash (ed.), *op. cit.,* p. 171; cf. too his, *Dooyeweerd and the Amsterdam Philosophy* (Grand Rapids, Mich.: Zondervan, 1962).
47. Clark, "The Axiom of Revelation," in Nash (ed), *op. cit.,* pp. 67-68; cf. too Clark, *Religion, Reason and Revelation* (Philadelphia: Presbyterian and Reformed Pub. Co., 1961).
48. *Ibid.,* p. 70; cf. S. O. Los, *Logika,* A. H. Koomans, Drukkerij en Boekhandel, Potchefstroom, South Africa, 1918, pp. 68, 81, 214, 225.

241

49. *Ibid.,* pp. 72, 74.
50. *Ibid.,* p. 76.
51. Cf. Fred H. Klooster, *The Incomprehensibility of God in the Orthodox Presbyterian Conflict* (Franeker, Netherlands: Wever, 1951).
52. Cf. Nash, "Gordon Clark's Theory of Knowledge," in Nash (ed.), *op. cit.,* p. 161.
53. Van Til, *An Introduction to Systematic Theology* (Philadelphia: Westminster Theological Seminary, 1966), pp. 168-173.
54. Clark, *A Christian View of Men and Things,* p. 34; cf. too his *The Philosophy of Science and Belief in God* (Nutley, N. J.: The Craig Press, 1964).
55. Clark, "Reply to Arthur F. Holmes," in Nash (ed.), *op. cit.,* p. 94.
56. *Ibid.,* p. 440.
57. Clark, "Several Implications: Dooyeweerd," in *ibid.,* p. 94.
58. *Ibid.,* pp. 96-97; cf. notes 45-50, *supra.*
59. Cf. notes 36 and 37, *supra,* and especially the text *in locis.*
60. Clark, "Several Implications," in Nash (ed.), *op. cit.,* p. 101.
61. David Hugh Freeman (part translator), *A New Critique of Theoretical Thought,* Vols. I-III (Philadelphia: Presbyterian and Reformed Pub. Co., 1953), being the English Translation and expansion of Herman Dooyeweerd's *De Wijsbegeerte der Wetsidee,* 3 Vols., 1935-1936.
62. Freeman (translator), *An Introduction to Christian Philosophy* (Philadelphia: Presbyterian and Reformed Pub. Co., 1954), being the English translation of J. M. Spier's *Inleiding in de Wijsbegeerte der Wetsidee* (Kampen, Netherlands: Kok, 1950).
63. Freeman, "The Neo-Augustinianism of Herman Dooyeweerd," in *Recent Studies in Philosophy and Theology* (Philadelphia: Presbyterian and Reformed Pub. Co., 1962). Cf. too his "Clark's Philosophy of Language," in Nash (ed.), *op. cit.,* pp. 257-275.
64. Freeman, *A Philosophical Study of Religion* (Nutley, N. J.: The Craig Press, 1954).
65. Freeman, *Logic: The Art of Reasoning* (New York: David McKay Pub. Co., 1967).
66. Cf. D. H. Th. Vollenhoven, *Logos en ratio, beider verhouding in de geschiedenis der Westersche kentheorie* (Inaugurale oratie), (Kampen, Netherlands: Kok, 1926); *De noodzskelijkheid eener Christelijke logica* (Amsterdam, Netherlands: H. J. Paris, 1932); and his *Hoofdlijnen der logica* (Kampen, Netherlands: Kok, 1948).
67. William S. Young, *Towards a Reformed Philosophy* (Grand Rapids, Mich., 1952), p. 137: "Discrete quantity, the simplest of Dooyeweerd's law spheres, itself is not so simple as Dooyeweerd represents it. For a number to be a discrete quantity, it must be, it must be itself, it must even be related to something other than itself. Being, sameness, other-

ness relation, are thus presupposed by numbers and by all more complex structures of reality. The most basic structures of reality are thus not numerical but ontological." Cf. too, *ibid.*, pp. 138, 143, in which Young respectively criticizes Dooyeweerd's classification of theology as a special science and labels Dooyeweerd's post-mortal "functionless soul" as an even "more shadowy spectre than the scholastic *anima rationalis.*" Cf. too A. L. Conradie, *The Neo Calvinistic Concept of Philosophy* (Pietermaritzburg, South Africa,: Natal University Press, 1960), pp. 81-95.

68. Young, *Foundations of Theory* (Nutley, N. J.: The Craig Press, 1967), p. ii. Cf. too his "Dooyeweerd," article in Philip Edgecumbe Hughes (ed.), *Creative Minds in Modern Theology* (Grand Rapids, Mich.: Eerdmans, 1966).

69. H. Evan Runner, *The Development of Aristotle illustrated from the earliest Books of the Physics* (Kampen, Netherlands: Kok, 1951).

70. Runner, "The Relations of the Bible to Learning," in *Christian Perspectives* (Pella, Iowa: Pella Pub. Co., 1960).

71. *Ibid.*, p. 117.

72. Runner, "Scientific and Pre-Scientific" and "Sphere-Sovereignty," both in *Christian Perspectives* (Hamilton, Ont., Canada: Guardian Pub. Co., Ltd., 1961).

73. Runner, "Scriptural Religion and Political Task," in *Christian Perspectives* (Hamilton, Ont., Canada: Guardian Pub. Co., Ltd., 1962).

74. D. J. Malan, *'n Kritiese studie van die wysbegeerte van H. G. Stoker vanuit die standpunt van H. Dooyeweerd* (Amsterdam, Netherlands: Buijten en Schipperheijn, 1968).

75. Calvin Seerveld, *Benedetto Croce's earlier aesthetic theories and literary criticism* (Kampen, Netherlands: Kok, 1958).

76. Seerveld, "A Christian Critique of Art," in *Christian Perspectives* (Ontario, Canada: Association for Reformed Scientific Studies, 1963).

77. Seerveld, "A Christian Critique of Literature," in *Christian Perspectives* (Ontario, Canada: Association for Reformed Scientific Studies, 1964).

78. Seerveld, *Christian Workers, Unite!* Cf. too his *The Rub to Christian Organization or . . . Christian Camel Drivers Unite?*, n.d. and his *Labor: A Burning Bush!* 1965 (all published by the Christian Labor Association of Canada, Rexdale, Ont., Canada).

79. Seerveld, *A Reformed Christian College* (Illinois: Trinity Christian College, 1960).

80. Seerveld, *What the Lord Requires of Trinity College* (Illinois: 1965).

81. Seerveld, *Cultural Objectives for the Christian Teacher* (Illinois: n.d.).

82. Seerveld, *The Song of Moses and the Lamb: The Joke of A.R.S.S. Education* (Hamilton, Ont., Canada: Association for Reformed Scientific Studies, 1965).

83. *Ibid.*, p. 26n.

243

84. Robert D. Knudsen, *The Idea of Transcendence in the Philosophy of Karl Jaspers* (Kampen, Netherlands: Kok, 1958); cf. too his *Dialectic and Synthesis in Contemporary Theology* (Philadelphia: Westminster Theological Seminary, 1967); and "Reflections on the Philosophy of Herman Dooyeweerd," *Journal of the American Scientific Affiliation* (June, 1954); and his *Sociology* (Philadelphia: Westminster Theological Seminary, 1966).

85. Cf. Paul G. Schrotenboer, numerous articles in *International Reformed Bulletin* (Grand Rapids, Mich.: "Motives of Ecumenism," in *Christian Perspectives* (1967); and "The Nature of Religion," in *Christian Perspectives* (1964).

86. Cf. Remkes Kooistra, *Facts and Values: A Christian Approach to Sociology* (Association for Reformed Scientific Studies, 1963); and his *The University and its Abolitions—A Christian Critique of University Education* (Association for Reformed Scientific Studies, 1965).

87. Hendrik Hart, *The Democratic Way of Death* (Rexdale, Ont., Canada: Committee for Justice and Liberty Foundation, 1967). Cf. too his doctoral dissertation on the philosophy of John Dewey, Free University of Amsterdam.

88. H. Van der Laan, *A Christian Appreciation of Physical Science* (Ontario, Canada: Association for Reformed Studies, 1966).

89. Arnold C. De Graaff, *Introduction to Psychology Syllabus* (Trinity Christian College, Illinois, 1967); *The Educational Ministry of the Church* (doctoral dissertation; and his *Understanding the Scriptures* (with Seerveld, [Ontario, Canada: Association for Reformed Scientific Studies, 1969]).

90. Cornelius Van Til, *The Defense of the Faith* (Philadelphia: Presbyterian and Reformed Pub. Co., 1963), p. 296ff.; and his *Bavinck the Theologian* (Presbyterian and Reformed Pub. Co., 1962). Cf. too his *Christian Philosophy* (Phillipsburg, N. J.: Grotenhuis, n.d.), p. 8; *Christianity in Modern Theology* (Philadelphia: Westminster Theological Seminary, 1964), pp. 81-83; and his *The Case for Calvinism* (Presbyterian and Reformed Pub. Co., 1964); his *Why I Believe in God* (Philadelphia: The Committee on Christian Education, The Orthodox Presbyterian Church, 7401 Old York Road, n.d.); his *The Triumph of Grace: The Heidelberg Catechism* (Westminster Theological Seminary, 1962); his *Christ and the Jews* (Presbyterian and Reformed Pub. Co., 1968); and his *The Dilemma of Education* (Presbyterian and Reformed Publishing Co., 1956). However, from personal conversations with Van Til, I seem to recall that he does not make the radical Dooyeweerdian distinction between naive and theoretical knowledge, nor the radical Dooyeweerdian distinction between the Creator's essence (God *is*) and the creature's existence (creation *is not* but merely *ex-ists* in God Who Alone *is* [Cf. Dooyeweerd, *A New Critique of Theoretical Thought*, I,

pp. 58, 73 n. 1, 96-97, 100, 508-509]). Interesting here is the resemblance which Dooyeweerd's *terminology* (alone!) bears to that of Tillich, *Systematic Theology*, Vol. I (University of Chicago Press, 1951), pp. 79-81, 110, 239. Moreover, it would also seem that Van Til and Dooyeweerd do have different views of the science of logic. Cf. Dooyeweerd, *A New Critique of Theoretical Thought*, II, p. 465, with Van Til, "Arminianisme in de logica," in *De Reformatie van het Calvinistich Denken* (ed.) C. P. Boodt (Uitgeverij Guido de Bres, 's-Gravenhage, Netherlands, 1936). Cf. too notes 44 *supra* and 112-115 *infra,* and especially the text *in locis.*

91. Rushdoony, *By What Standard? — An Analysis of the Philosophy of Cornelius Van Til* (Philadelphia: Presbyterian and Reformed Pub. Co., 1965).

92. Van Til, *The Intellectual Challenge of the Gospel* (Phillipsburg, N.J.: Grotenhuis, 1953); and cf. too his *Paul at Athens* (Grotenhuis, n. d.).

93. Van Til, "Arminianisme in de logica," in Boodt (ed.), *op. cit.*

94. Van Til, *The Later Heidegger and Theology* (Philadelphia: Westminster Theological Seminary, 1964).

95. Van Til, *Pierre Teilhard de Chardin: Evolution and Christ* (Philadelphia: Presbyterian and Reformed Pub. Co.), 1966.

96. Van Til, *Toynbee on Christianity* (Philadelphia: Westminster Theological Seminary, 1961). Cf. too in general his *Christianity and Idealism* (Philadelphia: Presbyterian and Reformed Pub. Co., 1955).

97. Van Til, *Has Karl Barth Become Orthodox?* (Philadelphia: Presbyterian and Reformed Pub. Co., 1954), p. 181; cf. too his *Christianity and Barthianism* (Presbyterian and Reformed, 1962).

98. Cf. G. C. Berkouwer, *The Triumph of Grace in the Theology of Karl Barth* (Grand Rapids, Mich.: Eerdmans), p. 390.

99. Van Til, *The Sovereignty of Grace: An Appraisal of G. C. Berkower's View of Dordt* (Nutley, N. J.: Presbyterian and Reformed Pub. Co., 1969).

100. Van Til, *The Theology of James Daane* (Philadelphia: Presbyterian and Reformed Pub. Co., 1959).

101. Van Til, *The Confession of 1967: Its Theological Background and Ecumenical Significance* (Philadelphia: Presbyterian and Reformed Pub. Co., 1967).

102. Van Til, "Significance of Dordt for Today," in De Jong (ed.), *Crisis in the Reformed Churches* (Grand Rapids, Mich.: Reformed Fellowship, Inc., 1968), p. 181ff.

103. Van Til to Lee, Letter, May 20, 1968, in respect of Lee's "How to Confess Christ in a Twentieth Century Expression of the Westminster Confession of Faith to a Changing Hostile Society" (Westminster Confession Address at Faith Theological Seminary, Philadelphia, March, 1968).

104. Van Til, *The Theology of James Daane.*
105. Van Til, *Common Grace* (Philadelphia: Presbyterian and Reformed Pub. Co., 1954), p. 93ff.
106. Van Til, "Nature and Scripture," in Stonehouse and Woolley (eds.), *The Infallible Word* (Philadelphia: Presbyterian Guardian Pub. Corp., 1946); cf. Van Til's, "Standard of Man in Paradise," in his *Christian Theistic Ethics* (Philadelphia: Westminster Theological Seminary, 1961), p. 104ff; cf. too "Christian Theistic Revelation," in his *An Introduction to Systematic Theology,* p. 62ff; and cf. his *Christian-Theistic Evidences* (Westminster Theological Seminary, 1961).
107. Van Til, *Particularism and Common Grace* (Phillipsburg, N.J.: Grotenhuis, n.d.), p. 20; cf. too his *Common Grace and Witness-bearing* and his *Paul at Athens* (both published by Grotenhuis).
108. Van Til, *The Doctrine of Scripture* and *A Survey of Christian Epistemology* (both published by the Den Dulk Christian Foundation, 1969). These two volumes are also entitled *In Defense of the Faith,* Vols. I and II—not to be confused with Van Til's other one-volume work, *The Defense of the Faith* (Presbyterian and Reformed Publishing Co., 1963).
109. Van Til, *A Survey of Christian Epistemology,* p. 224; cf. too his *An Introduction to Systematic Theology,* p. 176.
110. Van Til, *Apologetics* (Philadelphia: Westminster Theological Seminary, 1966), pp. 50-51.
111. Van Til, *Criticism of F. J. M. Potgieter's "Der Verhouding tussen die Teologie en die Filosofie by Calvyn" (Amsterdam, 1939),* Philosophia Reformata 5, 1940, p. 53. Here Potgieter (*op. cit.,* p. 219) argues that according to Dooyeweerd, "Not Revelation, but the regenerated heart, is posited as the foundation of philosophy." However, replies Potgieter, ". . . the fixed foundation of the *revelatio specialis* [may] never be exchanged for the instability and fallibility of the still sinful regenerated heart or *ego regeneratus*" (My translation—N. Lee). To this criticism of Dooyeweerd by Potgieter, Van Til replies: "Potgieter contends that a complete and constant submission of the *ego regeneratus* is nowhere found because no one is perfect. But surely such a submission does take place *in principle,* or there would be no more Christian theology any more than a Christian philosophy. Potgieter apparently desires that the Christian philosopher, instead of going directly to the Bible itself, should come to a 'bekwame *professor theologicus*' for a statement of what the Bible has to say to him. Are we then to understand that this is because this theological professor is perfect in degree as well as in principle? If the author had observed the simple distinction between perfection in principle and perfection in degree he could not have made the exceedingly serious charge of subjectivism against Dooyeweerd. . . .

[However,] Dooyeweerd has constantly subjected the *ego regeneratus* to the Scriptures. To be sure, Dooyeweerd finds in the *ego regeneratus* the *immediate* starting point and concentration point of philosophy. . . . But . . . it is the great virtue of the Wijsbegeerte der Wetsidee that . . . Dooyeweerd and Vollenhoven insist in all their writing that man should regard himself as a creature and a sinner and should therefore go to the Scriptures in order in the light of them to search out the meanings of the created world." But A. L. Conradie (*op cit.*, p. 122) agrees with Potgieter: "Van Til has not seen the real danger pointed out by Dooyeweerd's critics," she writes. "If theology is controlled by the cosmonomic idea, formulated by philosophy from the religious a priori, we are in fact making theology subject, not to the objective norm of Scripture, but to a *religio subjectiva* over which we have no control." However, D. F. M. Strauss (in his *Boekbespreking* of D. J. Malan's *'n Kritiese Studie van die wysbegeerte van H. G. Stoker vanuit die standpunt van H. Dooyeweerd* [in the *Tydskrif vir Christelike Wetenskap*, Association for Christian Higher Education, Bloemfontein, South Africa, 2de Kwartaal, 1969, pp. 70-71]) seems to agree with Van Til. "He who wishes to pass by the human selfhood in his faithful acceptance of Revelation," writes Strauss, "is engaged in putting and end to man's subjective (N.B., not subjectivistic) faith. Only the complete self-surrender of man to the central Scriptural basic motive brings about the radical conversion in the root of our existence by Christ's directedness towards the heart. . . . It is not Revelation which engages in philosophy, but man, and from his full selfhood under the control of some or other (religious) basic motive. Christian philosophy (and the special sciences) would only be grounded in the *religio subjectiva* if it [or they] exalted the full selfhood of man whence all acts of thought arise to the Archimedes point of philosophy. . . . [And] therefore Dooyeweerd writes: 'The Archimedian point of philosophy is chosen in the new root of mankind in Christ, in which by regeneration we have part in our reborn selfhood' (N.C., Vol. I, p. 99)." (My translation—N. Lee).

112. Van Til, "A Christian Theistic Theory of Knowledge," *The Banner* (Nov. 6, 1931), p. 2. Cf. B. J. van der Walt, "Wat is die verskil tussen 'n Christelike en 'n nie-Christelike wetenskap?" in *Bulletin van die Suid-Afrikaanse Vereniging vir die bevordering van Christelike wetenskap?* (Nov. 1968); cf. Ir. H. van Riessen, *Mondigheid en de machten,* Buijten en Schipperheijn, Amsterdam, Netherlands, 1967, pp. 200-202; "De Christen en Zijn Werk," in *Mens en Werk,* Buijten en Schipperheijn, 1966, p. 31ff.; and his "The Relation of the Bible to Science," in *Christian Perspectives* (Pella, Iowa: Pella Pub. Co., 1960), p. 3ff.

113. Van Til, *The Defense of the Faith,* p. 41.

114. Van Til, *A Survey of Christian Epistemology,* p. 226.

115. Clark, as quoted by Nash, "Gordon Clark's Theory of Knowledge," in Nash (ed), *op. cit.,* p. 167.
116. *Ibid.,* p. 169.
117. Van Til, "Arminianism in de logica," in Boodt (ed.), *op. cit;* cf. notes 58 and 109, *supra.* Cf. too Van Til, *Is God Dead?* (Philadelphia: Presbyterian and Reformed Pub. Co., 1966); and his *The Intellectual Challenge of the Gospel* (Phillipsburg, N.J.: Grotenhuis, 1953).
118. Gilbert Weaver, "Gordon Clark: Christian Apologist," in Nash (ed.), *op. cit.,* pp 304-305.
119. Cf. Rushdoony's "Introduction" to Dooyeweerd, *In the Twilight of Western Thought* (Nutley, N. J.: The Craig Press, 1965).
120. See note 91, *supra.*
121. Rushdoony, *The Foundations of Social Order* (Philadelphia: Presbyterian and Reformed Pub. Co., 1968); and his *The Mythology of Science* (Nutley, N. J.: The Craig Press, 1967).
122. Rushdoony, *The Messianic Character of American Education; Intellectellectual Schizophrenia—Culture, Crisis and Education,* 1961; *Freud,* 1965; and his "Clark's Philosophy of Education," in Nash (ed.), *op. cit.,* 1965 (all published by Presbyterian and Reformed Pub. Co.).
123. Rushdoony: *This Independent Republic* and *The Nature of the American System* (both Philadelphia: Presbyterian and Reformed Pub. Co.).
124. Rushdoony to Lee, Letter written *circa* June 1967.
125. Gary K. North, *Marx's Religion of Revolution* (Nutley, N. J.: The Craig Press, 1968).
126. North, "Social Antinomianism, *International Reformed Bulletin* (Mich., October, 1967).
127. Henry Van Til, *The Calvinist Concept of Culture* (Philadelphia: Presbyterian and Reformed Pub. Co., 1959).
128. Singer, "A Theological Interpretation of American History; Calvin and the Social Order," in Hoogstra (ed.), *John Calvin, Contemporary Prophet* (Grand Rapids, Mich.: 1959); *Calvinism: Its Roots and Fruits* (Presbyterian and Reformed Pub. Co.); "Gordon Clark's View of the State," in Nash (ed.), *op. cit.;* and *South Carolina in the Confederation* (Philadelphia: University of Pennsylvania Press).
129. W. Stanford Reid, "Absolute Truth and the Relativism of History," in *Christian Perspectives* (1961); "Calvin and the Political Order," in Hoogstra (ed.), *op. cit.;* and *Christianity and Scholarship* (Nutley, N. J.: The Craig Press, 1966).
130. Robert L. Reymond, *A Christian View of Modern Science* (1964) and *Introduductory Studies in Contemporary Theology* (1968 [both Philadelphia: Presbyterian and Reformed Publishing Co.]).
131. W. Masselink, "New Views Regarding Common Grace in the Light of

Historic Reformed Theology," in *The Calvin Forum* (Grand Rapids, Mich., 1954).

132. William K. Frankena, "Love and Principle in Christian Ethics" in Alvin Plantinga (ed.), *Faith and Philosophy—Festschrift for William Harry Jellema* (Grand Rapids, Mich.: Eerdmans, 1954).

133. D. Jellema, "The Philosophy of Vollenhoven and Dooyeweerd," in *The Calvin Forum* (1954).

134. Plantinga (ed.), *op. cit.;* and cf. his own "Necessary Being" in that volume.

135. William W. Paul, "Philosophy of Science," in *Christianity and the World of Thought*, ed. Armerding (Chicago: Moody Press, 1968); "The Interplay between Philosophy and Theology in Tillich's Thought," in *Bulletin of the Evangelical Theological Society* (1968); and his *What Can Religion Say to Its Cultured Despisers?* (Central College, Iowa, 1968).

136. Francis A. Schaeffer, *Death in the City* (Chicago: Inter-Varsity Press, 1969); *Escape from Reason;* and his *The God Who Is There.*

137. Hughes, ed. (see note 68, *supra*); and his own *Christianity and the Problems of Origins* (Philadelphia: Presbyterian and Reformed Pub. Co., 1964); and his "The Pen of the Prophet," in Hoogstra, *op. cit.*

138. E. L. Hebden Taylor, *The Christian Philosophy of Law, Politics and the State* (Philadelphia: Presbyterian and Reformed Pub. Co.); cf. too his smaller *The New Legality* (Nutley, N. J.: The Craig Press, 1967).

139. Taylor, *Evolution and the Reformation of Biology* (Nutley, N. J.: The Craig Press, 1967), p. v.